Marilyn in Manhattan

Also by Elizabeth Winder

Pain, Parties, Work:
Sylvia Plath in New York, Summer 1953

Marilyn
in Manhattan

Her Year of Joy

Elizabeth Winder

FLATIRON
BOOKS
NEW YORK

WWW.FLATIRONBOOKS.COM

Photograph of Marilyn Monroe in Fire Island © Eve Arnold/ Magnum Photos
Photograph of Marilyn Monroe in class at the Actors Studio by Roy Schatt courtesy of MPTV Images
Photograph of Marilyn Monroe dancing with Truman Capote courtesy Bridgeman Images
All other images used throughout courtesy of Getty Images

Library of Congress Cataloging-in-Publication Data

Names: Winder, Elizabeth author.
Title: Marilyn in Manhattan : her year of joy / Elizabeth Winder.
Description: First edition. | New York : Flatiron Books, 2017. | Includes bibliographical references.
Identifiers: LCCN 2016044104| ISBN 9781250064967 (hardcover) | ISBN 9781250064974 (e-book)
Subjects: LCSH: Monroe, Marilyn, 1926–1962. | Actors—United States—Biography. | Monroe, Marilyn, 1926–1962—Homes and haunts—New York (State)—New York. | Monroe, Marilyn, 1926–1962—Friends and associates.
Classification: LCC PN2287.M69 W56 2017 | DDC 791.4302/8092 [B]—dc23
LC record available at https://lccn.loc.gov/2016044104

Our books may be purchased in bulk for promotional, educational, or business use. Please contact your local bookseller or the Macmillan Corporate and Premium Sales Department at 1-800-221-7945, extension 5442, or by e-mail at MacmillanSpecialMarkets@ macmillan.com.

First Edition: March 2017

10 9 8 7 6 5 4 3 2 1

for Mary Angelo

Contents

Cast of Characters

(in order of appearance)

MILTON GREENE — Fashion photographer; Marilyn's best friend and business partner from 1954 to 1956

AMY FRANCO GREENE — Marilyn's close friend; married to Milton Greene

SHELLEY WINTERS — Hollywood friend of Marilyn's; a member of the Actors Studio and Marilyn's classmate in 1955

DARRYL ZANUCK — Executive producer and studio chief of Twentieth Century Fox

JANE RUSSELL — Marilyn's friend and costar in *Gentlemen Prefer Blondes*

JOE DIMAGGIO — Major League Baseball player; Marilyn's husband for nine months in 1954

CHARLIE FELDMAN — Marilyn's agent in 1954

BILLY WILDER — Directed Marilyn in *The Seven Year Itch*

JAY KANTER — Marilyn's agent from 1955 to 1956

FRANK DELANEY — Marilyn's lawyer in 1955 and 1956

MICHAEL CHEKHOV — Marilyn's Stanislavski-trained drama coach in 1953 and 1954

SAMMY DAVIS JR. — Actor, singer, entertainer, and friend of Marilyn's

ELSA MAXWELL — Gossip columnist, professional hostess, and friend of Marilyn's

KITTY OWENS — The Greenes' cook; befriended Marilyn in late 1954

GEORGE NARDIELLO — Fashion designer; met Marilyn in late 1954

NORMAN NORELL — Fashion designer; met Marilyn in late 1954

ELI WALLACH — Member of the Actors Studio; befriended Marilyn in 1955 and remained a close friend until her death

BEN GAZZARA — Member of the Actors Studio and Marilyn's classmate in 1955

DEAN MARTIN — Actor, singer, entertainer, and friend of Marilyn's

JERRY LEWIS — Actor, singer, entertainer, and friend of Marilyn's

MILTON BERLE — Actor, television personality; Marilyn's friend and former lover

CARSON MCCULLERS — American writer; befriended Marilyn in 1955

TRUMAN CAPOTE — New York author; befriended Marilyn in 1955

CONSTANCE COLLIER — English actress and theater coach; Marilyn's first drama coach in New York

CHERYL CRAWFORD — Influential theater producer and director; befriended Marilyn in 1955

LEE STRASBERG — Creative director of the Actors Studio and Marilyn's mentor

LEO LYONS — New York journalist; befriended Marilyn in 1955

EARL WILSON — New York journalist and a friend of Marilyn's

ROBERT STEIN — Journalist; spent time with Marilyn in March 1955

ED FEINGERSH — Photographer; spent time with Marilyn in March 1955

EDWARD R. MURROW — Prizewinning journalist and television personality; interviewed Marilyn in March 1955

ELLEN BURSTYN — Member of the Actors Studio; Marilyn's classmate in 1955

DELOS SMITH — Member of the Actors Studio; Marilyn's classmate in 1955

MARLON BRANDO — Member of the Actors Studio; Marilyn's friend and classmate in 1955

JACK GARFEIN — Member of the Actors Studio; Marilyn's classmate in 1955

CARROLL BAKER — Member of the Actors Studio; Marilyn's classmate in 1955

MAUREEN STAPLETON — Member of the Actors Studio; Marilyn's classmate in 1955

LOUIS GOSSETT JR. — Member of the Actors Studio; Marilyn's classmate in 1955

KIM STANLEY — Member of the Actors Studio; Marilyn's classmate in 1955

JACK LORD — Member of the Actors Studio; Marilyn's classmate in 1955

MARGARET HOHENBERG — Marilyn's psychoanalyst in 1955

PAULA STRASBERG — Former stage actress; married to Lee Strasberg; Marilyn's surrogate mother and confidante

SUSAN STRASBERG — American actress; daughter of Lee Strasberg and a friend of Marilyn's

JOHNNY STRASBERG — Lee and Paula Strasberg's son

SAM SHAW — New York photographer and a friend of Marilyn's; they met in 1954 while filming *The Seven Year Itch*

NORMAN ROSTEN — New York poet; friend of Arthur Miller's; befriended Marilyn in 1955

HEDDA ROSTEN — Norman's wife; befriended Marilyn in 1955

MAURICE ZOLOTOW — Journalist; interviewed Marilyn in spring and summer 1955

JIMMY HASPIEL — Teenage fan who befriended Marilyn in 1955

THE MONROE SIX — Six teenage fans who befriended Marilyn in 1955

ARTHUR MILLER — American playwright; Marilyn's lover in 1955 and her husband from 1956 to 1961

ELIA KAZAN — Stage and film director; Marilyn's friend and former lover

JOHN GILMORE — Actors Studio member; Marilyn's classmate in 1955

JOSHUA LOGAN — American stage and film director; directed Marilyn in the film adaptation of *Bus Stop*

JAYNE MANSFIELD — American actress and Marilyn's supposed blonde rival

TERENCE RATTIGAN — British dramatist, writer of *The Sleeping Prince*; met Marilyn in January 1956

LAURENCE OLIVIER — British actor; Marilyn's director and costar in *The Prince and the Showgirl*

CECIL BEATON — British fashion and portrait photographer; photographed Marilyn in February 1956

DON MURRAY — American actor; Marilyn's costar in *Bus Stop*

Preface

"In a dream you saw a way to survive and you
were full of joy."   JENNY HOLZER

In late November 1954, a woman who identified herself as Zelda
Zonk drove quietly to the LAX airport and boarded the evening's
last plane to New York. Accompanied by a young photographer
named Milton Greene, the woman wore no makeup, a man's oxford
shirt, and Jax cigarette pants under a full-length black mink.
She wore a black wig cut in a blunt pageboy and, though it was
nearly midnight, black Wayfarers. She lit cigarettes and bit her
nails like any other jittery twenty-eight-year-old about to jettison
marriage, home, and career in the course of one midnight flight.
Soothed by the revving engine, she slipped off the wig, revealing a tangle of fluffy blonde curls.

She was Marilyn Monroe.

As the plane took off, Marilyn watched LA's glitter diminish
beneath her and thought about all she had abandoned: Joe
DiMaggio and their broken fairy-tale marriage; her contract with
Twentieth Century Fox; her agent, Charlie Feldman; her acting
coach, Natasha Lytess; her Hollywood apartment and its closets
crammed with gabardine skirts and merry widows from Juel Park.
As the city shrank to a bright speck, Marilyn began to relax. Milton

poured her a drink, and they discussed their exciting new project—
an independent film company to be named Marilyn Monroe
Productions.

By the time they landed at Idlewild Airport, flush with scotch
and excitement, Zelda Zonk's true identity had been leaked. Fans
and photographers swarmed and screamed, though the temperature had dropped below freezing. Milton's wife, Amy Greene, was
waiting. She wrapped Marilyn in a blanket and rushed her into
the trunk of a black Cadillac. Lying on her side in the frozen dark,
Marilyn listened to the screams fade as Amy began the two-hour
drive past miles of forested rocky bluffs to her country house in
Connecticut.

The sun rose as Marilyn sank into the violet sheets and plummy
pillows of the Greenes' guest bedroom. She drifted to sleep, dreaming of her future. She's safe now. She's with friends. She's in
New York.

✎ Marilyn's year in New York was a magical time of artistic
discipline and self-discovery. It was about looking inward, taking
her power back, and determining the course of her own career. It
meant being a student again and learning the Method at the Actors Studio. It was also where she educated herself and developed
her tastes in literature, music, and art. She formed friendships
with writers and intellectuals such as Carson McCullers and Truman Capote. And it was where she began her relationship with
Arthur Miller.

Unlike the usual portrayals of childhood abuse and down-
ward spirals, this Marilyn isn't a victim. Nor is this the Hollywood Marilyn we know so well—dripping in diamonds and
swathed in mink. This is a furtive, fuzzier, happier Marilyn—clad
in dark Wayfarers, a bandeau scarf, and a boyish black polo coat.

This book lifts that veil to show the real, flesh and blood Marilyn—a strong, savvy woman who took control of her life. The New York Marilyn jogged undisturbed in Central Park and popped into Elizabeth Arden's Red Door Spa for a leg wax. She admired Rodin's *Hand of God* at the Met. She mewed and stretched on the floor, pretending to be a kitten in acting class. She dined at Gino's with Frank Sinatra, then swilled cheap scotch at the Subway Inn down the street. She stretched out in her bathrobe on the floor of the Waldorf-Astoria, scrawling poems on crisp hotel stationery.

New York centered Marilyn. It revitalized her and provided a stimulating haven for reinvention and self-inquiry. For the first time, Marilyn was living by herself, for herself. Each day was an adventure in reading, walking, seeing some new little thing. New York meant freedom to her—freedom from straitjackets such as "starlet" and "sex symbol" and "slut." This is Marilyn in Manhattan—a sensitive woman, the city she loved, and how she learned to love herself.

Marilyn in Manhattan

One

Miss Lonelyhearts

"Who can think about art in this miserable city?"

KATHY ACKER

Summer, 1953.

*O*f course, the surface looked sexy enough—parties on Doheny Drive, martini (no olives) in hand, wet red lips, hair like a platinum cloud, white halter top, skintight toreador pants, red peep-toe Ferragamos, and matching cherry polish. Always pale, a milkmaid among Malibu tans.

At twenty-seven, Marilyn Monroe was at the peak of her stardom. *Gentlemen Prefer Blondes*—her highest-grossing film to date—had launched her into the stratosphere of absolute icon. In less than five years, she'd gone from orphanage waif to child bride to factory girl to car model to GI pinup to studio underling to down-and-out extra to mogul's mistress to *Playboy* centerfold to BAFTA nominee. She'd been Sweetheart of the Month, Artichoke Queen, Miss Cheesecake of the Year, Girl Most Likely to Thaw Alaska, *Photoplay's* Fastest Rising Star, *Redbook's* Best Young Box Office Personality, *Look's* Most Promising Female Newcomer, and The Best Friend a Diamond Ever Had. She'd done twenty-one films, three hundred magazine covers, and won three Golden Globes. Marilyn was now Hollywood's most bankable actress. Not bad for a dirt-poor orphan who'd grown up in foster care and dropped out of high school at sixteen.

But grueling schedules, dawn call times, and constant travel were taking a toll on her. Breakfast of raw eggs whipped in hot milk with lashings of sherry, carrot-juice breaks at Stan's Drive-In. Giuseppa, her Chihuahua, soiling the carpet. Lonely lunches of raw hamburger and crackers, fights with her agent at Schwab's. Blowups with boyfriends at La Scala and Romanoff's. Nightly battles with insomnia, relieved only occasionally by Seconals and Nembutals.

After awards shows she'd flee like Cinderella, skipping the after-party and vanishing by midnight. Alone in her studio dressing room, she'd kick off her heels, strip off her gloves, and unzip a gown that wasn't hers to begin with. She'd peel off her false lashes, wipe off her makeup with tissues dipped in Pond's cold cream. Barefoot in jeans and a polo shirt, she'd throw her Ferragamos in the back of her car and drive west on an empty Wilshire Boulevard, speeding at up to 80 miles per hour. Safe at home, she'd drink a glass of sherry, pop a few pills, and sink into blurry sleep.

On set she was known as ditsy and distant, always darting away with a book between takes. Whenever someone would make a friendly overture, Marilyn would clam up. She was too earnest for idle chitchat and considered it a waste of time. As for gossip, she knew too well the havoc it wreaked. While sitting in hair and wardrobe, she'd tune out the whispers and jabs about who had bad skin and who was sleeping with whom and who had just had an abortion. Attempts to squeeze out juicy tidbits were shut down. "I don't know any," she'd say with a sigh, "because I don't get out."

Studio gossip and cocktail chatter were the pillars of Hollywood friendships, which were often forged at clannish house parties. Marilyn hated these—what would she even talk about?—it wasn't as if anyone was dying to know which Turgenev novel she was reading. "I didn't go out because I couldn't do polite conversation," Marilyn remarked. "I couldn't make table talk, small talk, so I said, 'What the hell, I'll just stay home.'" Whenever she did feel like socializing, Marilyn preferred nightclubs such as Crescendo and Mocambo, where she could slink in and out at will and avoid catty banter and boisterous parlor games.

This made for an especially lonely life in Hollywood—which was about cliques, connections, and friends of friends. In Manhattan it was fine to bar-hop on your own, check out your usual spots and see who's there. In LA, everyone went to people's houses: Charlie Chaplin's in Calabasas or Jack Warner's on Doheny Drive. They all seemed to have their own group—except Marilyn, who found herself alone even one New Year's Eve: "Everybody has a date tonight except me. If you're not doing anything, could we have dinner together?"

"Fundamentally unsure of herself, inclined to be suspicious of people because of past hurts she's suffered, Marilyn isn't easy to know," wrote Rita Malloy in *Motion Picture* magazine. And she wasn't. Hollywood would always be a bit baffled by her—skipping studio parties to ride roller coasters at Ocean Park or dreamily reading aloud from Kahlil Gibran's *The Prophet* whenever she broke for lunch. Who was this warm-blooded space creature who lugged around dictionaries, spoke like a drugged-up puppy, and looked like a French pastry? And how could they make sense of a girl who got lost on her way to the bathroom, took sixty takes to learn a line, then went home alone to read Heinrich Heine?

꧁ Like most other shy, imaginative misfits, Marilyn retreated into books. Back in '49 she opened her first charge account, at Martindale's bookshop, an odd choice for a starving starlet. Books kept her company during those long afternoons at Schwab's, spending her last nickel on a malted and eating it with a spoon to make it last. She'd leaf through *Walden* or *Camille,* waiting to be picked up by some modeling scout, then cab back to her dingy little room, switch on a lamp, and console herself with *Look Homeward, Angel.*

As her star power rose, Marilyn nourished her mind as best she could. She took yoga with Indra Devi, audited classes at UCLA—Backgrounds in Literature and Renaissance Art. Desperate to find her niche, she attended the Actor's Lab on Crescent Heights Boulevard. Even then she'd been an outsider—plopped in the back absorbed in a book, hungry, shoulder-length hair box-bleached and uncombed. Her classmates rarely invited her for coffee at Barney's Beanery or drinks at Musso & Frank's on Hollywood Boulevard. Perhaps the writer William Saroyan was right when he had prophesied, Grim Reaper–like, "You're a loner, Marilyn, and you'll always be alone."

Only one or two friends sensed Marilyn's depth, including the actress Shelley Winters, who shared an apartment with her in 1951. One late spring evening Dylan Thomas was in town, and Shelley volunteered to cook him dinner. She roasted a crispy pork loin with wedges of garlic, mashed some potatoes with green onions and sour cream, and tossed a salad with Roquefort dressing. She didn't expect much help from her roommate: "If you gave her a rack of lamb, she just stared at it." Shelley had assigned her the applesauce—open jar, pour in saucepan, heat, add dash of

Cointreau—but Marilyn got mixed up and poured in the whole bottle.

While Shelley cooked, Marilyn gathered white wildflowers from the empty lot next door, stuffed them in drinking glasses, and arranged them on the card tables she'd placed on their tiny balcony. She strung Japanese lanterns along the awning, lit candles, mixed gin martinis in milk bottles, and set out juice glasses to pour them in.

Marilyn and Shelley had one martini each—Dylan Thomas drank the rest straight out of the milk bottle. He downed a bottle of red wine, a bottle of white, and six bottles of beer he'd bought at a grocer's. (Back in Wales, grocers didn't sell cigarettes or alcohol—for this alone he might move to Los Angeles.) Naturally, Dylan didn't mind when they served the liquored-up applesauce as if it were a cocktail.

"Although Mr. Thomas teased and kidded me with his risqué Welsh wit," Shelley wrote, "he was quiet and respectful to Marilyn. Dylan Thomas seemed aware that behind the platinum hair and terrific body, there was a fragile and sensitive girl. . . . He was obviously a horny Welshman, but he never once made any kind of pass at Marilyn. Not even a verbal one. . . . I think this poet sensed that she very badly needed not to be thought of as just a tits-and-ass cutie." By the end of the meal Marilyn was smitten, though refused to jump into Dylan's green Hornet and join him at Chaplin's home in Calabasas. Before Dylan left that candlelit balcony, with its view of glittering Hollywood night, he sang a Welsh melody in minor key, which moved Marilyn to tears: "Come all ye fair and tender maids, who flourish in your prime/ Beware, beware, keep your garden fair, let no man steal your time/ A woman is a branch, a tree—a man a clinging vine/ And from her branches carelessly he takes what he can find, find, he takes what he can find."

——————

℘ If 1953 was Marilyn's breakout year, it was also the year she began to rebel. She had to beg for her own dressing room on the set of *Gentlemen Prefer Blondes,* and she was making far less than her costar, Jane Russell. The rigors of studio production were making her physically and psychically ill. She'd just finished filming *How to Marry a Millionaire,* her third major role in nine months. Battered by migraines, insomnia, viral infections, and bronchitis, Marilyn was visibly weakening. She'd wake up shaking, nerves already shot, gulp down a painkiller before rolling out of bed. Nausea was inevitable, and she was often vomiting, unable to keep down anything but orange juice mixed with gelatin. Like everyone else in Hollywood, she'd been diagnosed with anemia, which meant massive vitamin B injections and gagging down concoctions like tomato juice spiked with ground-up liver ("Even lime and Worcestershire sauce hardly mask the taste"). "I had no sense of satisfaction at all," Marilyn told *Modern Screen.* "And I was scared."

But Marilyn—the most popular actress in the world—was oddly powerless. America's sexy sweetheart was still the property of Twentieth Century Fox, and back in the early fifties, the studio controlled everything: from the roles you took on, to the directors you worked with, to how often you went to the bathroom, and sometimes even who you married. Studio heads had little respect for their actors—especially the women—and often tried to coax out publicity-boosting catfights. Directors often felt irrelevant and lashed out in frustration against their cast. On-set bullying was common, and Marilyn was an especially easy target. "They tell you to cry one tear," she complained, "and if you feel two and cry two, it's no good. If you change 'the' to 'a' in your lines, they correct you. An actress isn't a machine, but they treat you like one."

Marilyn knew she deserved better from Fox. This year alone she'd raked in heaps of glammed-up money. She was their sun, their power earner, yet they treated her like a dumb-blonde cash cow. Executive Darryl Zanuck claimed she had "emotions of a child" and was "ill-equipped" to determine the course of her career. (Not too ill-equipped to earn half their revenue.)

Fox had her lined up for *River of No Return,* a goofy Western with a slapdash script that was below even Zanuck's standards. Marilyn would play Kay, a honky-tonk floozy and saloon chanteuse. Roles like these made her sick—stumbling around in spiked shoes, slipping on sweat-slick floors, enduring snide cameramen's sneering and leers. She hated being bulldozed into the bimbo act. Most of all she hated Zanuck, who called her "Strawhead" behind her back, then cashed in fast to keep Fox afloat. But Marilyn was contractually stuck. Through gritted teeth, she accepted yet another role she knew was beneath her.

She longed for meaty roles such as Hedda Gabler or Grushenka from *The Brothers Karamazov.* She'd recently read Émile Zola's *Nana* and had fallen in love with the voluptuous French courtesan. Excited, she called George Cukor to see if he'd direct her in a film adaptation. Yet Cukor, a noted "women's director," declined. It was too risky, he said, and was there really an audience for decadent French novels from the nineteenth century?

Marilyn needed someone who believed in her. Her lawyers and agents would flatter her over salad and Dom Pérignon, then glaze over when she brought up her studio battles. She was beginning to lose hope. No one would take chances; no one would trust her talent. Fox, Paramount, MGM—even LA itself seemed to close in on her. She'd suffocate under its tawdry glare of misogyny, canned art, and smoggy money.

It would take a fellow outsider and artist, a soft-spoken photographer with a red-checked scarf and Brooklyn accent, to ignite

Marilyn's rebel flame and give her the strength to defy Darryl Zanuck and change the studio system forever.

✑ Marilyn had always known the power of image—starting from her first modeling shots in the late 1940s. She'd been a visual learner since childhood. At the orphanage she'd spend hours on her bed, lying on her stomach, leafing through the film magazines of the late thirties and forties: *Movie Mirror, Photoplay,* and *Screen Gems.* She'd been studying these images for years— the lowered lash, the parted lip, the plucked brow, and the dewy eye. By the time the cameras pointed at her, she was ready.

Unlike most other models and actresses, Marilyn worked closely with her photographers, makeup artists, and costume designers— and more often than not, they learned from her. She knew her chin looked weak in profile, her left side was prettier than her right, and that the halo of down on her face gave her a soft-focus Garbo glow. She practiced dropping her lip to make her smile less gummy. When she didn't like a picture, she gouged it with a hairpin. By 1953 she was dying to break loose from bloodless glamour shots, but she needed the right photographer. While she was browsing through stacks of picture portfolios, one in particular caught her eye. It belonged to a young fashion photographer named Milton Greene. His pictures were sensitive, spontaneous—especially the ones of Marlene Dietrich. She looked like a swan, with her arched back and snowy neck. "They're so beautiful," Marilyn breathed. "I want him to photograph me." She made a few phone calls, and soon enough Milton was boarding a plane to Los Angeles.

Jaded and skeptical, Milton was far from starstruck. At thirty-one, he'd photographed Liz Taylor, Ava Gardner, Cary Grant, both Hepburns; his pictures were featured in *Harper's Bazaar* and *Vogue.* He liked elegant women with a European flair, and he wasn't impressed by flashy screen queens: "Marilyn was not really what I would turn around for or call a whistle at, even though she turned on a lot of guys. I'd seen some of her movies, she looked interesting, but she didn't throw me. My style is more Dietrich, Garbo, Audrey and Katharine Hepburn, even Judy Garland in a different way." But when he met Marilyn, all that changed: "From the very beginning it was completely comfortable, like 'Let's make a date' or whatever. She put out her hand and said, 'You're just a boy' and I said, 'You're just a girl.' And from that moment on we sort of hit it off."

Milton Greene burst into Marilyn's life at just the right time, bringing with him a blast of icy East Coast air. Everything about him—his catlike way of moving, the blazers he had made in Rome, even his staccato Brooklynese—promised a fresh alternative to LA's ostentation. Unlike the big, blowsy Darryl Zanucks, Milton was unobtrusive, a beatnik among peacocks in his black turtlenecks, black linen jackets, black jeans, and black sneakers. A native New Yorker, Milton managed to live an almost European existence. His Midtown studio, at 480 Lexington Avenue, was pure Fellini, where writers, actors, and makeup artists played, drank sherry, and put on lipstick. He partied with jazz musicians, not models, and at night Max Roach and Gene Krupa would "come to the studio and jam." He wasn't sleazy (an anomaly among fashion photographers), nor was he formulaic. He didn't fuss around with lighting ("If you can't light it with one light, you can't light it."). Instead of overshooting or bossing around the models, he'd switch off the phones and break out the sherry, taking time to select the perfect record for the person and occasion (for Marlene Dietrich, it was always Stravinsky).

For their first shoot, Milton stripped off all that Hollywood pancake and shellacked hair to reveal a new Marilyn. "I took off lots of makeup, because it was caked," he said. "I made it much smoother for a fresh-scrubbed look. She wasn't used to that; she was used to a lot of makeup. Fellini maybe did films where he used a *bit* of pancake or powder, but most actors were used to lots of makeup out of habit." They shot in Laurel Canyon, but she could have been an Ivory Soap Vassar girl in her Peter Pan collar, flower-flocked cotton and almost-pageboy hair. She looked bright and bookishly sexy, not like some dial-a-goddess from a cheesecake mag. Marilyn loved the photos and immediately sent him two dozen roses.

By the time they met for their second shoot, Marilyn and Milton had bonded like school chums. They set up shop on a Fox back lot, ransacked the wardrobe rooms, and found the burlap skirt and wooden clogs Jennifer Jones had worn in *The Song of Bernadette*. ("It was the ultimate in joke," Amy Greene would later say with a laugh, "to put the world's leading sex symbol in Saint Bernadette's clothes.") The French village from *What Price Glory* provided the perfect backdrop—they'd later refer to it as *The French Peasant Sitting*. In scratchy black convent stockings and heavy nun's shoes, Marilyn seemed lit from within, blonde Hollywood saint, gorgeous and tired and not unlike Bernadette herself. Like a Cinderella in reverse, Marilyn went from Van Cleef to sackcloth— with Milton as her fairy godmother.

Somehow, Milton had done what no other photographer had: tease out the deepest underpinnings of Marilyn's personality. His photos were playful, puckish, and poles apart from the glossy brutality of her Hollywood images. "I wish he could photograph me always," Marilyn gushed. "I've had my pictures taken a lot, but with Milton Greene, it gave me new hope and a new outlook. I've never really liked the way I was photographed until I saw Milton's pictures. He has a way . . . he's not just a photographer, he's an artist, really. Even when he does fashions which are usually boring, he can make something so beautiful."

She was equally impressed with Milton's work methods: "It

was the first time I didn't have to pose. He just let me think, but he always kept the camera going . . . I wasn't aware of it." He spoke in soothing murmurs, listening to his subjects and subtly adjusting to their needs. He radiated calm—even Judy Garland mellowed out around him. "Some photographers either went overboard with 'lovey . . . honey,'" wrote one of Marilyn's press agents years later. "Or they maintained an aloofness. Milton had a way of making a star feel very comfortable, very relaxed, and someone like Marilyn had to feel cared for, had to feel relaxed."

She also had to feel safe, which was hard in a town where batches of girls were hauled in by the busload. For years she'd kept mute, emptying ashtrays and pimping herself out at parties on Doheny Drive. Before it was the talent scouts, now it was producers, but there was always some man gawking, eyeing her up and down like a prized hock of ham. "They treat me like a thing," she confided to Milton. "I hate being treated like a thing."

Milton didn't treat her like a thing. In fact, when she'd strip to change looks he'd turn politely around. ("I was surprised when they told me that everyone used to ball her on the set," he said. "I didn't believe it. I still don't.") He respected her as an equal—they worked together not just as photographer and model but as collaborators. Milton thought more like a filmmaker or director. Each shoot had a story behind it, a dynamic narrative he made up as he went along. His dress-up-box attitude gave Marilyn a safe space to get creative and play. And play she did, pulling peasant blouses and clangy bangles from wardrobe rooms, costume shops, and sometimes her own closet. For one shoot: a loose taupe sweater thrown over a shimmery peach negligee—worn barefoot as she strummed a balalaika against a black velvet background strewn with poppies and ostrich plumes dyed white, plum, and green. For another: a fox fur wrap and fisherman's hat. Or another: tumbled into a friend's unmade bed, drinking a glassful of juice. *The Dutch*

Girl Sitting, The Pekingese Dog Sitting, The Gypsy in the Window Sitting: Each picture is infused with glowing vulnerability, a candor and gentle humor specific to a rare kind of friendship—the friendship between two artists.

That summer, Milton and Marilyn forged an alliance that would change their lives. They met intermittently in Fox's back lots, romping among fabric scraps and Hollywood frocks, speaking the same private language, communicating in electrical little gestures like twins. Both battled childhood wounds (and childhood stutters); both shrank from crowds yet longed for companionship; both were moody but laughed easily and smiled even more. Both were otherworldly—more absorbed in their imaginations than in the concrete moment. Friends of Milton's said that chatting with him was like looking at an abstract painting. He'd get you talking about Greta Garbo's hair or the color of snow in Russia only to steal off to his studio and write. Beguiled by Milton's artistry and flair, Marilyn knew she'd found a kindred spirit: "He's so sensitive and introspective," she raved. "I work with other photographers, but this man is a great artist."

Throughout her life, Marilyn would be drawn to two types of men: the creative, emotive types she befriended, and the resolute, dignified hunks she married. Milton Greene belonged to the former category. But with his alley-cat hipness and soft-coal eyes, Milton had his own subtle lure over women—and Marilyn's lines between friendship and romance were always fuzzy. They may not have been each other's type, but the sparks were mutual. "I think," Milton mused after Marilyn's death, "I had the feeling that we were going to make it. It's easy to say this now, but between exchanged looks and handshakes, there was a feeling that we were going to get together. It was just a feeling."

Milton's hunch was confirmed one midsummer photo shoot in 1953 on assignment for *Look*. First he rubbed her with body makeup, coaxing her vanilla-matte pallor into warm, wet honey. Marilyn posed naked under a borrowed black cardigan, gently parted to reveal an unzipped slice of silky bare skin. The sweater belonged to Amy Franco, Milton's Cuban-model fiancée, who was back in New York planning the perfect September wedding.

Still flushed from the intimacy of the afternoon's shoot, they dined at a quiet little bistro on Sunset with private rooms and candlelit tables. They talked about art, New York City, Marlene Dietrich—all their usual subjects—but this time the conversation was charged with urgency. Milton was flying back east that night, and Marilyn offered to drive him to LAX. "When I was ready to leave she gave me a kiss," Milton admitted. "And then she pulled back and gave me another kiss. Then I said, 'Wait a moment, now it's my turn,' and gave her a kiss and said, 'Gee, I don't really feel like leaving.' And she said—you know, the way she talks—'I really wish you wouldn't,' and I said, 'I wish I didn't have to either, but I'll be back.' I left, and I kept thinking of her on the way back to New York."

Two weeks later, Milton went back to LA on an unrelated assignment for *Look*. This time he spent every free moment with Marilyn, holed up in her duplex below the Sunset Strip, drinking scotch, listening to records, and lounging around in bed with her neurotic black cat. "I really got to know her, and that was different," he explained. "The feeling was different; the movement was different; we liked each other; I couldn't help it."

On Milton's last weekend in LA, they drove to Palm Springs, taking photos along the way. "We slept together in Palm Springs," he remembered, "then drove back to her house and went to bed again. Then we got dressed and went to a party. Everyone was there, including Frank Sinatra. Everyone heard Marilyn was taking singing lessons, and everyone wanted to hear her sing, so she sang a song from *River of No Return*. She was fantastic, because she was so sexy. She never sang like Judy Garland, she never turned it out like Frank Sinatra, but she had this voice like 'I wanna eat you. . . .' Her voice would go high, and then glow, and it was really sexy. It wasn't the greatest voice in the world, but it was sexy."

Sexy or not, Milton was due back in New York to marry Amy, who was already two months pregnant. Marilyn was devastated: "She was sad; she was very upset. I said, 'Look, we'll always be friends; we'll always love each other.'" Marilyn doubted that, but there wasn't much she could do. She wondered if she'd ever see her new friend again.

Milton had given her hope when she'd needed it most. She was closing in on that dreaded age: thirty. As an actress you went from kitten to crone, begging for fringe roles as lunatic spinsters and murderous aunts. Marilyn lost faith in Hollywood—but not in herself. All along she'd been smiling for the camera with Thomas Paine's *Rights of Man* hidden behind her script, lolling around pools in Beverly Hills, actually reading the books everyone thought were just dopey props. For years she'd kept *Leaves of Grass* on her night tables, dreaming of change. Like Whitman, she knew she contained multitudes.

❧ When she met Milton, in 1953, Marilyn was heavily involved with her boyfriend, Joe DiMaggio. For eighteen months he'd been courting her, visiting her on set, taking her for drinks at Villa Capri or Chinese at Bruce Wong's. He spent weekends sprawled out in her duplex, commandeering the TV until her gargantuan crystal ashtrays overflowed with Camel stubs. Their chemistry was fierce, buttressed by tenderness and respect. With his Old World manners and quiet devotion, Joe shielded her from the vulgarities of Hollywood—its ugly narcissism and cheap fame.

Marilyn knew Joe wanted to marry her, but something was holding her back. She worried they didn't have enough in common, didn't have enough to talk about. His silences bored her—and even frightened her. Addicted to television with no interest in art, Joe rarely cracked open the many books she kept giving him—Saint-Exupéry, Jules Verne. Ambivalent at best toward her acting career, Joe brushed off her creative struggles as Hollywood nonsense. "I don't know if I can take all your crazy publicity," Joe said to her early on in their courtship. Marilyn told him he didn't have to be part of it. "I am," he snapped back, "and it bothers me."

On August 8, 1953, Marilyn flew to Canada to film *River of No Return*. From the very beginning, she was out of her element. In addition to singing and playing guitar, Marilyn was forced to do her own stunts—horse riding, gunfights, and whitewater rafting. The director, Otto Preminger, bullied her, slapping her ass, teasing her as she struggled with the harrowing stuntwork. During an action-packed scene in the Athabasca River, Marilyn's raft tipped over, filling her boots with icy water. She sprained her leg, nearly drowned, and spent the rest of the summer in a cast and crutches. When DiMaggio heard of her accident, he flew to Canada immediately and kept watch over her for the rest of production. After the film wrapped, Joe whisked her away to San Francisco, where she met his mother, cooked pasta with his sister, and watched him fish for perch from the Fisherman's Wharf pier. Reluctant to race back to LA, Marilyn stayed on in San Francisco, a decision that pleased Joe endlessly. When she did return to Hollywood, Joe came with her, and they rented a home together on North Palm Drive.

On November 4, 1953, *How to Marry a Millionaire* premiered at the Wilshire Theatre in Beverly Hills. A hit with the critics and box office alike, the film earned $8 million worldwide—Fox's second-highest-grossing film of the year. More important, it cemented Marilyn's status as a gifted comedienne. Now, she hoped, Fox would finally give her the respect she deserved.

But Zanuck already had her next film picked out—*The Girl in Pink Tights*—another bimbo role with an idiotic storyline. When he sent her the script, Marilyn promptly returned it—with TRASH scrawled in marker on the title page. Zanuck reminded her that she was under contract and advised her to be a good girl and learn her lines.

With DiMaggio's support, Marilyn flatly refused to consider the script. On December 15, she failed to show up for her first day of filming. True to his word, Zanuck suspended Marilyn for having violated her contract. Jobless and directionless, Marilyn braced herself for another lonely holiday at the Beverly Hills Hotel.

On Christmas Day, Joe surprised her with a blazing fire and decorated tree, flank steaks and buckets of ice and Dom Pérignon. He flung a black mink round her shoulders and gave her a thirty-five-baguette eternity ring. This time when he asked her to marry him, she said yes.

꙰ In the spring of 1954, Marilyn warily renewed her contract with Fox. Her agent, Charlie Feldman, had negotiated a substantial salary spike and secured her the lead in Billy Wilder's exciting new comedy, *The Seven Year Itch*. But first she had to do one last musical: *There's No Business Like Show Business*. Marilyn winced at the thought of more lip-synching and shimmying, but she was under contract again and was forced to accept.

Within weeks, Marilyn was seriously regretting her choice to return to Fox. Once more, it was working her like a dog—fifteen hours a day, seven days a week, on another throwaway musical Zanuck thought would make him rich. She'd wake at dawn, stuff herself into sequins and plastic paste flowers, and prance around in huge hoops and high-plumed headgear like some deranged cockatiel. She flubbed her way through campy dances under the Fox

lot's Technicolor glare, sweating under the hot klieg lights, dripping body makeup. Inwardly she seethed at Feldman for having
pushed her into accepting Zanuck's terms.

Joe wasn't much help. He'd gone from supportive to outright
surly, spending his evenings glued to TV Westerns or out all night
at poker games. He made no effort with her Hollywood crowd—
glowering in the dark when she brought back friends, hissing to
himself about "that bunch of phonies." When he did deign to visit
the *Show Business* set, Joe seemed to prefer the jaunty vigor of Ethel
Merman to Marilyn's exasperating drama. Off set she was spotted wandering down Sunset Boulevard, wrapped in minks in
ninety-degree heat, weeping softly. Five months in, their marriage
was foundering. She thought he'd never tire of taking care of her—
all those midnight flights and financial advice and pretending to
like her attempts at cooking lasagna. Here was a man who'd fly
across the country when she'd twisted her foot yet wouldn't talk
to her at dinner.

Twenty-four hours after wrapping up *Show Business,* Marilyn
flew to New York to begin *The Seven Year Itch.* She begged Joe to
explore the city with her: the Met, the jazz spots, even Central
Park. Joe blew her off and spent his days at Toots Shor's gabbing
with friends about the 1952 pennant races. By now, the cracks in
their marriage were obvious. The hacks hovered, ready to pounce,
steno pads poised for the next slammed door, the next dressing
room shouting match.

The final blow came at two in the morning on September 15.
A crowd of 4,000 had gathered at Lexington and 52nd to watch
Marilyn Monroe's skirt blow up. The vanilla halter, electric fans,
flashing cameras, and screaming men made for a frenzied publicity stunt, and an explosive scene between Marilyn and Joe. With
each whoosh of the subway DiMaggio's blood boiled hotter. Smirky
gossip hound Walter Winchell poked him in the ribs and said,

"What're you gonna do about it, Joe?" Fuming, Joe stormed off to get drunk at Toots Shor's. He caught the earliest flight to San Francisco, and Marilyn returned to LA alone.

Distraught, she sought advice from "Old Jane" Russell. Must she give up her own identity in marriage? How did she manage an acting career along with a husband and children? Jane advised her to leave studio worries at work and concentrate on Joe when she was at home. But Marilyn couldn't switch off like that nor would she want to. Even if she did, she would have had to numb out with Nembutals and Sinatra records to clear her head. Marilyn was beginning to see irreconcilable differences—not just between herself and Joe but between family and career.

Some actresses mean it when they say they want to focus on family, that all they want to do now is cook, nurse babies, and change nappies. Marilyn didn't. She meant that she was deeply invested in her relationship, and that she wanted to make her husband happy. For Joe—and for most mid-century American men—that wasn't enough. As one studio insider predicted, "If it's ever a question with Marilyn of marriage or career, the marriage may go."

The marriage did go. On October 22, 1954, dressed in a LeMaire suit of black gabardine and a strand of Mikimoto pearls from Emperor Hirohito, a puffy-eyed Marilyn stood on the steps of Santa Monica Municipal Court and announced her split from the Yankee Clipper.

⁊ Marilyn's career had already been teetering, and now divorce flung her into the media hailstorm. Dogged by photographers, hounded by journalists, and emotionally shattered by the breakup of the century, Marilyn needed another champion.

Days after the breakup, Marilyn got a phone call from Milton

Greene. He was back in town with Amy; would she meet them at a party at Gene Kelly's? Marilyn paused. The last thing she needed was another trade party, all the puffed-up banter and inside gibes. Charades was an institution at Gene's, and the very thought paralyzed her. Sensing her hesitations, Milton offered a solution: He'd take her to dinner first, then they'd slink into the party late and undetected. (He'd never got the hang of charades, either—the game was too literal for them both.)

Charades was in full swing by the time they arrived. Amy waved Marilyn over and greeted her warmly. Makeup-free, camel coat thrown over a black Capezio leotard, hair still wet from her bath, Marilyn was hardly the siren Amy had expected: "I've never seen anyone so bedraggled. She looked like a wet chicken."

Marilyn shrank into a corner with Milton. After nearly a year apart, they clicked right back into high gear, heads bent together in catlike conspiracy. This bright-kerchiefed boy and shy little chicken were planning something big.

꙳ With her professional and personal life in upheaval, Marilyn needed a plan. She'd been battling Fox for more than a year and still didn't have the one thing she wanted: creative control. Even a powerhouse such as Feldman couldn't deliver her that. He managed to squeeze more money from Fox, but failed to grasp Marilyn's ultimate goal. Milton understood the importance of script, director, and cinematographer approval. Why not strike out on her own, he suggested, move to New York and start her own production company? It was a concept they'd been bouncing around for months. Now those vague conversations took a serious turn. Within days, Marilyn moved into the Voltaire Apartments on Sunset Boulevard, where she and Milton smoked and snacked and schemed about their secret coup. "The idea was to create an independent production company for Marilyn so that she could break out of her typecasting and make films that she wanted to make," recalled Amy, who was part of the plan from the start. "She loved it. She preened. She said, 'I'm gonna be the head?!'"

From the very beginning, part of the appeal was New York itself. "Los Angeles is without the cultural and intellectual ferment which is to be found in any other large city in the world," wrote Marilyn's friend Maurice Zolotow, who hated LA as much as she did and claimed that the city's major cultural achievements were "the square-block supermarket, the one level and multi-level ranch house, the backyard barbeque, laundromats, and drive-in hamburger joints." (Marilyn did like the drive-in hamburger joints.) LA's chlorinated grottoes and fake Florentine fountains were all she knew.

So far, her trips to New York had been disappointingly flat: overnight rides on the 20th Century Limited, huddled in her bunk reading *Swann's Way* while she was supposed to be learning the script for *Love Happy.* Toothbrush, powders, and lipsticks crammed into her cheap plastic travel case, blouses and bras stuffed in the trunk of white rawhide she'd bought on credit to look luxe and city-chic. For years she'd glimpsed Manhattan in frustrating little fragments. Now it was about to become her home.

Milton sprang into action immediately. "The plan was to speak to the lawyers," he explained decades later, "find out what was what, create a new deal and fight Fox." He mailed Marilyn's contract to his lawyer, Frank Delaney, who denounced it as a "slave labor agreement." Even better, Delaney spotted a few loopholes that might give them an out. Milton was thrilled, but Marilyn still fretted over possible consequences. "Eventually, they're gonna give in," he assured her. "That's how it works."

Within days, Marilyn's Hollywood team was replaced by a crew of New Yorkers. Frank Delaney signed on as her lawyer. Superagent Charlie Feldman was jettisoned in favor of Milton's friend Jay Kanter. As for housing, she would stay with the Greenes in their Connecticut country home, beyond the reach of Zanuck's henchmen. Milton would take care of everything; she could leave all the business dealings to him. Milton's lack of experience didn't seem to bother her. He had boundless enthusiasm, impeccable taste, and a quiet, street-smart confidence in his creativity and wit. "She was lost and alone," he said. "Who's she gonna trust—not Zanuck, not Charlie Feldman, not DiMaggio. She had no one she could trust except me. Because I'm gonna give her a straight answer. I'm not gonna fuck around." He believed in Marilyn: "She wasn't dumb—she was intelligent, and she had a good head. I always thought she was quick. There were times when something was way over my head, I just couldn't believe it, and she'd come up with a suggestion or make a remark about something and I thought, 'Well shit, why didn't I think of that?'"

In late November Milton resigned from his position at *Look* and committed to Marilyn exclusively. Both had faith in their art, and were ready to risk it all to realize their vision. "All any of us have," Marilyn reflected months later, "is what we carry with us, the satisfaction we get from doing what we're doing and the way we're doing it." She trusted Milton and his talents entirely. "I didn't have much experience," Milton admitted later, "but if I had to do it all over again, I don't think I could do better."

❧ By December the whole town was buzzing with rumors of these enfants terribles and their haphazard plan. Friends called frantically, desperate to talk some sense into Marilyn, begging her not to risk her future on an inexperienced kid. How could she be so impulsive, so reckless? But Marilyn didn't leave impulsively. Her LA friends didn't realize she'd been planning her escape for years.

In her personal life she flitted about capriciously—she was notoriously myopic in matters of the heart. But when it came to her career—the thing that mattered most—Marilyn never lost sight of the larger picture. *Pink Tights* and *There's No Business Like Show Business* weren't the first jobs that bored her. Instead of diva tantrums and tears, she rebelled on the stealth, stashing Lincoln Steffens' books in her red Gucci bag, hidden under peanut brittle and plastic curlers. She quietly made choices that advanced and empowered her, such as firing her drama coach and signing on with Michael Chekhov. He affirmed what she had always intuitively sensed—the value of looking inward. Rather than battle her "weaknesses," Chekhov showed her how to work with her gifts. Under his guidance, Marilyn channeled her own intelligence rather than acting like a trained monkey. "You can do anything," Chekhov told her. "Don't let them trap you into what they want."

As much as she wanted to bolt, Marilyn was savvy enough to wait for her moment. *The Seven Year Itch* wrapped that fall, and she sensed it was going to be big. This would be the fourteenth film she'd cranked out for Fox, and if she had it her way, the last.

Zanuck and his cronies were oblivious. For years Marilyn had been playing the ditz, churning out money, all the while burning her dumb blonde effigy in secret.

$\wp$ Knowing she'd be free from the pressures of Hollywood, Marilyn relaxed into her final weeks in LA. An atmosphere of unusual warmth and merriment lit up the city. Sammy Davis Jr. was back at Ciro's after the car wreck that nearly blinded him, and everyone was out toasting him at the Mocambo and the Crescendo, wearing jeweled eye patches in support, brandishing highballs like pirates. For the first time in years, Marilyn let loose, carousing the clubs with Sammy D. and his crew. You'd find her draped on a striped banquette feeding petits fours to Tony Curtis, or on the floor with Milton petting someone's bichon frise, a rhinestone barrette clipped to its fur. At parties they hung on each other like two teenage beatniks—Milton in Roman black and Marilyn in those dark slip dresses she wore all the time. "The two of them were just giggly," a friend remembers. "It was almost like a sister and brother between them. I don't know if there was a romance there."

On her last day in LA, Marilyn threw open two Louis Vuitton trunks and gathered the scraps of her life that still mattered to her: a framed picture of Abraham Lincoln, a triptych of Eleonora Duse, a Vassarette bra, The Sonnets of Edna St. Vincent Millay. Dirt to diamonds, LA was all Marilyn had ever known, dating from the orphanage that looked out over RKO. From her window she could see Mount Lee, with HOLLYWOOD spelled in those boxy wooden letters. Her bleached-out childhood was California through and through—all smudge pots and shantytowns, shacks of tin clapboard and chain-linked yards littered with crosses of white plastic. Backyard preachers kicked up fire and brimstone under sad little orange groves. They terrified her—the doomsayers and soothsayers with their larders full of wheatgrass, their aversion to Tylenol and long conversations about God and what it really meant to eat grapes as a Christian Scientist.

Still, there was something raw and lovely about Los Angeles—the lights twinkling over Catalina Island, West Hollywood's scent of overripe flower pulp, amphetamine, and exhaust fuel. Departures crash into you with spiky intensity, throwing daily mundanities into high relief. Suddenly the ding of an elevator, the glint of a teaspoon on a room service tray, or the last snack you buy at your favorite bodega moves you to tears and you're flung into nostalgia for a place you haven't left yet and didn't even think you could miss.

What was she thinking on that last day, when she snapped shut her trunks, hailed a taxi, and rode down Sunset Strip for the last time? There was the Villa Nova, all stained glass windows and hacienda wood beams, where she'd met Joe DiMaggio for their first date. There was the Polo Lounge, where you could order a palm reading along with your Tom Collins, and the Garden of Allah, where she'd languished waiting for Joe Schenck or Sydney Chaplin to buy her a drink. And of course, there was Schwab's, where she'd suck down pills and iced coffee with Sidney Skolsky, gawking at "the real beautiful call girls," the air thick with nicotine, watered-down ice cream, and perfume.

"It must have taken great courage to quit Hollywood as you did, to give up all the luxury, the money, the importance—after being so very poor," said Elsa Maxwell, who spoke to her months later.

"No," she said softly. "No, Elsa, it didn't take any courage at all. To have stayed took more courage than I had."

The Fugitive

"Recently somebody asked me, 'What are you
trying to do in New York? What do you honestly
want to be?' I told them, 'I want to be an artist.'"

MARILYN MONROE

*T*he Greenes lived in a hilltop country house in the idyllic town
of Weston, Connecticut. The house had been built around an
eighteenth-century stable, with towering ceilings and airy walls and
a massive log fireplace flanked by custom-made sofas. Milton had
remodeled it, putting French glass where the barn doors had been,
adding on darkrooms and studios with culkwood floors. There were
sixteen rooms, including a plant-filled conservatory connected to
a huge Colonial kitchen rigged with modern appliances. The guest

room had been revamped and freshly painted just for Marilyn. "We did the guest room over for her," Amy Greene told *Photoplay*. "It's in purple, pink and white. The curtains and dust ruffles are crisp white organdy. The wallpaper is lavender with a small purple figure and the rug just matches the purple. There's a pink quilted bedspread and dark purple velvet throw pillows. The chest is an old one with a white marble top and I put pink china lamps on it. It's a simple and sort of old fashioned room, but it is as dainty as she is and suits her exactly. Marilyn loves it."

Eleven acres. Vegetable gardens. Stretches of wild woodland like something out of a fairy tale or the old Russian books she loved. In lower Connecticut, forty miles from New York, this was as close to nature as she'd ever been. She took daily walks in the woods, bundling up in Milton's coats and stomping through the snow with the terriers like a little Grushenka or Lara. Her first snow—she loved the sounds of the snow crunching under her boots. She'd never seen a tree without leaves—or even changing seasons. "I remember one day we were driving home from a friend's house," Amy remarked. "Marilyn looked up at the hillside and remarked that the trees were just dead, bare sticks. Then, the next week, they began to turn green. To her, it seemed like a miracle."

That magical winter when her focus turned inward, Marilyn woke up when she wanted to, wandering from her bed to a balcony that overlooked birchwoods and mountains. She lived in her white bathrobe and spent hours soaking in bubble baths—soapy blonde hair piled on her head, skin pink and rosy as a Boucher cherub. "You look like a strawberry soda," Amy observed to Marilyn's delight.

Surprisingly, Marilyn adjusted immediately to the rhythms of family life. Amy—half-expecting prima donna antics—was delighted with her houseguest: "She made her own bed, kept her room tidy, brought down her clothes on wash day. If she slept late, she would make her own breakfast, rinse off the dishes and put them in the dishwasher. Neither our maid nor I had to wait on her."

The Greenes' cook, Kitty Owens, liked Marilyn immediately, detecting no diva or starlet tendencies. Each evening she'd pop into the kitchen ready to peel potatoes or snap string beans ("Is this the right size?"). They'd chat about men, and Marilyn confessed her crush on Abraham Lincoln. "He was such a great guy," she'd sigh as if he'd taken her on a date to the Clambake Club. "When I see a man like that, I would love to just sit on his lap."

With no immediate projects, Marilyn could enjoy Kitty's home cooking without worrying about gaining half an ounce. After years of raw egg concoctions and lone liver chops broiled in hotel kitch-enettes, Marilyn ate with relish. She preferred savory to sweet and loved vegetables—stewed tomatoes, stewed corn, string beans, red cabbage with apples, and winter squash. On cold nights she'd warm up with hot bowls of chili or her favorite late-night snack—eggs scrambled with anchovies and capers. Kitty kept plenty of spinach on hand for Marilyn's iron-rich diet. Once she found her tiptoe on the counter scraping spinach off the ceiling ("Kitty, I had a little accident. . . ."). She'd opened the pressure cooker too soon.

The Greene household took Marilyn's bizarre habits in stride. Each morning Kitty's husband Clyde would haul a bag of ice up-stairs and pour it in a basin. Marilyn would stand on it: "It will make my legs firm!"

Milton worried that she'd get restless, so he took her for long drives on his German motorcycle or sometimes drove her into Man-hattan for ritzy nights on the town. She even saw Joe again. "I re-member the first time the telephone rang in Connecticut and it was DiMaggio inviting us to dinner that night," remembered Amy. "I went gaga. We went to the old El Morocco. I sat there and talked baseball with Joe and he was ecstatic. Marilyn never had any interest in all that. He held my hand in his—it was like putting your hand in a giant muff. It was a wonderful evening."

For the most part, Marilyn was quite happy to stay at home. Trimming the Christmas tree, roasting carrots with Kitty, morning jogs with Amy—these rituals were new to her and delightful. She adored the Greenes' baby, Joshua, always offering to feed him or give him his nightly bath, wrap him in one of her terrycloth robes, and surround him with a nest of pillows. She lavished him with gifts including a pajama bag called Ethel and a huge stuffed teddy bear named Socko. "If the rest of us are busy," Amy Greene told *Photoplay,* "she's always down on the floor playing with him." For the first time Marilyn had stability—and more important, time.

Meanwhile, the press still reeled from her shattered marriage. Headlines such as I'LL ALWAYS BE ALONE and DON'T BLAME YOUR-SELF, MARILYN popped up, including an open letter to the newly divorced actress. Threatened by her choices, they turned the tables and hinted of "a nameless fear that has ruled her all her life." The exploding popularity of psychoanalysis led to trendy diagnoses and renewed interest in Marilyn's troubled past. The stain of divorce had knocked back their goddess to her dirty roots. Suddenly Marilyn was back to being an orphan—one with "no real worth of her own," a "frightened, lonely, and thoroughly insecure young woman." They riffed on tired clichés—poor little glamour girl, alone for the holidays.

While the press spun hackneyed tales of a cheerless Christmas season, Marilyn met a new set of creative personalities. The Greenes kept open house on the weekends, filling their rooms with Josh and Nedda Logan, Mike Todd, literary agent Audrey Wood, Leonard Bernstein, and Richard Rodgers. Initially Marilyn shrank from it all, the piano sing-alongs and theater gossip. She'd hide for hours in the bath before padding downstairs in slacks and a sweater, curling into a chair with a vague smile on her bare face. Sometimes she'd linger on the lower stairwell, swinging her legs over the slate blue carpet, baby Josh holding a tumbler of bourbon to her mouth. Some nights she wouldn't emerge at all: "Do you mind if I don't come out tonight?" she'd whisper to Amy through the bathroom door.

"At a party she never sat in a corner playing regal and expecting guests to come to her," wrote Amy Greene. "More likely, I'd find her emptying ash trays or picking up glasses. A lot of people in show business and advertising and publishing live up here and she was just one of us. And she knows how to listen, that girl. To women as well as to men. It didn't take the girls long to see that Marilyn wasn't after anyone's husband. She just simply fit into our crowd and everyone loved her."

Amy was quick to dismiss the sly jabs at Marilyn's temptress reputation: "They must have thought Marilyn was a combination of Theda Bara and Mata Hari—the vamp and the threat. Many times people would say to me, 'Oh, how can you have her in your house, in your life, blah?' I trusted her completely. As a woman, I trusted her. I was secure in my marriage and I was secure with her."

Watching America's favorite pin-up queen lounge around her house in a robe triggered no insecurity in Amy: "It was the other way around—I intimidated her. She said to me once, 'You intimidate me.' I said that's good—everyone should be afraid of somebody." She had yet to realize that Marilyn was afraid of everyone.

Many feel the opposite when they say "I'm a very secure person," but Amy was telling the truth. At twenty-five, she was already startlingly confident, with the crisp tone and assured mannerisms of someone much older. It helped that Amy was just as gorgeous, albeit in a sleeker, darker way. She was five feet and ninety-five pounds with a pert little nose and a dusting of tawny freckles

that made her look about fifteen. She barely wore any makeup—
Marilyn had to teach her how to apply eyeliner. What's more, Amy
inhabited the rarefied world Marilyn could only dream of. She'd
grown up on the Upper West Side; she'd posed for Richard Avedon;
she'd been to convent school; she knew Anne Klein and fit into
sample sizes; and she'd been suckled by a Cuban witch as a baby.

"You're so lucky to have a man like Milton love you and marry
you," Marilyn remarked with a wistful little look. "I know," Amy
shot back, "but he's also lucky to have me." Marilyn giggled. She'd
never heard a woman say *that* before.

With Milton working in the city, Marilyn and Amy spent afternoons antiquing or driving to Westport for coffee and eclairs at
the Daily Corner, a café owned by Milton's sister Heny. "She liked
to drive," Amy recalled. "We'd take the convertible and go sailing
along the highway with the top down. We both liked to feel the
wind on our faces and the warmth of the heater on our legs."

Amy wasn't just "putting up" with Marilyn—she liked her. "We'd
discuss everything from clothes to housekeeping to babies to
headlines. Sometimes we'd giggle like a couple of school kids.
Others, we'd come up with some sure-fire formula for saving
the world. You know the way women do. . . . I thought it was just
great that she could come to visit us. It would be nice to have a
girl around the house. I grew up in boarding schools, and although
we have lots of friends, there's just so much distance and we're all
so busy that I don't get much chance to sit down to talk with other
women." The feeling was mutual. Marilyn had few close girlfriends in the Hollywood years—it was all backbiting starlets in
the Beverly Hills Hotel.

In her starch-white collars and convent-chic ponytails, Amy was
the type of woman inevitably described as "together" or "polished"—
quite the opposite of Marilyn's slippery straps and misplaced bras.

But she admired Amy's self-possession and even acquired some of it during her winter sabbatical. "She was so impressed with anyone who is efficient," wrote Jane Russell, another friend who managed to balance glamour with practicality. Well-meaning friends would give Marilyn address books and desk calendars, but she'd use them as journals and scrap paper, jotting down little poems or ideas for a script. Important phone numbers and contacts were often scrawled on a crumpled Kleenex and tossed into the back of her car along with girdles, old plane boarding passes, unmatched shoes, and traffic tickets.

Left to her own devices Marilyn was sloppy in epic proportions. But under Amy's roof she was "neat, clean, and no problem whatsoever." Amy enjoyed taking charge of Marilyn, immediately addressing practical issues such as wardrobe. Like most other native Californians, Marilyn had no real winter clothes. "My friend, Annie Klein, who was a wonderful dress designer, had a 'magic' closet in her office on Seventh Avenue where she put all the fabrics that buyers were afraid to buy, too avant-garde or whatever, and there were only three people allowed in that closet. Annie one, me two, and a model that she had, called Reggie. It was Christmastime when Marilyn came to us, and I said, 'Listen, I have a friend and she's an actress—I never told Annie who it was—and I need some clothes because she has no fashion sense and I have to dress her up.' And Annie said, 'Come and get what you want.' So I went to the offices, and I took about eight outfits, had them send to Connecticut. It went under the Christmas tree. And Christmas morning, she opened it up, and she was aghast. No one had ever done this for her before, ever. No one."

"On Christmas Eve I took her into New York," Milton remembered. "She saw all the stores, all the Christmas trees, all the lights. It was her first Christmas here. We started at Lord & Taylor, then worked our way up Fifth Avenue. It was very touching—she was like a little girl. She wore a coat and scarf, no makeup. She looked wonderful."

On Christmas morning, Marilyn shuffled downstairs in furry winter slippers, wrapped in a baggy crewneck and a pair of Milton's pants. Boxes, ribbons, and shiny paper were strewn under a bauble-laden tree. The phone rang off the hook with calls from LA—Frank Sinatra, Sidney Skolsky, Billy Wilder, and Bob Hope. Amy answered with feigned innocence while Marilyn and Milton giggled in the background. "Tell me, Mr. Hope," she inquired coolly, "is Marilyn lost?" She hung up the phone and joined Marilyn on the floor, rolling and hooting with laughter.

The phone was still ringing when Milton formalized Marilyn Monroe Productions on New Year's Eve 1954. It was official: Marilyn was in hiding.

༃ After Milton Greene, Amy was Marilyn's strongest supporter. Not only had Milton quit his steady job at *Look*—he had mortgaged his house and maxed out his credit to support Marilyn and their new production company. With a wife and a one-year-old son, this was the gamble of a lifetime, and Amy never batted an eye. MMP was their future, and she was ready to do whatever she could to help.

Her first order of business was giving Marilyn a makeover. Milton had long been exasperated with Marilyn's wardrobe, which ricocheted from skintight to slovenly with little in between. "That looks like a schmatta," he'd moan whenever she'd show him a dress. He begged her to stop passing out in her makeup and cajoled her into using the gold-plated hairbrush Sinatra had given her on her birthday. "Instead of being a slob," he ordered, "act like a woman."

"Look," he insisted. "You have something that looks fantastic on screen, but you walk around like a slob. You want to be a great actress and you already are, but you have to carry yourself a certain way. Look at Katharine Hepburn—she has a certain style or class. You need a certain something, something other than cheap blonde sexpot. Now let's go out and buy some clothes."

So he drove her into Manhattan, hitting up Bergdorf's, Bonwit Teller, and Saks. "She bought a dress at Bergdorf's with a sheer panel that looked great. But then she'd never really wear it. She'd just go back to the old clothes she was used to—slacks cut too short that never really fit, blouses that never really had the right lines."

Frustrated by wasting money on unworn clothes, Milton enlisted Amy's help. A former model—who tucked her pearls into her neckline years before Jackie would—Amy was the ideal style mentor. Typical fashionista, she started with shoes: "I was the one who got her out of those dreadful shoes she always wore—round in front, closed in back, with a two-inch gap on the instep. Every star at Twentieth Century Fox wore those. I got her fifty pairs of Italian shoes at Dalco. Identical closed pump with a high spiked heel, maybe three-and-a-half inches long. I paid twenty bucks a pair for them, and she wore them for the rest of her life."

Clothes were a little more complicated. The paltry trunk Marilyn had taken to New York failed to impress Amy—jeans from J.C. Penney and the Army surplus shop, puffed-sleeved dresses with babyish yokes, skintight sweaters thrown in with beige Don Loper suits and the bugle-beaded Cecil Chapman dress she'd worn onstage in Korea. To the sophisticated East Coast Amy, these clothes were nothing short of pitiful, though she soon realized why—Marilyn had barely updated her wardrobe since her starlet days. "Whenever she needed something to go out, she'd go to her friend in the wardrobe department at Twentieth. She'd borrow something, and then the next morning she'd bring it back with a $50 bill slipped in." It would have been cheaper to buy her own dresses—but Marilyn didn't plan that far ahead, and she knew she'd probably lose them anyway.

Amy thought it best to start with the basics. "I wanted to buy her cashmere sweaters, so I took her to a shop called the Separates Shop that my friend Bootsy Moffat ran in Westport. And she very quietly said, 'Bring me one in 34, 36, and 38.' Thirty-eight for a soft shapeless sweater, 36 for dinner parties, and 34 for national television. I said, 'Christ, just take the 38.' The tight sweaters—she always called those her 'work clothes.' I thought it was all nonsense."

Marilyn had been dressing like this for years—squeezing into too-tight sizes, stitching marbles into her bra. "She'd try dresses on in size twelve, and if she liked it she'd buy it in a size ten," wrote Shelley Winters, who went shopping with her in Hollywood. Shelley went hoarse begging Marilyn to buy the size that fit, but she'd always protest with "I'm bloated" or "I just drank three Cokes."

Now here in Westport, Connecticut, Marilyn was up to her old tricks. "She would look at me out of the corner of her eye and say, 'What don't you like about it?' And I'd say, 'Well the ass is too tight, or the skirt is too short.' She'd take my advice but with a grain of salt, and only up to a certain point. Then the 'work clothes' would come out again."

"You're already a star," Amy would plead. "You can wear anything you want. You don't have to show your ass; you don't have to show your tits." But Marilyn felt alienated by "respectable" high fashion, which tended to favor trim nymphs like Amy. She knew she'd never be "classy" or "elegant." She knew she'd never be in *Vogue*. At the same time, she had zero interest in following trends—she was almost too beautiful to be a fashion icon. With mid-century trendsetters like Diana Vreeland, Wallis Simpson, Babe Paley, or even Jackie Kennedy in the early years, you always noticed the clothes before the woman. Marilyn knew instinctively how to flip that around. A dress, however beautiful, would always just be a flattering frame. It was her face, her body, her hair and skin that were on show. That's why she always favored neutrals—even her tartiest frocks were in black, creamy whites, or camel with touches of bronze. Likewise, jewelry was just another distraction. "I don't own even a little diamond the size of a pinhead," she boasted to *Modern Screen*. In a time when short chokers were practically mandatory, Marilyn left her neck bare. The foundations for a classic style were already there. Amy just had to tease them out.

With her usual directness, Amy went straight to the source: the designers themselves. She invited George Nardiello and Norman Norell for dinner, and together they created Marilyn's new wardrobe from scratch.

By the time he met Marilyn Monroe, Norman Norell had become one of the country's top designers, equal to Cassini, Dior, and Balenciaga. His shapes were sexy but understated—shirtwaists, mermaid dresses, high-necked sheaths, and nautical flourishes— worlds away from the painted-on lamé and plunging cleavage Marilyn was used to. At first Norell was appalled by her trampy taste. "She wanted everything to look like a slip," he said. "Everything had to be skintight; you had to reinforce every seam or everything would break."

But he bonded with Marilyn over a mutual interest: theater. Back in the thirties, he'd dressed Gertrude Lawrence and Ilka Chase. "He would tell her about all the clothes and they'd discuss theater," said Amy. "Norell and Marilyn spent hours together— they adored each other." George Nardiello also loved dressing Marilyn: "She looked even more gorgeous without any makeup on, sitting around in this beat-up terrycloth bathrobe. I used to make her pancakes with caviar and sour cream."

Every Sunday they'd meet by the Greenes' roaring fire and work with Marilyn on her signature look. First they addressed figure problems, which Marilyn didn't mind discussing openly. "She had a very long back and a very long waist," remarked Amy, "which is interesting because she didn't have a neck to speak of. But her thighs were lovely; she had really long tapering thighs. Norell once said to me, 'She really has a wonderful body, but she doesn't belong in this century.' And he's right—she's totally a turn-of-the-century-type woman." But Marilyn needed a modern wardrobe: tight but still classy, washable, packable, and neutral enough to allow for spontaneity.

The result was a capsule collection of black sheaths and slips, sexy but simple and perfectly in tune with Marilyn's aesthetics. Each dress was skintight, just the way she liked it, but in Norell's "slipper satin" sober black mattes they looked refreshingly natural—more curvy selkie than wanton bombshell. She liked them so much she had copies made, supplementing the couture originals with cheaper versions sewn by Seventh Avenue dressmakers. She loved the ease of a uniform, and though she'd mix in capris and skirts snagged from Anne Klein, she spent the next few months living in identical black slips.

Marilyn may have needed Amy's fashion expertise, but with makeup she was pure maven. She'd been perfecting her beauty routine since her starving-model days—shampooing and setting her own hair, bleaching it with peroxide paste, disguising her botched nose job with layers of gray contour. She watched backstage stylists and tweaked what she'd learned, going rogue against the trends of the day. Instead of powdering her face to a faddish matte, she coated her cheekbones with Vaseline, lanolin, and olive oil. She approached makeup with the technical skill of an artist—it made sense that the director she loved best was a painter. The

way Marilyn highlighted her eyes had more in common with da
Vinci's *Madonna of the Rocks* than with shadow tutorials in
Vogue.

That winter Marilyn and Amy whiled away the hours giving
each other makeovers. Cross-legged on the floor, they rummaged
through Marilyn's leatherette beauty kits—lipsticks by Max
Factor, bobby pins, mini–squeeze bottles of Helena Rubinstein
lash glue, white highlighter sticks, Liz Arden shadows in Autumn
Smoke and Pearly Blue, Revlon nail polish in Hot Coral and
Cherries à la Mode, and bristly brow brushes in robin-egg blue.
Under the ambery glow of her portable beauty lamp, Marilyn
lined Amy's eyes with umber pencils and separated her lashes
with tiny gold lash combs. As she worked on Amy, Marilyn refined her own look.

Away from iron-lacquered Hollywood, Marilyn cultivated a
natural style. Lipstick went from Russian Red to pale pink. Con-
toured cheeks gave way to soft peachy blush and light flicks of mascara that let her natural beauty shine. She blonded her hair even
paler, but gave it gravitas with plain black turtlenecks. She paired
Amy's effortless chic with *Wuthering Heights* meets Jean Harlow
hair. Marilyn was confident, and she glowed.

While the fashion team worked on beauty and wardrobe, Milton took charge of media image. His barn studio flooded with natural light that matched Marilyn's relaxed, off-duty bloom. She found
freedom in the winter-lit barn; she didn't have to be sexy or aloof
for the camera. Unguarded, she let her emotions shine through
and illuminate her. What emerged was a playful, vulnerable sensuality that was much more compelling than diamonds and cheesecake. He shot her invisibly naked under Amy's loose pullover, red
rayon fabric stretched over her knees; or feigning slumber in a tennis sweater, palms pressed together like a child's. She posed

between two sawhorses in a pinstriped button-up, hands clasped behind her neck.

Sometimes they worked in his Manhattan studio, a nineteenth-century office building surrounded by Condé Nast offices and swank hotels. A friend once described Milton's studio as "a cat burglar's dream," with its balconies, twenty-foot crenellated ceilings, and floor-length windows that swung open over bustling Midtown streets. More like Rome than New York, 480 Lex was a space full of Old World romance, where you could sip cocktails on the balcony or host long, Italian-peasant-style lunches. (Milton did both.) He'd pasted the walls with his photos from *Vogue* and *Look,* stuffed trunks with costume props full of old magic— the perfect environment for creating with Marilyn.

Their first photoshoot at 480 Lex—*The Ballerina Sitting*— occurred by happy accident. Marilyn was struggling with the zipper of an organza dress—one of the too-tight Anne Kleins Amy had given her. Inspired, Milton perched her on a wicker stool between horizontal rods that looked like dancers' bars. Clutching the gauzy bodice to her milky skin, Marilyn looked like a sleepy ballerina.

This was Marilyn and Milton at their collaborative best— impromptu offhand glamour, cheeky but sweet. Barefoot and unzipped, Marilyn embodied the rough sensuality of offstage ballet: pink ribbons and leather, tights, old leotards and dusty practice rooms. Her naked feet look slightly swollen, her rolled shoulders suggest tired, touchable flesh. The zipper marks on her exposed back are red, raw, and provocative. In a time when women were groomed to perfection, this was sexy, undone, and completely modern.

Milton and Marilyn were ahead of their time, and they knew it. How soon would it take the world to catch up?

❧ With Milton and Amy by her side, Marilyn revamped her public image. After dinner they'd sit round the fire with tumblers of scotch, planning their first press conference. What would she wear? Whom should they invite? And then there was the business side, with all its technicalities. "Almost every evening there were meetings with attorneys," wrote Amy. "Marilyn had a good understanding of the business, but I wouldn't know. I'd just get out of the room."

Milton did the real dirty work—fielding calls from lawyers and agents, keeping furious Fox moguls at bay. Marilyn often stayed behind whenever he drove into town, answering the phone from the bath when he'd call to consult on publicity offers or delinquent traffic tickets. There were telephones scattered all over the house— Milton liked to roam as he talked, dragging fifteen-yard cords behind him. Marilyn loved doing business from the tub. Charlie Feldman called daily, making halfhearted threats. Journalists, columnists, and trade tattlers demanded to know—where was Marilyn, what was she doing? Where was their gorgeous fugitive, and when were they getting her back?

For now, she preferred to stay in the snowy country. Cut loose from the confines of Fox and Hollywood, Marilyn's mind was free to roam, and roam it did. She plunged into the Greenes' extensive library, starting with a list from Michael Chekhov then quickly moving on to her own preferences. She read voraciously— especially biographies—Josephine Bonaparte, Lady Emma Hamilton, Marie Antoinette, and Eleonora Duse—bold women who invented themselves, seized control of their image; women whose personalities defined the age they lived in and glittered out from the past.

"She was fascinated," said Amy, "by women who had made it." Sometimes Amy found her sitting on the stairs, gazing at a portrait of Lady Hamilton, a coal miner's daughter who launched herself into the highest echelon of eighteenth-century society. Then she discovered Josephine and scooped up every book she could find about her, chattering at dinner about the empress and her friends. She regaled them with stories about Juliette Récamier, a brainy beauty who commissioned a nude statue of herself. When Juliette's breasts began to age she smashed the girlish marble ones—controlling her image just like Marilyn.

"She was like a child about stories," Amy recalled. "She said nobody had told her stories in her childhood, so when anybody told her a story, she was hooked." One day Marilyn was preparing for a drive, wrapping a long white scarf around her neck. Amy noticed and made a joke about the dancer Isadora Duncan, strangled to death by her own silky scarf. "Who's Isadora Duncan?" Marilyn asked, already enthralled. "It was," Amy would note with a laugh years later, "Isadora Duncan Week in Connecticut."

Like Marilyn's first role model Eleonora Duse, whose framed picture she kept by her bedside, she had little formal education and read compulsively to make up for it. "Books were her Harvard," claimed Amy, who sensed the depth behind Marilyn's girlish enthusiasm. The Greenes marveled at her peculiar tastes and realized that their pinup girl was really an Old Soul. She zeroed in on their records of Bach, Mozart, and Shostakovich, and pored over their books on Renaissance art. "The feelings she had about old, old paintings," mused Milton, "Michelangelo, Rubens, Van Dyck—that period. Not Monet, Renoir, Cézanne, or Picasso. It was the old ones she liked. I have a print downstairs she gave me of a head that looks like it came from the Michelangelo period. She bought it at an auction. There are certain old things that she heard about and liked, and she went after them personally." For years she'd been honing her curatorial instincts, and this was the moment she'd been waiting for: the gift of quiet and time.

In New York, Marilyn became a compulsive writer, a habit she retained for the duration of her life. She loved classic composition books and always had several going at once, their black-and-white marbled covers scattered throughout the Greenes' house. Many ended up near the bathtub.

From the snowy cocoon of the Greenes' country home, Marilyn cultivated her image—and herself. At night the Greenes heard her pacing upstairs, switching on the radio, opening books and then slamming them shut. She stayed up late, her mind active and churning until she drifted to sleep in the wintry-pink Connecticut morning.

December rolled into January, and Hollywood still had no idea where Marilyn was hiding. Twenty-nine days after her midnight flight, she was ready to emerge. It had taken Fox a month to realize their star was actually gone.

Three

Blonde on (Subdued) Blonde

"I'm for the individual as opposed to the corporation. The way it is, the individual is the underdog, and with all the things a corporation has going for them an individual comes out banged on the head. The artist is nothing. It's really tragic."
MARILYN MONROE

*O*n the evening of January 7, Marilyn's attorney, Frank Delaney, flung open his doors on East 64th Street to flocks of photographers. Tonight, Marilyn would unveil herself to the public and announce the formation of Marilyn Monroe Productions. As usual, she was late. Reporters and cameramen blocked the sidewalk. Inside the press had been humming since five, sipping cocktails with Marlene Dietrich and Tony Curtis, checking their watches and craning their necks for a glimpse of the "new Monroe."

It was 7 p.m. before Marilyn blew in like some skittish snowflake. She wore a tight white sheath with loose spaghetti straps, white satin slingbacks, white stockings (Milton had to run out to a nurse-uniform store), a fluffy white ermine, and diamond chandelier earrings on loan from Van Cleef & Arpels.

Flanked by Delaney and Greene, Marilyn sat down for the press. "I have formed my own corporation so I can play the kinds of roles I want," she declared. "I'm tired of sex roles. People have scope, you know. . . . And I have a dream of sometime playing in Dostoyevsky's *The Brothers Karamazov*."

Then came personal questions and their obligatory responses: "We are very good friends, Joe and I. We always will be. . . ." Some pert journalist shouted about Marilyn's being under contract with Fox, but Delaney shot back that she was "a free agent."

By midnight a crowd still milled around the door, with Milton trying to round up Amy and Marilyn. "Sinatra was playing at the Copa," remembers Amy Greene. "I had a crush on him, and I really wanted to go. But I knew there was no way anyone could get in. As we were getting in the limo to go home, Marilyn said, 'Do you really want to go to the Copa?' I said, 'Yes.' She said, 'Follow me.'"

Marilyn—who felt like a nuisance most of the time—loved when she could actually be helpful. She led them through a clattery kitchen (the Copacabana's VIP entrance) into a smoky room where Sinatra was playing to a full house. Sinatra, annoyed at being interrupted mid-song, stopped the orchestra—only to look up and see his friend Marilyn swathed in white mink like some polar angel. "It was like a scene out of a movie," Amy recalls. "A table and three chairs materialized down front, right under Sinatra's nose.

We sat down and Marilyn said, 'Is there any other problem you'd like me to take care of?'"

After the show, Sinatra invited the group to his dressing room. "It seemed to me most of the audience decided to go along," remembered Amy, who panicked at the thought of being crushed by a stampede. "The passageway wasn't built for mass movement. At the steps there was a terrible jam." Marilyn happily took charge, pushing her friend toward a bouncer and instructing her to wrap her arms around his thick neck. The bouncer carried Amy to safety as she swung from his neck like a pendant. "It was the most amazing thing. In all that pushing and shoving Marilyn kept on smiling and talking to people. She wasn't scared a bit. When we're in a crowd, it was me she worried about." Meanwhile, Milton fought back the stragglers and handled Marilyn.

After a late-night dinner with Sinatra at the 21 Club, they piled into the limo for a nightcap at Marlene Dietrich's on Park Avenue. It was well past three by the time Marilyn stumbled in, lightly drunk, Guerlain lipstick in Rouge Diabolique smudged on her ermine collar. Dietrich found the red smudge "maddeningly erotic" and fell asleep dreaming of this tipsy, kittenish creature—whose fluffy white fur and platinum whiskers reminded her of Jean Harlow.

The sun was rising by the time they staggered back to 480 Lex. Still wired, Marilyn asked Amy for a Seconal. (She'd given her stash to Amy and told her to act as warden.) She'd earned her right to a sound sleep—they all had.

Neither Marilyn nor Milton realized how badly it had gone. The Jean Harlow ensemble had been a miscalculation—blinding the reporters with platinum curves. To make matters worse, Marilyn had reverted to glib frippery when bombarded by the press. But who wouldn't when asked questions of such hostile inanity?

PRESS: "Marilyn, we heard there's something new about you? What is it?"

MARILYN: "Well, my hair is new. I used to be platinum, but I dyed it. Now I'm a subdued platinum."

PRESS: "Do you want to play the Brothers Karamazov?"

MARILYN: "I don't want to play the brothers. I want to play Grushenka. She's a girl."

One of the friendlier skeptics was Billy Wilder, who loved her warmth but considered her more a calendar girl with perfect comedic timing. "I say they're trying to elevate her to a level she can't aspire to," he said. "Mae West knew where she stood—but somebody talked Monroe into thinking that she's much better, and that she has so much to give to so many people. A human being has to know his limitations. She should know her speed limit, and not attempt 180 when she can only do 60. It's like herring à la mode," he added. "You put the chocolate ice cream on the herring and the herring ain't gonna taste good, and you'll spoil the ice cream too."

Even Elsa Maxwell sensed that Marilyn was holding back: "She reminds me, so often, of the girl who stays on and on in the powder room, fluffing her dress, combing her hair and repairing her makeup—to postpone the moment she must join the party and sink or swim." Elsa was also thrown off by Marilyn's outfit, and puzzled over her choice of tight white satin. "'Why,' I wondered irritably, 'don't the Milton Greenes, who are her good friends—with Milton being a fine fashion photographer—help with the clothes?' Then I forgot she was dressed all wrong, because—curiously enough—she wasn't vulgar in this costume. She was more like a little girl, in spite of her twenty-eight years, who was trying to appear sophisticated and grown-up. She reminds me of a fawn, without really looking like one. She radiates health and vitality. And I find something wistful in her eyes and remember her years as an orphan when she was boarded out with different families and many times treated as a little slave."

"You're a fool to be photographed with Monroe," one Fox mogul warned Elsa after that disastrous first press conference. "You keep writing about her in your newspaper column too! You don't seem to get the idea that she's on the way out. A year off the screen and she'll be washed up! We can find a dozen like her!"

Elsa laughed in his face. "You'll never find a dozen like her! You may find a dozen beautiful hunks of photoplasm topped off with blonde hair. But they won't be Marilyn Monroes. Wait and see—you'll be glad to have Marilyn back on her own terms."

☙ When the Sunday papers arrived, Marilyn was humiliated. "Miss Monroe has a firm contract with us," Fox stated, "and we have her exclusive services until August 8, 1958." Headlines such as DIFFERENT? PRETTY MUCH THE SAME . . . were typical. "Marilyn Monroe is a stupid girl and is being fed some stupid advice," sneered the *Hollywood Reporter*. Even worse, if she dares to take on "long hair, art theaterish" roles such as Grushenka, "some of her attractiveness will have been lost."

As usual, Milton and Marilyn had overestimated the intelligence of their audience. She was always a little too smart for the press, who were too busy mocking her to ever really hear her. They had no idea who Grushenka was—if they'd actually read *The Brothers Karamazov,* if the book had any meaning to them other than a reference point for something brainy and Russian, they'd have known that Marilyn was perfect for the role. Instead of being taken seriously, she was dismissed—again—as a sugary joke. (Years later, she'd blame the press for ruining her chances to play Grushenka—a role she'd always been drawn to.)

From the moment of her late arrival, the press had been poised to punish her—ready to record her next blonde blunder. Still ditsy, still late, she was the "same old Marilyn," a bimbo with delusions of grandeur. How dare this bratty bleached-out starlet leave Hollywood—and couldn't Fox crush her as fast as they had raised her? The press didn't get it yet. Blinded by their own jabber and squawk, they missed the magic. Like a butterfly sealed in its silk-tapered swaddle, Marilyn was still priming herself, cocooned in her tight white satin. New York was waiting.

* * After the press conference came more shaky starts. She was offered the lead in *Guys and Dolls,* but issues with Fox made it impossible to accept. She was out of work, out of money, and entirely dependent on Milton's cash handouts. Doubt and insecurity gnawed at her. Maybe the *Hollywood Reporter* was right—maybe she was a silly starlet.

Meanwhile, Milton had begun to realize just how much he'd taken on—phones ringing off the hook, piles of telegrams, offers from columnists and magazines he'd never even heard of. The floodgates had opened, and the press was bombarding him with questions: What were their plans? Had Fox really fired Marilyn? Milton was a photographer, not a publicist, and now he was at the center of a media hurricane.

He quickly hired a press agent, two handlers, and a secretary—all of whom cost much more than they could afford. MMP was still waiting for funding, and Fox was threatening lawsuits, scaring away potential investors. Their only hope was Henry Rosenfeld—millionaire dressmaker and "Dior of the Bronx." Henry and Marilyn had an ongoing flirtation; he'd send her love letters and cash presents. Milton begged Marilyn to dash to Rosenfeld's Boston home and work her magic. But the thought of sashaying around, luring him for money made her queasy. It was a relapse back to those Hollywood days she had fought so hard to escape.

Her faith in Milton momentarily slipping, Marilyn turned to Joe, who was still her confidant and would be for the next six months. Joe was always there, and she still trusted him, with his wary protectiveness, sound financial advice, and his "steel magnate" suits of gray flannel. He insisted on escorting Marilyn to Boston. Joe liked Milton but didn't trust him with business. Who knew what this Rosenfeld guy would try to pull over them both?

Joe drove Marilyn to Boston himself, stopping on the way to meet his brother Dominic for dinner. Soon the small Wellesley restaurant was mobbed with reporters. One reporter fought his way to their backroom table. "Is this a reconciliation," he asked, shoving a microphone in Joe's face. Joe turned to Marilyn: "Is it, honey?" Marilyn shot him down coolly. "No, let's just call it a visit." So Joe blocked out his hurt and focused on his current task—carrying minks, trunks, and red leather Gucci bags, shielding her from flashing cameras and nosy reporters.

The next morning Marilyn met with Rosenfeld, clad in his classic red tie and worn suit of navy blue. As charmed as he was by Marilyn, he refused to sponsor MMP. (He would, however, give Marilyn checks, love letters, the odd diamond bracelet, and free reign over his factory shop in the Bronx, which she merrily raided with friends, hauling back armfuls of dresses and suits.) Joe drove Marilyn back to New York under clouds of doubt. She'd uprooted her whole life and taken enormous risks, only to degrade herself Hollywood style—flaunting her curves and batting her eyes for wealthy men.

Despite this setback, Marilyn remained positive, energetic, and determined. Never once did she doubt her decision to team up with Milton Greene, and she was in no mood to come crawling back to Fox and Co. Two days after returning from her failed Boston trip, Marilyn rejected another flimsy script with a bold pink telegram addressed to Darryl Zanuck: "AM EXCEEDINGLY SORRY BUT I DO NOT LIKE IT. SINCERELY, MARILYN MONROE."

Besides, money was the last thing on her mind. She'd moved East to learn, explore, and dive deep into New York's world of art and theater. For Marilyn, theater was the ultimate challenge. Actors she admired, such as Marlon Brando and Eli Wallach, slipped gracefully between screen and stage, toughening up and expanding in the process. Last September while wrapping up *The Seven Year Itch,* she'd managed to catch a performance of *The Teahouse of the August Moon.* Backstage she met Wallach, whom she immediately christened Teacake.

"After that night's performance," wrote Wallach, "a press agent had ushered her into my dressing room—I remember that she looked nothing like the movie star I'd seen on screen—she wore a simple dress and had short blond hair. She was pale, shy, and wore no lipstick. The first thing she said to me was 'How do you do a whole play?' Though she was by now perhaps the world's most famous movie star, she had never appeared in a play, and she seemed both awed and curious about it. I had the impression that she might not have ever seen a stage production. After we'd talked for a while, she asked if she could come see the show again and watch from backstage. I told her I was afraid that the management wouldn't allow it, so she said she'd watch from the balcony, which she did many times after our meeting."

Emboldened, Marilyn dropped in on more plays, at times wandering backstage by herself. There she met and impressed another Method actor, Ben Gazzara: "The time she came backstage, she wore no makeup, her hair was windblown, she was girlish and very pretty, and she was ecstatic about what she'd seen." Marilyn found herself relaxing around these actors, smoking out the window of their dressing rooms, the chilly city air mixing with the carnation-y scent of stage makeup. She could see herself thriving in a group like this—where women had roles as expansive as men did and joined them at Sardi's over tumblers of Chianti.

It's not hard to imagine why stage acting appealed to her. The mid-fifties were still Broadway's golden age, when theater was closer to high art than was film. More important, stage actors enjoyed a real creative freedom—a freedom that eluded her during all her years in Hollywood. "Movie actors are held stiffly to position," explained director Josh Logan, who worked in theater as well as film. "Much, much more than in plays, you're prescribed by the limitations of the camera—if you move sideways, you'll get out of the frame, or your arm will be cut off. You have to be constantly thinking, 'Am I on my mark; am I in my frame?'" Marilyn watched these plays with growing interest. Cut loose from the rigor of budgets and call times, she knew that she could reach unimagined heights as an actress. Who knew how much she could accomplish, how much she could do?

Meanwhile, Milton was working hard. Keeping track of Marilyn was a full-time job—constant appointments, dress fittings, and platinum touch-ups. There were always bills to be paid, prescriptions to be filled, letters to be answered. Evenings were spent gliding around on her arm at movie premieres and late-night parties. On top of all that, Milton was still maintaining his photography business—sole provider for himself, his family, Marilyn, and MMP.

"We always had a plan of attack," Amy pointed out. "I'd mention a play and say, 'When do you want to see it,' and she'd say,

'Well, let's do it next Wednesday or Thursday.' I had a very scheduled regime for her. I would make her go to the theater at least
once a week; I would take her to movies at least once a week; I
would take her to the right parties at least once a week."

Throughout her life, Marilyn would attract people who believed
in her—busy people with packed lives of their own who still supported her past the point of exhaustion—but no one as much as
Milton Greene. Milton usually slept three hours a night if he was
lucky. He could stay up all night working or at the Copa, but he
always woke at the crack of dawn. If he and Amy had crashed at
the studio, he'd wake her up and send her to the Kanters' with a
coat thrown over her pajamas. Jay—who was also responsible for
Marilyn—would already be shaving in the bathroom, and Amy
would crawl into bed with Judy for a few more hours of sleep.

"At that point when we went to parties and theater and stayed
over, we slept in the studio," said Amy. "He had this wonderful
big studio—but she couldn't sleep there because there was only
one bed. I said to Milton, 'We have to get her a pied-à-terre in New
York. She's a young woman with two old married people and she
needs a life.'" Lured by its hot meals, helpful staff, and proximity
to Milton's studio (and Elizabeth Arden's Red Door Spa), Marilyn
settled on the Gladstone Hotel.

On the morning of January 19, Joe DiMaggio was spotted hauling stacks of Louis Vuitton trunks down East 52nd Street through
the Gladstone's revolving glass doors. Gloria Swanson had lived
there in the twenties, but now there were bats, creaky hallways, and
small, stuffy apartments—hardly the epitome of chic. Marilyn's
suite was dark and poky, crammed with shabby Victorian furniture.
But she had her own parlor and kitchenette stocked with gin,
bourbon, and sherry. Carl Sandburg's bio of Abraham Lincoln was
displayed proudly on the coffee table. (Marilyn would often treat

a book as a centerpiece, more weighty and worthy than a Tiffany vase.)

Photographers camped outside the revolving doors, snapping her pulling on a pair of gloves or chatting on the pay phone in the gloomy little lobby. They caught her in glimpses—slinking out in her winter mink, Garbo hat hiding half her face as if she weren't quite ready to be seen. For now, Marilyn wanted to protect her fuzzy, fledging life—so downy and vulnerable and wonderfully different from the pageantry of Sunset Boulevard. She loved huddling round the fire sipping sherry with Milton or ducking past the cameras for a late-night walk in Central Park.

Marilyn was much more generous with her teenage fans, who skipped school to wait hours outside the Gladstone, shivering with their Kodak Brownie cameras. To give them a little thrill, she'd whirl through the door, twirling runway style and blowing a kiss.

Sometimes Joe could be seen striding through the Gladstone lobby. They may have been separated, but DiMaggio was still the man Marilyn trusted the most. Marilyn continued to join Joe on day trips to Boston, dinners out with Dominic, and drinks at the Sherry-Netherland hotel. It was not uncommon to see Joe pulling up by the Gladstone in his blue Cadillac, with Marilyn flying out the lobby door, paparazzi ready to pounce. "What's next, Marilyn?" "Are you back on with Joe, Marilyn?" It was all on such shaky ground—Marilyn had no answers, not even for herself. Neither did Joe. He could only hope, as he sped off like a fugitive chased by the flashing pack.

❧ Now that Marilyn had finally emerged, she needed a private driver, leg waxes at Elizabeth Arden, bleaching at Enrico Caruso's, and chaperones to bring her to meetings or shows. At this point, most of her wardrobe was still stashed in Connecticut, and Milton would frantically drive back and forth from Weston, slips, minks, opera gloves, and handbags strewn in the backseat.

Marilyn still clung to Milton in those wintry early months, slipping a gloved hand through the crook of his arm as he guided her through the Astor or the Elmo. She had a few old friends in New York that winter, mostly the Rat Pack, who were friends of Milton's, too. There was Milton Berle, a lover turned friend from her chorus-girl days. Back then she was just another blonde cutlet, but Berle sensed that "there was nothing cheap about her. She wasn't one of those starlets around town that you put one meal into then throw in the sack. . . . She had respect for herself. Marilyn was a lady."

Jerry Lewis and Dean Martin were also in town doing their weekly show at the Copa. "Both Jerry and Dean are always yelling and falling all over the place when they see me," Marilyn said with a giggle, "and I love them for it. Other people have criticized me for the way I dress and the way I walk, but Dean and Jerry never do." So was Sammy Davis Jr., another affectionate prankster who treated her with that brotherly mix of teasing protectiveness. Back in LA there'd been a rumor she and Sammy had slept together, a rumor they both found hilarious. To the Rat Pack guys she was just Marilyn—no starlet and certainly no piece of studio meat.

Supportive as they were, these friendships paled in comparison to Marilyn's devotion to Milton Greene. Their creative collaboration showed no signs of slowing down. That winter they spent nearly every day together bustling around his Lexington studio, rooting through magazine stacks and clothing racks, hatching up plans for quirky new photo shoots. Tables heaped with screenshots, ashtrays, old copies of *Look,* and black Bakelite telephones that never stopped ringing. Sinatra would be playing on the phonograph;

Sammy Davis Jr. would stop by for a drink. You might catch them pasting tissue-thin flowers to a white paper background, or with their heads bent together at the worktable, discussing their plans to collaborate on a book. He'd crouch on the floor, straightening the seams of her stockings, fiddling with his Nikon, and humming along to a bebop record, while she'd vamp around in rosary beads or played with a litter of Pekingese puppies. With every click of the camera, Marilyn's confidence swelled. "There was a kind of magic between them, something that you could tell was clicking," wrote Jay Kanter. "It was fun to watch."

Those months, it was always Marilyn and Milton and Milton and Marilyn. Winter snapshots reveal a catalog of intimacy—nestled together at the Astor or sprawled out on the floor of 480 Lex pouring nightcaps after a movie premiere. They finished each other's sentences, drank from the same glass like twins. Norman Mailer described their relationship as haunted by "some wistful longing of the past," and if Marilyn ever fell in love at first sight, it was surely with Milton. Whether clipping rhinestone barrettes to celebrity dogs or collapsing in giggles over proposals from Prince Rainier, their bond went far deeper than shiny urban frolics. "The two of them knew a secret," observed Amy. "When they planned and schemed they would be on the sofa and I would be in a chair next to them and they went right off into their own world that only the two of them understood."

That winter, she and Amy planned a surprise party for Milton's thirty-third birthday. Marilyn and Jay Kanter called a three o'clock meeting at the Gladstone, while Amy filled the studio with drinks, guests, and decorations. ("Keep him out till six thirty," Amy instructed.) "We had a hard time with Milton," Jay remembered later. "We transacted all the business in a couple hours, but we had to keep him another hour. So Marilyn would say, 'Oh, that reminds me of something else I've been wanting to take up.' We'd dispose of that in a few minutes and Milton would say, 'I've got to be going.' Then I'd say, 'Oh, here's something else to worry about.'"

They kept Milton busy until six forty-five, then walked him to the studio, where everyone burst out "Surprise!" Marilyn beamed, watching Milton's face light up with joy. "Marilyn was wondrously happy," said Amy, "for she felt she had put it over—and she had. It's the first time she ever had a surprise party for anyone."

The loves of our lives aren't always our lovers, and Marilyn's great romance never ended in marriage. Joe DiMaggio and Arthur Miller loved Marilyn, but Milton understood her. For Marilyn, who said she felt like "a fish out of water," being understood was everything. Milton was the closest she came to those elusive words "soul mate"—a concept she believed in until the day she died.

By this point, Marilyn had been dodging the press for months. But journalist George Carpozi Jr. coaxed her into an interview by suggesting a walk in Central Park—he'd read that she loved long walks in the woods. He arrived at the Gladstone with photographer George Miller in the late afternoon of January 27. Miller bullied Marilyn as if he were some major director— ordering her to touch her toes, get on her back and cycle in the air, drop to the floor and do ten push-ups. Emboldened by bourbon, he asked her to switch out her tennis sweater for a camisole.

MILLER: "Now, Marilyn, can you drop the strap please?"

MARILYN (*uneasy whisper*): "I don't think the strap will come down. . . ."

MILLER: "Aw, come on, Marilyn, you can make it fall. Give it another shake."

It was as if she were back at Fox—forced to shimmy like a stripper till the strap inched down her shoulder.

Sensing that Marilyn needed to be rescued, Carpozi stepped

in: Why don't they take that walk in Central Park? He'd parked his Buick outside. Marilyn changed into a black slip ("Do I need a coat?") and threw a bowler hat over her messy hair. She grabbed her mink and Carpozi's hand.

Central Park was pitch black. Wind snarled through the leafless trees, whipping Marilyn's bare, stilettoed legs. She smiled broadly, heedless of the frigid air. This was her new home, New York in its glittering darkness. Freed from the strain of his sleazy photographer, Carpozi tried once more to open Marilyn up. This time she didn't dodge him with batted lashes or jokes. She took his arm and began, "I was born Norma Jean Mortensen in Los Angeles County General . . ."

❧ Carpozi was shocked by Marilyn's optimism. How could she seem so happy? She'd left Hollywood for a chilly, ramshackle suite swarming with rats, paparazzi, and greasy teens. Bad press, lawsuit threats, and Darryl Zanuck still breathing down her neck. With MMP teetering and no investors in sight, her situation was tenuous—even her clothes were still in LA. She had no money, no relationship, no future—at least not one she could see. But she had her freedom, she had Milton, and for now that was all that mattered.

One late January morning, Marilyn emerged from the Gladstone arm in arm with Milton and George Nardiello. A dark-eyed fourteen-year-old named Peter Mangone shivered by the door, fiddling with a Revere movie camera he'd borrowed from his brother. Marilyn turned on her heel to blow Peter a kiss, and Milton gamely allowed the boy to follow. Perhaps Peter reminded him of his younger self—a shy kid from the Bronx, skipping school to stake out his favorite star.

For the next few hours, Peter followed the trio as they sauntered down Fifth Avenue, making stops at Elizabeth Arden and I. Miller & Sons. Sometimes she'd pause to adjust her fur collar or to whisper and giggle into Milton's ear. Sometimes she'd gaze skyward and yawn, lashes lowered like a cat's. The late-morning light cast a lo-fi haze. She looked like a blonde peach.

Marilyn looked particularly beautiful in those first months of 1955, her tousled locks skimming her chocolate collar, her skin iridescent against the city's gray matte. She cut a stark hourglass figure in fitted black cashmere—and for once her figure looked elegant, not exaggerated. Cars screeched to a halt on the curb. Somewhere on 54th Street a Checker cab crashed into the back of a delivery truck, its dazed driver grinning out the window: "Marilyn!!!"

She squeezed Milton's arm tighter, smiling in the frosty air. They marched at a merry clip—Lexington Avenue still glittered with ice, but a giddy thaw hung in the air. Winter was halfway over, and all it took was one balmy gust to unleash spring's woozy levity. They might end up bankrupt and disgraced, but spring was coming, and it looked bubbly and blonde and dizzy with promise. Like a bottle of champagne straight from the freezer—the one you were saving for Sunday but open on Tuesday. Because you no longer feel worried and woolen—just clear, smooth, and synthetic as a Lucite bauble. Because of the creamy camellias in the Liz Arden window. Because you're going to share the bottle with your best friend—the one who makes you curious as a teenager, and you want that high to last all night, all week. You want it to last forever.

Were they foolish? Many were impressed by their boldness, but few actually believed in them. "I don't think Milton really knew how powerful these men were," said their friend Jess Rand. "You could win the battle, but you never won the war."

Four

Liquor, Literati,
Lee Strasberg

"When she came to New York she began to
perceive the possibilities of really accomplishing
her dream."   LEE STRASBERG

*T*hat winter, an unlikely friendship provided Marilyn with a
welcome distraction. Novelist Carson McCullers had been
holed up at the Gladstone for months, surviving on coffee, liquor, and cigarettes. At thirty-seven, Carson was eighty-five
pounds, half paralyzed, and addicted to alcohol and "pinkies"
(pills). Her husband had committed suicide the year before, and
she herself had spent time in the Payne Whitney Psychiatric

Clinic, where Marilyn would endure her own harrowing ordeal six years later.

Like Marilyn, Carson was dreamily feckless and struggled with practical things such as cooking and laundry—basically born for hotel living with its housekeeping, hors d'oeuvres, and room service. It was freezing that winter, and the two of them often sat in the lobby warming up over double shots of whiskey or cognac. Carson was never without her signature drink—the Sonny Boy, a Thermos of tea and sherry—with a flask of whiskey sloshing around in her purse just in case. On the party circuit she was known as an adorable show-off. She'd brandish her cane, outdrink everyone, then flounce home to drink more—leaving New York's literati staggering off to sleep.

Through Carson, Marilyn met other prominent writers such as Tennessee Williams and Truman Capote. By the time he met Marilyn, Truman was mascot of the ladies-who-lunch set, whispering over shrimp salad at the Plaza Hotel. Babe Paley, Gloria Guinness, and C.Z. Guest flocked to him despite his backwoods pedigree. But Marilyn was no WASP-y swan—like Truman, she'd been abandoned by both parents, passed between relatives and foster homes. She was as lovely as Gloria and Babe but irreverent, passionate, and a true artist.

Marilyn and Truman both loathed LA and quickly bonded over their love of Manhattan. They'd stroll down Third Avenue, peering into antique stores, examining garnet rings and grandfather clocks. On a whim they once popped in a palm reader's shop, then fled at the sight of a beaky lady knitting baby-booties. He'd take her to the Oak Room for drinks and discuss his new project: *Breakfast at Tiffany's*. Or they'd go to the Waldorf but never P.J. Clarke's—Dorothy Kilgallen was always in there, as Marilyn put it, "getting bombed."

Of course, Truman loved Marilyn—her Good Humor giggle,

her "dairy-fresh" skin set off by those black slips that were quickly becoming her New York uniform. Both were talkers, charmers, champagne bunnies, and secret workaholics. Truman—a self-declared "horizontal writer"—shared Marilyn's deceptively louche habits. He'd spend days supine, martini in hand, pounding his Corona typewriter like a drunk Little Lord Fauntleroy. He understood Marilyn's messy perfectionism: unanswered telephones, tubes of Russian Red lipstick collecting lint in her purse. When you love your work so much, it spills into your life and makes you lose track of pills, appointments, lovers, and friends.

Unlike Marilyn, Truman gossiped—which married producer kept secret girlfriends and quite possibly boyfriends, too. The rumors often involved his "friends" or even Marilyn herself. Babe Paley was convinced that her husband—William S. Paley of CBS News—was sleeping with Marilyn. "She's awfully jealous of you," Truman baited with glee, leaning over their table of crab legs and daiquiris.

But Marilyn wasn't interested in mean-spirited banter. She'd rather dig deep into individual personalities—especially Elizabeth Taylor's. ("But what is she reeeally like," she'd press.) She'd wave her hand to hush Truman when he tried to switch back to the sordid bits. "If you can't say something nice about someone, don't say anything all," she'd chime, with all the sweet sincerity in the world. (Capote would go on to pen a portrait of Marilyn that was druggy, vulgar, blowsy, and inane. Years later he'd boast that his snapshot was the best celebrity piece he ever did. Was he aware that he—like Arthur Miller, Darryl Zanuck, and so many other men to come—was selling her out?)

Through Truman, Marilyn met her first New York drama coach, the renowned Shakespearean actress Constance Collier. Born in 1878, she made her stage debut at three as Peaseblossom in

A *Midsummer Night's Dream*. She'd started out as a Gaiety Girl before moving on to dramatic theater. By the 1930s she was living in New York, throwing lesbian lunches, holding court like a Parisian salonnière, telling tales of her engagement to Sir Herbert Beerbohm Tree, or nights carousing with Oscar Wilde. Everything about Miss Collier—from her wicked humor to her witchy black wraps and velveteen toques—seemed steeped in Edwardian London, as if she'd stepped off the Apollo stage and right onto Madison Avenue.

For the past two decades, Miss Collier had been coaching Vivien Leigh, Greta Garbo, and both Hepburns. Marilyn would never resemble the Katharines and the Audreys, with their finespun cheekbones and aristocratic chins, their respectable measurements and invisible cleavage, the ones who cast an admiring hush at award ceremonies, graciously accepting their Oscars in mellow tones. They were never breathless or overexcited, never needed colonics to squeeze into their dresses, were never side-eyed by Zsa Zsa Gabor or slut-shamed by Joan Crawford. (Nor did they inspire Jerry Lewis to crawl onstage at the Redbook Film Awards, baying like a teenage monkey.) With her pancake face and sugar lisp, Marilyn couldn't play patrician if she tried. Her soft-serve figure was too ripe to glide into English riding jodhpurs. She'd look better snapped in a polyester frock pouring coffee at Howard Johnson's or draped in showgirl boas handing out poker chips at the Lido. Could Miss Collier accept a starlet into her rarified fold?

"She had seen none of Marilyn's movies," wrote Truman, who loved to push together polar opposites, then watch them combust or fall in love. "She really knew nothing about her except that she was some sort of platinum sex-explosion who had achieved global notoriety; in short, she seemed hardly suitable clay for Miss Collier's stern classical shaping. But I thought they might make a stimulating combination."

This time Truman got it right—it was love at first sight. Perhaps it was her music hall past, but Constance adored Marilyn immediately. (According to Amy Greene, she once tried to seduce Marilyn at a dance.) She fawned over her, called her "my special problem," and compared her talent to a fluttering butterfly. Marilyn's technical training was irrelevant to her—what mattered was that "flickering intelligence . . . like a hummingbird in flight." At nearly eighty, Miss Collier's eyesight was weak, and all she could see of Marilyn was her fuzzy blonde halo—a blur of bright butter glittering in the gloom.

For her part, Marilyn loved Miss Collier, just as she loved all "tough old grannies." Even her murky parlor—oil rich and dark as the Tintoretto paintings she adored. Between lessons at Miss Collier's and nightcaps with Carson in the Gladstone lobby, Marilyn found solace in Victorian gloom, a welcome tonic to Hollywood's saccharine flash.

They worked on Ophelia—Constance thought she was made for the role: "I was talking to Greta last week, and I told her about Marilyn's Ophelia, and Greta said yes, she could believe that because she had seen two of her films, very bad and vulgar stuff, but nevertheless she had glimpsed Marilyn's possibilities. Actually, Greta has an amusing idea. You know that she wants to make a film of Dorian Gray? With her playing Dorian, of course. Well, she said she would like to have Marilyn opposite her as one of the girls Dorian seduces and destroys. Greta!"

Marilyn longed to meet Collier's celebrated femmes, especially Katharine Hepburn. "I'd love to just call her up," she confessed to Capote. But she was insecure—she was still just a movie star, not a real actress, not yet. In a matter of days, this would change.

❧ On February 1, Carson McCullers took Marilyn to a dinner party hosted by Paul Bigelow. A self-dubbed "professional catalyst,"

Bigelow was known for making things happen, and could be a powerful ally for Marilyn if he liked her. Theater producer Cheryl Crawford would also be attending, another potential advocate and a close friend of Carson's. Thin-lipped and flinty, Cheryl was Broadway's hard-tack captain. She'd done *Porgy and Bess, Brigadoon,* and Tennessee Williams's *Rose Tattoo.* Most importantly, Cheryl was a founder of the Actors Studio, the prestigious workshop based on the teachings of Konstantin Stanislavski. Shelley Winters, Marlon Brando, and Maureen Stapleton were all members, and Marilyn hoped to join them.

Still skittish around such high-powered figures, she begged Milton to meet her for moral support. After her recent spate of bad publicity, Marilyn was wary of how she came off and was sensitive to any slight or snark. Broadway often looked down on Hollywood types, especially comedy blondes with kitschy-vamp walks. How would Cheryl—in her masculine ascots, close-cropped hair, and sensible shoes—respond to a starlet like her? Worse yet, Cheryl was a close friend of Charlie Feldman's, the agent Marilyn had split with in December. Marilyn wanted to bail on the party, but Carson McCullers bucked her up with double whiskeys by the fire. Liquor-warmed and bundled up, they set off for Paul's home on East 54th, a skinny brownstone crammed between the Elmo and a prosthetic-limb shop.

As luck would have it, Marilyn was seated opposite Cheryl Crawford, who immediately started questioning her about her dealings with Feldman. When Milton piped up in Marilyn's defense, Cheryl lashed back, calling him "evil and just no good."

With Milton stunned into silence, Marilyn was forced to speak for herself: Feldman hadn't fought hard enough for the creative input she needed and was miffed when she wasn't satisfied with less. As a woman who'd clawed her way up in a field ruled by men, Cheryl could sympathize.

Somehow, the unthinkable had happened—Marilyn had melted the implacable Cheryl Crawford. After dinner, the two women huddled up in a happy chat about acting. Cheryl vowed to advance Marilyn's career. They made a date for the following day. Cheryl would take Marilyn to observe her first session at Lee Strasberg's Actors Studio.

At nine thirty-five the next morning, Cheryl met Marilyn at the Gladstone Hotel. They took a crosstown cab to West 46th—Cheryl in tailored wool, Marilyn in her mink, sunglasses, and black scarf—and slipped in through the back entrance. Marilyn lowered her dark glasses in awe—it was as if she had stepped into an unfinished cathedral. Perched attentively on rickety-crammed chairs, this group looked more French Resistance than Chateau Marmont. There was Marlon Brando in his tight-rolled white tee and loafers, Jack Lord in a dark pullover and fluffy pompadour, Kim Stanley and Anne Jackson in simple skirts and blouses in creams and blacks. They sat in rapt attention, lit cigarettes, and drank coffee in a ritual hush, all in thrall to their mentor, Lee Strasberg.

Cigarettes ashed out and coffee went cold while Lee stalked the room in his billowy blazers—like some seductive monk beguiling his flock with the promise of enlightenment. He spoke of the "choice" of art and "the supreme essence of feeling." The actor creates her own imaginary realities; she must inhabit the role to coax it to life. Actors, not directors, force scenes into being, and the actor creates with her own flesh and blood. He stressed feeling over reason, urging his students to look endlessly inward. "If you start with logic," Lee warned, "you might as well give up." This was the validation she'd been desperately searching for. Far from Hollywood's glitterati in a cold little room on West 46th Street, Marilyn had finally found her Shangri-la.

Immediately, Marilyn arranged a meeting with Lee. Within days, she was dining at his home on Central Park West. She left the meeting with clear goals—and, perhaps more importantly, structure. One of Lee's requirements for his students was therapy, a task Marilyn embraced wholeheartedly—she'd been deep into Freud for years. Five times a week she saw Dr. Margaret Hohenberg, a Hungarian psychiatrist with blonde braids wrapped in a crown round her head. Three nights a week Strasberg coached her alone in his Midtown apartment—she was still too shy to attend regular workshops. Marilyn's days went from haphazard to highly scheduled, and the aimless anxiety of the previous weeks began to dissipate.

Already, Marilyn was far from the lost little girl she'd been in LA. She had a suite in Manhattan, supportive friends, two renowned acting coaches, and a good-natured analyst who looked like a buxom milkmaid. She had house calls from stylist Richard Caruso, crates of unopened Chanel No 5, and Seventh Avenue dressmakers churning out slips by the dozen. She had dinners at Sardi's, cocktails with Capote, and wintry nightcaps with Carson McCullers. She had plans to play Ophelia and had an entrée into the Actors Studio. She had her own production company. She had Milton Greene and the creative alliance of her dreams.

The press, however, continued to obsess over what she didn't have: a husband. As late as March the press was more concerned with DiMaggio's comings and goings at the Gladstone than with Marilyn's acting plans. "Let's face it," *Photoplay* proclaimed. "There is no substitute for being loved. Absorbing work is not sufficient." Back in Hollywood Marilyn was thought of as a rambunctious, misbehaving child. Studio lackeys belittled her to hide how shaken they really were. She'd worked them into a frenzy—they had no idea what she'd do next or what she had brewing out East. Marilyn may have risked it all, but Zanuck and his cronies were far more frightened than she was.

Women who veer off course are dangerous. They disrupt status quo, rattle power structures to their brittle cores. They might have expected this from Katharine Hepburn, a swaggery baritone rebel who could drink with the boys in her trousers and fedoras. But Marilyn belonged to *men*—she was their chirpy little bird, cheap and easy as baby powder. What do you do when Miss Cheesecake goes rogue, divorces a national hero, and defies the most powerful men in Los Angeles? Zanuck and his team were the closest you could come to sultans and kings. By cracking the fortress of Studio Hollywood, Marilyn had struck an early blow at the patriarchy itself.

Like it or not, the world was changing, the backlash poised and ready to strike. Tactics ranged from warning and fearmongering to outright humiliation, with studio-controlled magazines like *Motion Picture* leading the charge: "The truth may well be that thousands of housewives, living unspectacularly in little towns across the land have found more genuine peace of mind than Marilyn Monroe knows at this moment . . . or may ever know."

How did *Motion Picture* know what brought Marilyn peace of mind? And did those thousands of "unspectacular" housewives breathe a collective sigh of relief?

Five

Infatuation

"I think Marilyn knows exactly where she's
going—and that's forward. It's just possible that
she'll turn out to be not only the sexiest but
smartest blonde of our time."   EARL WILSON

After months of hibernation, Marilyn's spirit was beginning
to rouse. She needed to be seen again but not by the tabloids'
flashes and hacks. No more press conferences with their cheap
quips and sound bites. This time she'd do it her way, but she
needed the right venue, the perfect backdrop for her own potent
glow. A place rich with history, where Dorothy Parker and Bob
Benchley swilled scotch and passed out over plates of roast

partridge. Those first frigid months of '55, Marilyn's real coming out happened slowly, smokily, in a former speakeasy called the 21 Club.

Warmed by whiskey, Marilyn eased her way back into visibility. She loved 21's single-malt, Old World mood. Somehow the stacks of pewter tankards in diamond-shaped lattices, glazed black leather banquettes, red Persian rugs, and oak walls hung with fox and hound prints suited Marilyn even more than the tinsel and swank of the Copa. Wrapped in black mink, neck bare, she looked fresher than she had weeks ago at Frank Delaney's. Her milkshake skin glinted off silver wine buckets and foil-topped bottles of Dom Pérignon. Club owner Bob Kriendler showed off his rare trophies. Pulitzer playwright Sid Kingsley bought her drinks. Richard Adler immediately demanded that she star in his musical, *The Pajama Game*.

Her confidence growing, Marilyn was eager to mingle with the New York press, and the 21 Club was the perfect place to do it. Media tycoon Leo Lyons held court at his regular table, while the *New York Post*'s Earl Wilson made the rounds until 3 a.m., gathering gossip for his column, It Happened Last Night. Despite the star-studded banter that filled their columns, Leo and Earl were respected as real writers, a label that attracted Marilyn immediately. Unlike the Hollywood hacks, they genuinely loved their subjects, saw them as friends, and would never betray them for a new Cadillac or a trip to Palm Beach. Bob Kriendler was strict about press he let in—media brute Walter Winchell was banned from the club and so was the gossipy Dorothy Kilgallen.

Away from bullies, Marilyn could spar with the best of them. Leo Lyons and Earl Wilson saw past her vampy walk and sex-doll coo. They loved her easy banter, how she held her liquor, how she'd actually blush when she shook your hand and made no move to disguise it. These were her kind of men—table-hopping till three and typing past dawn for the sheer fun of it. Like her they were curious and genuinely loved people and culture. Leo talked about his interviews with George Bernard Shaw; Earl asked about her connection to Dostoyevsky's Grushenka. Earl in particular was struck by the change in Marilyn. He'd met her years ago and found her sexy but "wooden." This time she bewitched him with warmth and wit, not bare cleavage or the powdery mix of perfume.

Marilyn thrived in snug groups like these—crammed into banquettes, ordering round after round over late-night snacks of caviar in pastry cups. Nestled in 21's leathery haze, she'd gab late into the night with her newfound friends. Before she braved the icy street's blast of cold air, she'd grab Leo or Earl's arm. "Hold a good thought for me," she'd whisper as she slid into her mink. At this point, she still needed all the blessings she could get.

༄ Just down the block from the posh 21 was a sports saloon ran by the lovable carouser Toots Shor. On February 26, Marilyn arrived on DiMaggio's arm—swathed in white ermine and signing autographs. The occasion was to celebrate Jackie Gleason's thirty-ninth birthday, but as Earl Wilson reported the next day, "at times it seemed like a party for Marilyn."

Toots Shor was all backslapping swagger, where men literally drank each other under the table (sometimes you'd have to step over Jackie Gleason). No caviar—just chopped chicken livers, steaks, and slabs of roast beef. But Marilyn loved the boozy bonhomie, the red-checked tablecloths cluttered with ashtrays, cheap drippy candles, and tumblers of whiskey and soda. She shimmered through the thick liquor haze and smoke, stopping to perch on a chair for a chat. Pert shoulders framed her face like two downy light bulbs. Stripped of jewelry in spaghetti-strap black, Marilyn looked like some touchable bunny—just like her heroine, Jean Harlow, who resembled a soaped-up lamb no matter what strappy couture she was wearing.

"She was the ultimate Homecoming Queen," recalled Audrey Meadows, "bathing in tidal waves of affection." She kissed and chatted with John Huston. (He was on her "men to sleep with" list—and why not—with his three-piece suits and cigars, all Havana and cowboy leather.) Leo Lyons spent most of the night gazing up at her adoringly. Jackie Gleason kept one meaty hand clasped round her waist—the other clutching his snifter of brandy. The rowdier men made a failed attempt to hoist Marilyn onto a table, which resulted in her yelping and scampering off to the powder room: "Ladies, I wonder if you could help me. I seem to have gotten a splinter up my ass." The crisis was averted with a straight pin sterilized by Audrey's cigarette lighter.

"It was a drama lesson just to watch her shine," remembered Audrey. "Despite the fact that a Monroe entrance had the effect of transforming every other woman in the place into a soft boy, we women liked her too." "EVERYONE loved her," Earl Wilson reported, "even the girls."

Despite this frenzy of men—stampeding for her, begging her for interviews, photo ops, and kisses—Joe remained unruffled. The notoriously jealous DiMaggio just sat there beaming, arm flung round his ex-wife, smoking cigarettes and ashing over plates of half-eaten strawberry shortcake. He glanced up to admire Earl Wilson's striped tie. "Marilyn bought me a tie like that," he said, grinning. "It seemed to all who watched the couple in New York that Joe was wooing Marilyn as he did in the early days of their courtship," *TV and Movie Screen* noted. "At this writing, there seems to be a good chance of reconciliation."

Marilyn looked happy and dewy as the evening wore on. She loved these kinds of parties—parties where you could actually have fun, where you could watch some sexy little drama unfold in a corner or maybe be part of one yourself. Compared to all this, LA was "just dull."

Happily, the feeling was mutual—Manhattan loved her back. "Marilyn is so enormously popular here," Earl boasted triumphantly in his next-day column. "She should stay in New York—this is Her Town."

❧ All winter long, Marilyn bloomed in the dizzying glitz of her new social life. She dated Marlon Brando. She had pillow fights with Truman Capote. She drank gin at the Subway Inn with Sinatra, drank wine with Milton Greene at La Petite Cuvée, and danced with Prince Serge Obolensky at the Hotel Astor. She attended movie premieres and late-night revelries, where she was always, according to reports, "the hit of the party." A far cry from the mute "wet chicken" at Gene Kelly's.

"I didn't realize how much she really loved people until we started going out around New York," marveled Amy Greene, who watched Marilyn charm the most jaded Manhattanites. "She was having the best time ever. We took her to Dick and Dorothy Rodgers' twenty-fifth wedding anniversary, where everyone was dressed to the nines, with all the dresses and the diamonds. Oh, honey, everybody was there—Truman Capote, John and Elaine Steinbeck, Gloria Vanderbilt, Carol Saroyan, Dorothy and Oscar Hammerstein—everyone who was in the arts at the time. Marie Harriman, who was married to Averill at the time, was there—she couldn't see her hand in front of her face and was also very vain and didn't want to wear her glasses with an evening dress and all her jewelry. Marilyn was approaching, and all she saw was this blonde vision coming towards her, and she said to Dick Rodgers, 'Who is *that*?' When he said Marilyn Monroe, she screamed, 'Oh, my God, she's *gorgeous*!' It was the only person in the world who couldn't recognize her because she literally couldn't see. When Marilyn heard that story she loved it and went over to Marie and gave her a big kiss. Marilyn was very shy with women, but she was also very giving—the type to throw her arms around this lady who didn't recognize her and kiss her. She loved that sort of thing. That night someone snapped a very lovely picture of Marilyn in profile with Marie Harriman, and they sort of have their arms around each other, which is charming."

The Broadway crowd warmed up to her quickly, showering her with invites to their star-studded parties. Back in her Hollywood days, Marilyn would have fled, burying herself in blankets with Sinatra records and the telephone. In Manhattan her social confidence and lively spirit bloomed. "Between acts everyone talks to her," marveled Amy, who accompanied Marilyn to plays and premieres. "People will call down from the balcony to say they either like her dress or that they don't like it. Or that her hair looks lovely." Even more astonishing was Marilyn's response. "She answers them just as though she had known each one, personally, all her life. That magnetism, believe me, is a two-way current." It was undeniable—Marilyn was becoming a PR expert.

Milton was the gatekeeper—at least initially. He'd pour the bourbon, apologize for Marilyn, and vet the journalists—he didn't want them attacking her with questions about her divorce. But gradually, Marilyn relaxed with the press and even began to enjoy herself. She held interviews at bars, ordering thimblefuls of Harveys

Bristol, which she'd promptly spill in her lap. "Oops," she'd say with a giggle, dabbing her lap with a napkin and calmly moving on to the next question. Instead of shying away from the personal, Marilyn was warm, expansive, and playful. "Nobody can write dialogue for her which could possibly sound half as much like her as the dialogue she thinks up for herself," wrote Pete Martin, a New York journalist who was charmed by Marilyn's "Monroese." "I've never been able to wear pajamas or creepy nightgowns," she'd quip, or "I sleep with my eyes half open, dreaming of a man." Even her simplest statements were shot through with some deeper, mysterious truth. "I think I'm a mixture," she said to Pete Martin. "Of what I don't know. One thing, I'm continually off balance." On the screen or on the page, Marilyn wanted to give her fans something worthwhile: "I have a certain sort of stupid sincerity. I mean I don't want to tell everybody who interviews me the same thing. I want them all to have something new and different and exclusive. When I worry about that, I start to get sick to my stomach."

The Manhattan press was inclined to humor Marilyn. And why not? They reveled in her oddities, which she played up instinctively. She begged reporters to use pencils and notebooks and forbade recording machines: "It would make me nervous to see that thing going round and round." Instead of getting angry at her inevitable delays, the press felt sorry for her. "She thinks the maid must have gone off with the top of her tapered slacks," her secretary would report to columnists waiting in the foyer. "She's running around without a top on."

Gone was the insecure Hollywood waif, plotting early escapes from pool parties in the Canyons. Her candor with journalists paid off—public opinion began to turn back her way. "Never underestimate this gal," warned Earl in his cover story "In Defense of

Marilyn." He wrote, "What other actress—during a suspension—has gone about making a million or so new friends?"

❧ On February 22, Marilyn attended a Navy gala at the Hotel Astor and was crowned Ship's Sweetheart for the USS *Bennington*. "True to her reputation," recalled sailor Paul Lazzaro, "she showed up at our party at almost 11 p.m. After chugalugging a whiskey sour that appeared out of nowhere backstage, Marilyn took the stage. By then 3,000 sailors had been drinking for three hours and Marilyn Monroe shows up! It was total chaos."

A nervous Jay Kanter ushered her through the street exit to a thronged Times Square. There was no clawing or pawing—the sailors treated her far more respectfully than the press hounds ever did. Coat-free in black spaghetti straps, Marilyn lingered in the cold with the men, bumming their cigarettes, kissing their cheeks, clutching a USS *Bennington* sweatshirt to her bare neck and chest.

"I asked if we could get a picture of her kissing a sailor goodnight," explained Lazzaro. "She said in her whispery voice 'Why certainly!' A band of sailors stood in awe in a respectful circle around her, but no one was close enough for a picture. I called for a sailor to step in. However, my only response was from one of the ship's Marines who stepped up to Marilyn's right arm and said 'How about a Marine?' 'Well OK, I said, but I want a sailor too.' 'How about you,' Marilyn whispered to me. She reached up, grabbed both our cheeks and drew us in, blonde hair, black satin dress—you get the picture. Flashbulbs popped along with a couple of sailors."

The most famous woman on earth was no haughty Hitchcock blonde. Marilyn chatted up her leg waxer, gossiped with shopgirls, and waved hello to the garbage men on 57th Street. If you met her in the powder room of the Copa she'd probably lend you her lipstick. And she remembered faces—a stewardess who was nice to her on a plane, a war widow on crutches from a skiing accident. After all, her fans had made her a star, "no studio, no person, the people did."

"The people" were the mechanics, nuns, cabbies, and busboys who hung on her fluttery strut and glittering hips. "The working men" she described in a touching interview. "I'll go by and they'll whistle, and then they'll say, 'Gosh, it's Marilyn Monroe!' You know, those are the times it's nice, people knowing who you are and all that, and feeling like you meant something to them."

Paparazzi, literati, directors, and designers were fleeting. She shared Capote and Sinatra with Liz Taylor and Ava Gardner. But the fans—the waiters, teenagers, and factory workers; the "popcorn and huzzah crowd"—belonged to her.

✑ March 9, 1955. Gladstone Hotel, 7 p.m. *East of Eden* premiere. Fishtail sheath in biscuit brocade. Exposed shoulders, fox fur wrap, white opera gloves. By now she's learned the magic of fabrics. Taupes and creams near the face to set off her pneumatic skin. Silk fawn collars, sanded satin. Dozens of buff kid gloves. She keeps the dusting of fuzz that covers her face—side effect from Laszlo's hormone cream—for its soft focus glow. (Elizabeth Taylor shaves hers off.) She daubs her cheekbones with Vaseline. Not that she needs it—the temperature has spiked into the mid-60s. Will she sweat through her heavy brocade? Does she even need her fur wrap? She peeks out the window—wooden police horses flank the exit. Milton and Amy wait in the limousine parked curbside. (Amy like a dainty Lara in her black fur hood, Milton adorably childish in his dinner suit, a boy playing dress-up.) John Steinbeck will be there—what will she say to this gruff imposing man?—she loves *Tortilla Flat*. Director Elia Kazan will be there with his wife. Milton Berle will be there with his wife. And has anyone guessed about her and Brando? She's already late—she's supposed to usher with Marlon—will he be annoyed? (He will be annoyed, and he will forgive her.)

This is the Actors Studio's first major benefit, and even Margaret Truman is a guest usherette. Thousands have gathered round the Astor Theatre, a mounting frenzy in the balmy air. Martin Block is perched on high with his microphone, interviewing celebrities as they arrive. Milton Berle approaches Block with his wife, Ruth, in tow. Everyone knows he has a thing for blondes, and everyone knows he has slept with Marilyn. He's extra-solicitous of Ruth that night—"Doesn't she look great, Martin?"—one hand at her back while nervously scanning the crowd and flashing bulbs for signs of Marilyn. (By the end of the night he'll be wrapped in complicit little chats with Marilyn—pulling her onto his lap, kissing her cheek, prancing for the camera.)

Everyone is there. Kazan is jittery. John Steinbeck looks like he needs a drink. Margaret Truman is looking for Marilyn. Martin Block is looking for Marilyn. Marlon Brando is looking for Marilyn. Everyone is looking for Marilyn: "I heard a rumor Marilyn Monroe was ushering." "Has Marilyn arrived yet?" "We expect Marilyn to walk in with Joe any minute." The crowd swells up with a roar. "Okay, I guess Marilyn's arrived."

The streets jammed, mad fans lurching forward, tears streaming down their cheeks: "I touched her! I touched her!"

Marilyn emerges—not on Joe's arm but on Milton Greene's.

James Dean is a no-show at his own premiere. Somehow, everyone forgets to notice.

❧ Milton takes her to the Friars Club on March 17, where her pals Dean and Jerry are being honored with a roast. The only woman in a group of fifty bawdy men, Marilyn sits sandwiched at a banquet between Bobby Clark and Eddie Fisher. She's Belle of the Boys Club Ball, miles away from Hollywood's slick leers and chintzy grins. Dean and Jerry clown for the crowd; Marilyn giggles in the background, a glistening bubble at Eddie's shoulder ("I've always had a thing for Eddie Fisher"). He's lapping up her synthetic-kitten look, but years later—broken and embittered by Liz Taylor—he will declare her beauty spoiled, ravaged by pills and booze. Sammy Davis Jr. leans on Marilyn's chair, smelling of Aramis and Marlboro Reds. Tonight they look like a puckish couple, batting around inside jokes. She's looking up at him, one jaunty brow cocked, her fuzzy blonde halo diffusing the vamp. Milton Berle whispers in Marilyn's ear, his gold wedding band conspicuous and benign. He's close enough to catch the scent of her neck—hard sparkle of aldehydes and skin-warmed styrax. They both love this sort of thing and are good at it, too—carving out chunks of school-girl intimacy no matter how grand the gala. Berle's barely drinking, just plowing through Havana cigars, and Marilyn loves the vanilla aroma. (He'll soon give her a box of his favorite Cubans—they're so much better for her than the cigarettes she smokes.) Dean and Jerry are waving her over, and she poses, arms flung round their shoulders as if she's tamed them, as if they're hers. Dean grasps her fingertips. He's quick to claim her, too. Jerry's eyes are wide and sooty as a puppy's. (Marilyn on Jerry: "I just think he's sexy. You know, I can't quite analyze it but it's there.") The poses get crazier: Even in black ties and Chanel No 5 there's this pajama party vibe. Dean chews on her pearly palm and Jerry bites into her arm like a lamb chop. Someday Jerry will blame the press for her death ("She was kind, she was good, she was beautiful"). And seven years from now—three days after "Happy Birthday, Mr. President" and eight weeks before she finally passes out in her Brentwood bed, phone in hand, when Fox has their final revenge and punishes her for her success and fires her for the last time, Dean will risk his career and walk out in protest. This will be the last act of respect, the last act of kindness, the last acknowledgment of her talent and her genius. The last to happen while she's still alive.

❧ The Broadway crowd found themselves protecting—her. At the Friars Roast, comedian Joey Adams had planned to crack a joke about DiMaggio, then thought the better of it, stopping himself for Marilyn's sake. Carol Channing, who'd been urged to trap Marilyn into singing "Diamonds Are a Girl's Best Friend" at a post-premiere party, wisely talked herself out of it. "I decided it wouldn't be fair. I just know that I'd kill anybody who'd do it to me, so why should I do it to her?"

"Marilyn discovered that New York show people—supposedly hard and tough—have real respect for her," wrote Earl Wilson. "She hasn't had one bad experience with them." The whole town seemed to fall in love with her collectively. They loved everything about Marilyn—her firm handshake (no matter how weak she was at the end of the night), the warm way she remembered everyone's name. "We're going to be good friends," she'd say, with a squeeze of the hand by the elevator door. And she'd mean it.

Manhattan continued to offer fresh pleasures. She delighted in the highbrow as well as the low, responding to Tolstoy and hot dogs with the same innocent rapture. "She's so hungry—greedy almost, but not quite—for all the wonderful things in the world," wrote Elsa Maxwell of Marilyn's disarming curiosity. "Things like association with stimulating people, fascinating books, a chance to see the planet she lives on, a knowledge of music and art and food and wine. Like a child with a big box of candy, she can't quite decide which treat to sample first."

She'd sleep past noon, order grapefruit juice, soak in an ice bath spiked with Chanel. Then the flurry of calls—cocktails and jazz on Swing Street, or a midnight feast of cold borscht and steak at Manny Wolf's Chop House. She loved the El Morocco: the limousines lined up on 54th Street, the strong martinis, the Cuban band. She'd kick off her shoes and samba for hours. Marilyn was beginning to enjoy herself, and it showed.

Fox had mocked her for daring to change, sizing her up as the "same old Marilyn." But this Marilyn—tipsily dancing with Truman at the Elmo, barefoot in that black Norell slip, pumps flung under a zebra-striped banquette—was a new Marilyn. Stripped down, she glowed: roots freshly blonded baby-silk at the temple, waves at the nape as if damp from a nap. Stiff curls and stuffed satin had loosened, softened. Nails glossed clear—not Cruella red—and filed to oval points. No jewelry, just bare, creamy skin. She grinned over her shoulder at the in-house photographer. Capote clutched her wrist like a sweaty cherub.

Dancing with Truman, gliding through the Astor Theatre on Marlon Brando's arm, or frolicking *La Dolce Vita*–style in Central Park's Bethesda Fountain, Marilyn was the toast of her adopted town. Every day was a new adventure. Every night was her coming-out ball. And though she had never lived in New York, it felt like she had come home.

Six

Flesh Impact

"Only Marilyn would've done it—an important
movie star getting on top of a huge elephant. She
was like God in drag."   RAY MYERS

*O*n March 21, actress Sheree North appeared on the cover of
Life in a spangly leotard and showgirl pose. Fox had just signed
her to a four-year contract, screen-tested her for *The Girl in Pink
Tights* and cast her in *How to Be Very, Very Popular,* two films
Marilyn had rejected. Zanuck had been grooming Sheree to re-
place Marilyn for months. Now he taunted her with this headline:
SHEREE NORTH TAKES OVER FOR MARILYN MONROE. As usual, Elsa
Maxwell came to Marilyn's defense. She dismissed Sheree as one
of the "ersatz Monroes," identifiable by their exaggerated (padded)

curves and peroxide hair. To Elsa, these were cheap copies to be batted away like flies: "They may successfully have imitated Marilyn's walk and other physical characteristics. But there—take my word for it—all resemblance ends. In mind and spirit—which are the very essence of any human being—Marilyn and the ersatz Monroes are as far removed as I am from the Venus de Milo." Elsa was right: Sheree couldn't replace Marilyn Monroe. Both films were box office duds.

Marilyn wasn't threatened by Sheree, but she was shaken enough to get proactive with publicity. This time she'd play by her own rules and show them something raw and authentic. This time she'd be herself.

The next day, she woke late, threw on a coat and darted into a dim little cocktail lounge on 57th Street. She slumped into a chair across from her friend Sam Shaw, *Look* photographer Ed Feingersh, and *Redbook* editor Robert Stein. She ordered a scotch mist and sat mutely until it arrived. Wearing no makeup, she looked pale and vulnerable, like a child who had overslept. She fixed her eyes on Robert and asked, "Why do they print things about me that aren't true?"

Robert shot her a bleary look—he'd already downed five panicky scotches. This was his first time seeing Marilyn up close, and he was struck by the pearly lightness of her skin. He was feeling pretty fragile himself—it'd been three days since he'd flown in from LA, and Marilyn had only just surfaced. He'd been warned she never made small talk, that she never asked rhetorical questions. Robert could tell she was waiting for an answer.

"They don't mean to hurt you—just use you."

Marilyn smiled at his honesty. So far she'd been flitting and flirting with the press, occasionally flinging morsels at Leo or Earl. But she wasn't playing hard to get. She was doing what she always did, waiting for the right moment.

Robert sympathized with Marilyn, with her escape to New York, her longing for art and personal fulfillment: "After two dozen movies, a headline marriage, and a headline divorce, she was in New York to prepare for parts like Grushenka in *The Brothers Karamazov*. The papers dug out all the clichés about comedians who want to play Hamlet, underlining their ridicule with photos from *The Seven Year Itch*. Marilyn on the subway grate, an updraft billowing the white dress over her hips."

Ed Feingersh—a wiry risk-taker who lived in saloons—was a great match for Marilyn. He spent more time photographing patrols in Korea and Irish Horan's Hell Drivers than fashion models. He worshipped Cartier-Bresson, Fellini, grainy movable images seen from the inside out. He had no use for static, fluffed-up glamour shots, and neither did Marilyn. Right away the three made a pact over scotches. There'd be no posing, no blowing kisses, no studio setups—just a "straight look" at Marilyn's new life in Manhattan.

"A line flashed through my head," remembered Robert Stein. "The Marilyn Monroe You've Never Seen." Why not shoot in the gritty heart of workaday Manhattan—the underground platform at Grand Central Terminal? The Starlet in the Subway—Marilyn was delighted.

Just before they left, a tanned, good-humored DiMaggio breezed in, his face lit by a "schoolboy smile." "Sam, how are you," he said, clapping him on the shoulder, telling him how relieved he was that Marilyn had left "that movie crowd." He nodded and grinned at Robert and Ed, told Sam to take Marilyn antiquing again, then strode out of the dark little lounge into the bright noise of 57th Street.

❧ She arrived the next morning on the Grand Central platform, with her agent Dick Shepherd tagging along. Marilyn was nervous. This was her first subway experience—she took taxis everywhere—and besides, the gridlocked throng would have been unbearable. But in an oversize camel coat and tousled hair, she looked like your average city girl—buying coffee and *Vogue* at a kiosk or waiting on the platform for the IRT, clutching her copy of the *Post*. "Nobody recognized her. Eddie's camera kept clicking while she stood strap-hanging on the uptown local. No heads turned."

Marilyn certainly wasn't dressed like a fashion plate, but that was the whole point. In fact, it was her lack of interest in fashion that gave her such a wonderful sense of style—a style she solidified in New York City. She wore black pullovers and toreador pants to dive bars with Frank Sinatra, flung minks over slips for midnight walks in Central Park. She paired cocktail frocks with plain trenches from Jax, mixed couture with sportswear, and wore sober wool suits with gloves of black fishnet. In a time when women matched their polish to their purses, Marilyn usually had a strap slipping off her shoulder, slept-in hair, or a bare leg in winter. She rarely wore hats—her head was too huge for silly veiled flowerpots. She wore a terrycloth bathrobe with the same aplomb as white ermine. And she threw on Army-Navy jeans for runs to the 42nd St. Smoke Shop.

A woman at her most beautiful is a woman living authentically. Like Jackie Kennedy—more gorgeous at fifty than twenty in her Henleys, jeans, and windswept hair—Marilyn seemed to age backward. At twenty-eight, she was living by herself, for herself—even her shabby little room at the Gladstone brimmed with the delicious vertigo of possibility. The heady high of feeling yourself change in a way you can't quite see yet.

Now living alone, Marilyn began to break away from Amy's sartorial influence. She lounged around in plaid pants and scuffed-up loafers, paired bedhead with plunging gowns by Oleg Cassini.

1955 was the year she went rogue with her hair, mussing it up even after Caruso's pricey cuts. As with James Dean, the crazier her hair, the better she looked. "Marilyn was the first star of any magnitude to appear in public unconcerned with the state of her tresses," wrote Caruso himself. "As if to say all this beauty just thrown together." The screen queen in quiet rebellion. This was Marilyn's new brand of sex appeal—more arresting and alluring than the pop-shockers and hippies that came decades later.

In New York, Marilyn became her own stylist—expertly projecting her unique image. Her casual glamour looks just as chic today—more relevant than Audrey Hepburn's shirtwaists and Grace Kelly's pearls. Her style remained unchanged from 1955 to her death, in 1962—a time when fashions and fads moved at warp speed. Yet she never looked dated. She still doesn't—a shot of her in pigtails, jeans, and cowboy boots on the set of *The Misfits* could have been taken yesterday. In a ratty white robe on Venice Beach or strapped in Cecil Chapman satin, she was always unmistakably Marilyn. Beaming in her loose camel coat, she glowed like a fresh deli daffodil. She loved her scruffy disguise.

Of course, no matter what she wore, Marilyn was noticed—even on the subway in New York City. A man on the platform spotted her and turned around, obviously attempting to place her face. Did he know her? Perhaps last week's cute blonde from the Copa? Playing along, Marilyn tried to look serious, then broke into a broad smile. Slack-jawed the man gasped aloud: "It's her."

Arm in arm with Dick Shepherd, she took the street exit, walking past signs for matzo balls, twenty-five-cent hamburgers and ten-cent ice cream cones. Hot subway air gushed up behind her. Marilyn unbuttoned her coat, the scent of her perfume mixing with newsprint, street hot dogs, petrol, and tire rubber. Spring had arrived, with Manhattan's haphazard beauty in bloom. These may have been the happiest weeks of her life.

———

❧ For eight days, Ed and Robert trailed Marilyn through New York, documenting the details of her new city life. They rented a suite at the Ambassador Hotel—her rooms at the Gladstone were too shabby. The suite was bright and springlike, with white wicker furniture, floor-to-ceiling windows, and loose undone curtains in gauzy white.

If Milton Greene was the first to show Marilyn's playful vulnerability, Ed Feingersh was the one who captured her very real need to be alone. That first morning Ed shot her reading, sprawled out on a wicker chaise with copies of *Motion Picture Daily* and Lee Strasberg's *An Actor Prepares*. Marilyn had often been photographed reading, but this was the first time it didn't seem like a joke—as if you'd actually caught her in the act of some private thought you were desperate to know. In striped capris and a black sleeveless blouse, Marilyn embodied an undone, low-key sexiness. She twirled her hair absently, absorbed in her book, then kicked off her shoes, feet flexed like a dancer's. Even barefoot she always seemed to be wearing invisible stilettos or flesh-toned heels.

By late afternoon, they were wrapping up. The sun lowered, casting pointy black shadows in the white airy room. Marilyn didn't want to be alone—she was liking this creative, collaborative feeling. She asked Robert and Ed what they did at the end of the day, so they took her to Costello's, a dank little dive bar on Third Avenue.

Just the kind of place Marilyn loved: full of history, exclusive but decidedly untrendy. Wood panels murky with age and cigarette smoke. James Thurber's comics scrawled on the wall. (Marilyn loved James Thurber; she'd bought *Thurber Country* a couple of years earlier.) Dogs being chased by rabbits. Scrawny men cowering under towering wives ("I'm leaving you, Myra, you might as well get used to the idea"). Writers from the nearby *New Yorker* were always stopping by for steak sandwiches and cheap gin. Yanko, the bartender, was often too hungover to tie his shoelaces. ("If I bend over to tie them, it feels like the sides of my head's going to pop out on me.") Propped beside the register was a blackthorn walking stick that Ernest Hemingway had cracked over John O'Hara's head. The bar's owner, Tim Costello, kept watch and drank tea in the back.

Marilyn slid into a chair across from the bar. She looked luminous against the dark paneled wood, her raw blonde hair fluffed up in a beachy pompadour. She gazed up at the loopy drawings of henpecked men and pensive little dogs, smoke curling from the dwindling cigarette clasped in her hand. She'd never seen anything like this before—the blackthorn stick and the literary past, the rough-hewn saloon mood that wrapped you in a cozy, permanent dusk.

Robert Stein found the afternoon especially memorable: "Tim, usually wary of strangers, was clearly intrigued by the blaze of blond hair at our table, and in a rare gesture, came over to take the orders himself."

"A screwdriver, please," Marilyn said.

Tim was expressionless.

"Vodka and orange juice," she added.

Tim kept looking at her. "We don't serve breakfast here," he said.

"Okay," Marilyn said agreeably. "Vodka on the rocks."

Tim gave the order to his brother Joe at the bar and went back to reading his paper. Later, as Ed Feingersh was heading to the men's room, Tim stopped him.

"Who is she?"

Ed smiled. "Marilyn Monroe."

Tim's face darkened. "I ask you a civil question and you get smart."

Ed flashed his Cheshire grin and continued to shuffle around, mixing drinks at the bar like he owned the place. (Sometimes you'd forget that he didn't own the place—he had his mail delivered there, and that's where he entertained guests.) Every now and then he'd put down his camera and scrawl his own version of a Thurber dog on a cocktail napkin. Hours passed—more drinks and more cigarettes, sun sinking lower and the Third Avenue El rattling above. No one gave Marilyn more than a quick look. As she was leaving, a photographer at the bar tapped Ed on the arm. "If you come back later," he stage-whispered, "bring your little friend."

Marilyn wanted to stay—this murky subterranean nook offered her a freedom she had never found in California, with its relentless sunshine and solar blankness. Before the year was out, the Third Avenue El would be torn down, along with the pillars the regulars used to steady themselves while hailing cabs in the morning hours. Ed would take a turn for the worse, drinking more and photographing less. And Marilyn would be teetering on the edge of a new life.

They took more street photos near the Gladstone suite, this time in sleek black and her favorite fur collar. This was her classic movie star "disguise"—though the rhinestone-studded cat eyes didn't fool anyone. They walked down 57th Street, sweet pollen mingling with the scent of wet mink. She paused by the window of Liz Arden's salon, with its flower display and cool bottles of beauty. The glass door swung open in a gust of setting lotion, behind it a woman—stiff and tall as a mannequin, dressed like Marilyn in all black and tailored wool. In her pillbox hat with starchy veil and sprayed-stiff curls pinned tight to the scalp, she looked like a ghost from a different time. If she recognized Marilyn, she didn't show it and continued her glide down Fifth Avenue.

Marilyn had little in common with the dark femmes, ice queens, scrubbed virgins, and gamines of her era. She anticipated the exciting, complicated women of the French New Wave who were just beginning to emerge at the time of her death. They were passionate rebels who grinned through wine-stained teeth, reveled in their kinks, and were all the more gorgeous for it. It's ironic that Marilyn—icon of hard-spackled glamour—was actually a pioneer for the restless flesh-and-blood beauties who surfaced in the sixties.

In one of her most progressive shoots yet, Marilyn posed dishabille in her rooms at the Ambassador. When a seamstress came to fit her for another Norell dress, Ed whipped out his camera, eager to catch the classic Marilyn moment. Each shot is intimate, with a delightfully subversive feel. We see her fastening a garter or striking a cheeky pose in an Ambassador monogrammed bathrobe. We see her relaxed and in control, perched on the arm of an upholstered chair, drinking wine from an old-fashioned coupe. (She rarely used furniture as it was meant to be used.) We see her unmade bed, her chaotic suite—mink flung on the chaise, bras and books strewn over the carpet, vanity cluttered with half-drunk wineglasses, Glorene lashes and square compacts in black lacquer. The white wicker furniture and floral wallpaper look more like a teenage bedroom than a movie star suite. You can breathe the smoke curling up from her cigarette, inhale her skin as she anoints her cleavage with hot drops of Chanel.

Reduced to mascot of the ultra-femme fifties, few people realize how progressive Marilyn really was. None of her contemporaries would have allowed themselves to be photographed bare-faced and hungover, joking with the dressmaker, passing out in full makeup, or simply lolling around their own messy hotel room. Grace Kelly was pure patrician ice. Liz Taylor was warm-blooded but Hollywood flawless. And Audrey Hepburn played the artless ingenue but rarely dropped her gamine polish—at least not for the camera.

On March 24, Eddie Feingersh photographed her getting ready for the *Cat on a Hot Tin Roof* premiere—lining her eyes with Liz Arden pencils, dusting her nose with peachy finishing powder. She fluffed her hair, sipped wine from a tumbler balanced on the dresser corner. Then the lavish finish: "Before going out, she put on a performance with the stopper from a bottle of Chanel No 5," wrote Robert Stein, "stroking her skin in sensuous delight."

She arrived at the Morosco Theatre in a cloud of white ermine, glowing like a bronze doll in her sheath. She'd paired couture and fur with rockabilly hair, her hands ringless under her opera gloves, nails clear, lustrous, and rubbed with lanolin. Her bare swathe of neck was more arresting than the sea of chokers and chandelier earrings glittering around her. She might have been the only woman there without a single piece of jewelry.

Milton Greene was there to shepherd her through the crowd. They spent most of the night together, whispering and giggling during intermission. She engaged her fans with touchable ease, slipping off her mule and using its sole as a surface for autographing *Playbills*. Tennessee Williams fluttered around, inviting everyone to the after-party on the St. Regis rooftop.

His mother, Miss Edwina, held court on the roof, in her garden-party frock and bonnet swathed in flowers. Gore Vidal and Truman Capote milled around clutching highballs, teacups, and cucumber sandwiches. Writer Elaine Dundy described the moment Marilyn arrived.

At that moment a buzz and a rustle ripped through the crowd. Everybody stopped what they were doing, freeze-framed with their drinks, hors d'oeuvres or cigarettes halfway to their mouths. They were all looking in one direction. A path had been cleared, and walking through it was Marilyn Monroe. She was wearing what anyone else would have called an underslip, a simple, unadorned black silk slip with thin shoulder straps and clearly nothing under it. Her skin was a luminous alabaster with pearly blue and rose tints such as I have never seen outside paintings by the Old Masters. She was more astonishingly beautiful in the flesh than on celluloid and we all stared silently in our reverence.

Eventually the party started up again. By then I had worked my way around to her part of the room and was rewarded with the following tableau vivant: blonde Marilyn was seated in an armchair. On one of its arms perched Carson McCullers, her brown hair chopped short and uneven as if she'd taken an ax to it, her body fierce in tomboy tension and twisted like a pretzel. Sitting in a chair on the other side of Marilyn-In-Her-Slip was Edwina-Williams-In-Her-Hat. They were conversing with each other, all three with heads inclined. The Three Fates, I decided; Beauty, Brains and Motherhood. Whose destiny were they spinning out at that very moment?

Eddie was waiting at the Gladstone when Marilyn staggered back, collapsing by the fire in a threadbare chair. He took one last shot of her drifting to sleep in white fox fur. She slept upright in the lobby that night while bats beat their lullaby in the rafters above.

As their week together drew to a close, Marilyn grew quieter, more reflective. She took off her peach Pucci dress and wrapped herself in a white terry bathrobe. Without a word she stepped onto the balcony, lit a cigarette, and stared out at the Manhattan skyline. "Eddie's shutter just kept clicking, and rolls of 35 mm film filled up," wrote Robert Stein. "He never asked her to pose. She hardly knew he was there."

This was a Marilyn the world hadn't seen yet—alone, withdrawn but dazzlingly happy.

Eddie's photos of Marilyn are infused with some quiet magic, which Robert Stein attributes to the resemblance between photographer and subject. "In their days together," wrote Stein, "despite their disparity in looks, I could see Eddie and Marilyn were much alike. Like Marilyn, Eddie was given to self-parody to mask the pain of being defenseless against daily living and, like her, desperate to make full use of the gifts such an open nature provides. Just as Marilyn dreaded looking less than perfect in front of the cameras and was always late, so Eddie obsessed over what he did behind the camera and would let no one else develop or print his pictures. . . . They both were somehow more directly connected to life than the rest of us, and more vulnerable. Each held on to an ideal of Art as if it were life itself, and, as it turned out for both of them, it was. Marilyn's movies and Eddie's pictures made those who saw them feel more alive but at the same time fear for their safety, sensing the price that would have to be paid for their luminous openness."

But it was Marilyn's luminous openness that made her such a hit in New York. For the first time, she felt accepted, welcomed. Unlike glassy, judgmental Hollywood, New York embraced her quirks and creativity, and she couldn't imagine going back. "If I close my eyes and picture LA," she said at this time, "all I see is one big varicose vein."

℘ After months of lying low, Milton was anxious to stir up publicity for Marilyn. The fans should see for themselves that their star had not dimmed, that she wasn't in exile cowering under the thumb of the mighty Darryl Zanuck. They needed a stunt, a spectacle, with all the razzle-dazzle Marilyn deserved. This could be tricky—her contract with Fox forbade paid appearances except for charity events. Mike Todd would soon be hosting a Ringling Bros. gala to raise funds for the Arthritis and Rheumatism Foundation. With a celebrity guest list, Madison Square Garden location and Milton Berle as ringmaster, this could be the perfect high-profile debut. As a longtime supporter of charities, Marilyn leaped at the chance to appear in the circus—riding an elephant, preferably a small, female one, with a rhinestone saddle and pink bow on its tail.

The fitting at Brooks Costume Company was a disaster. She'd been given a charcoal bodice to match the elephant's skin, but Marilyn hated charcoal and demanded a black one. Besides, it was too tight—the seams dug into her flesh and hurt. Tailors and seamstresses bustled around her. Costume fitter Mary Smith was there, so was Dick Shepherd, Milton Greene, Eddie Feingersh and Robert Stein. Reporter H.D. Quigg slipped in, eager to brag about seeing Marilyn naked. Half-dressed, humiliated, and surrounded by gawkers, Marilyn began to cry.

"At the costume fitting she arrived as the Star," wrote Stein, who was alarmed by Marilyn's sudden outburst, "until the Other abruptly emerged and burst into tears of frustration." What Stein misidentified as some schizoid fit was really a normal reaction to being poked, prodded, sewn up, and stripped in a roomful of gaping men. She might as well be back in the Fox wardrobe room with the bitchy wardrobe assistants, tape measures, straight pins, and scratchy fabrics. It all felt like one giant step backward—she'd tottered around in five-inch heels, tripped on her train, and had fallen smack on her million-dollar ass. She hadn't put her career on the line to be cut up into cheesecake again.

On March 31, she prepared to ride her elephant through Madison Square Garden. Backstage, Milton donned his dinner jacket and pinned her into the black velvet bodice. Stagehands frantically painted the elephant pink while someone hoisted Marilyn onto its back and pushed her into the crowd of 8,000 raucous fans.

"The place went absolutely ape," Amy Greene told *Photoplay*. "I have never experienced anything like the hysteria and the din that came out of those mouths all the way up the stands. I'm telling you, I had goosebumps. Everyone cheered her, and when I looked up toward the balcony, it was the strangest sight. All I could see were the open mouths, right up to the rafters."

Everything worked beautifully. The elephant was tender and tame, pausing to bow at the cheering audience. (Milton: "Afterwards she talked about how sweet and nice the elephant was. She called it a 'sweet baby.'") Marilyn smiled and waved in spangled glory, all the while bleeding from a straight pin that had punctured her thigh.

With its fishnet tights and heaps of cleavage, Marilyn's costume was far more revealing than the halter necks and thin robes that had enraged Joe last year. Yet Joe seemed unruffled. In fact, when the elephant stopped in front of his box, Joe beamed "as if to let everyone know that Marilyn is still the one girl in his life." Bedecked in her feathered can-can outfit, Marilyn waved from her perch. She was, quite literally, on top of the world.

The tide was beginning to turn—Marilyn had been wooing the press spectacularly. Journalists reported "peace offerings" from Zanuck, including dramatic roles in *Anastasia* and *The Girl on the Red Velvet Swing.* "If true," predicted one reporter, "it seems that Marilyn's revolt has begun to reap dividends."

Milton and Amy basked in the glow of Marilyn's wild triumph. It was as if they were all rebel teenagers, thumbing their noses at Hollywood. "It was like a cannon had been shot in Old Madison Square Garden," remembers Amy Greene. "It was a moment in all our lives that we were David and Goliath—and we were loving every minute of it."

Seven

Ingenue

"Marilyn was a field of wild flowers, a gamboling
puppy in the backyard, a pink sunset in June.
She was glorious, and we had to look."

MARLON BRANDO

*M*arilyn's pink elephant entrance had the effect she'd been
hoping for. "It was international coverage," explained Amy. "Newspapers, magazines—nothing that was printable at that point didn't
carry a huge picture of her. So now Zanuck is freaking out. The
stockholders are saying, 'Darryl, this lady is looking good, why isn't
she making pictures?'"

She soon caught the attention of Edward R. Murrow, an

award-winning journalist who'd taken down McCarthy. He wanted Marilyn for his TV series, *Person to Person,* and arranged to meet with her and Milton at the Ambassador Hotel. Ed talked shop with Milton, lit Marilyn's cigarettes, joked about the fast one she'd pulled on Zanuck and crew. Marilyn beamed in her marten fur. Ed's show, with its massive audience, was a chance to launch her dream into the world.

But when Murrow and his crew descended on the Greenes' home for filming, something shifted. Marilyn watched the technicians rush around the living room, fiddling with their cables and cameras. Milton looked on anxiously—he recognized the look of panic flickering across her face. He hoped they'd finish up the preparations in time for a quick rehearsal to ease Marilyn's nerves. "I took her for a ride on my motorcycle to distract her," he said. "We talked, and she was nervous. That comes off on the show—a certain kind of nervousness that she's trying to shake off."

Even her outfit—a straight wool skirt and white short-sleeved sweater—seemed stiff and awkward. It didn't suit Marilyn at all— nor was it remotely typical of her easy style. She'd had use for those sorts of plainer outfits in Connecticut, but in the city she'd been living in black slips and bathrobes. She gave subsequent interviews on her own louche terms—in a suite at the Waldorf wearing nothing but a robe. Needless to say, those interviews were far more successful.

At the time it seemed novel to film her *en famille,* but the whole setup cast her as a dependent little girl. In spite of her closeness with the Greenes, she was still their guest. It would have been bold and unnatural for her to march around the house like she owned the place. In Weston, Amy reigned as a confident queen—it was her domain, not Marilyn's. Amy jumped in whenever Marilyn faltered—and that day Marilyn faltered a lot. She sat mutely on the couch, looking to the Greenes for cues and approval, stroking the dog's fur when she saw Amy petting it. Everything seemed to go wrong—even Ed Murrow's opening question—"How's Marilyn as a houseguest; does she clean up after herself . . . ?"—was infantilizing. How could she answer a question like that? Marilyn sighed, raising a sweet but exasperated eyebrow.

In Murrow's defense, it was a valid question. Marilyn was about as domesticated as a baby cheetah—and just as rare in a Connecticut country home. But it wasn't a cheetah Marilyn resembled that day—more like a plasticky, petrified doll, eyes darting under a thick fringe of panicky lashes. Gone was the usual witty minx who could catch a reporter's banter and throw it right back at them. In fact, Marilyn seemed less like herself and more like those delightful ditzes Lorelei Lee and The Girl from *The Seven Year Itch*. At a time when everyone was waiting with bated breath for the "New Marilyn" to emerge, this was the worst possible outcome.

What happened? Milton, too, seemed mysteriously off. During rehearsals with Ed he'd been bright and talkative, but withdrawn and tentative today during filming. Marilyn and Milton could be moody and changeable, just as likely to dash out of a party as to rush to it. Amy called it "Russian gloom," and it surfaced in them both, especially Milton, who could be strangely— though charmingly—absent. They had similar insecurities—the shyness, the childhood stutters—and they dealt with them in different ways. Milton would detach into blasé coolness, while Marilyn would lapse into fuzzed-out vagaries. Like many creative types, they were too dreamy to be sharp. Why chain yourself to the moment when you could be slipping in and out of Technicolor?

During cocktail parties or interviews, Marilyn was always clutching at a connection—frantic for something genuine, something substantial to say. She'd never be snappy and pert like Amy, nor would she ever get the hang of small talk. For Marilyn, words were much more than surface banter. That's why she rehearsed so much for her roles—going over the lines until they became her own. If you changed a line (as directors often do) she couldn't snap back and adjust; she was already too invested. She'd never be an ad-libber or improv comic—words were too weighted, too important for that.

Marilyn was at her best in the long-form interviews she gave later in life—where she could dig deep into subjects and steep in them. But short interviews and rapid-fire press conferences put her on the spot. She saw them as miniature confrontations, and protected herself with evasive quips.

Reactions were mixed when the interview aired on *Person to Person*. Reporter Richard Heller thought Marilyn presented "beautifully, modestly and with her famous smile charming as ever." Others weren't so kind, gleefully snarking about the "same old Marilyn." Milton and Marilyn had hoped to convince the naysayers that they had the upper hand, that MMP would win this battle with Fox. For the second time that year, they fell short.

To make matters worse, Amy had made such an impression on screen that one headline read FORGET MARILYN, WHAT ABOUT AMY GREENE? Hollywood director Jean Negulesco called the next day, offering Amy the lead in *Bonjour Tristesse*. Amy was kind enough to dismiss these offers and brush off the attention, crediting her performance to what she called The Ed Murrow Effect: "I was terrific because I was making googly eyes at this wonderful man."

Negulesco was one of the few directors Marilyn actually trusted. He'd directed her in *Millionaire* and immediately recognized her sensitivity and intelligence. He took her to long dinners where they'd discuss Matisse, Chagall, Braque, and Gauguin, and lent her books such as *The Old Man and the Sea* and W.H. Hudson's *Green Mansions*. He even painted her portrait on oil canvas, a special gift that she kept by her bed at the Gladstone. That this man was now offering roles to Amy must have struck Marilyn as a terrible blow.

The next hit came when Milton shot down an NBC offer for

$2 million and six TV shows. "I turned it down because I knew she didn't belong on television," Milton insisted years later. "She belonged in cinema. Really, I turned it down because I believed in her."

He didn't explain his reasoning to Marilyn, nor did he consult her before answering no. "She turned to me and said, 'You don't think I can do it.' I said, 'No, you can do it. But you belong in cinema, not television. Cinema—period.' So then she agreed, because I had turned down 2 million bucks for myself, so what kind of a bastard could I be? But she felt, after I turned down the TV thing, that I didn't believe in her as an actress. That's why she turned to Lee Strasberg and leaned on him so much."

Her trust in Milton permanently rattled, Marilyn threw herself into working with Lee, who'd been coaching her privately for weeks. She'd been making excellent progress, impressing him with her openness and keen emotional sensors. With Lee, she never stuttered or stammered. He found her incisive and articulate, never ditsy. "I find her quite brilliant," gushed Lee, already enraptured with Marilyn's potential. "It's rare to find that underlying personality so close to the top and so anxious to get out, so quick to respond. It was almost as if a person was waiting for a button to be pushed, and you push it and a door opens, and you see gold and jewels and so on." Lee was convinced she was ready to take the next step—classes at the formidable Malin Studios.

It was time to dive deep into acting again.

✍ By 1955, Lee Strasberg's Actors Studio had become the inner sanctum of quality acting, whether you admitted it or not. Thanks to members such as Brando and Dean, the industry's "sweatshirt school of acting" went mainstream—not just on Broadway but in Hollywood, too. Lee wanted to expand, bring his bohemian little tribe into the future. Most of all, he wanted Marilyn, who seemed to drop from floaty Hollywood Candyland into the dusty rooms of Malin Studios at just the right moment. He already loved her.

Whether his students would was another matter. Clannish and bohemian, they clung to T-shirt-and-jeans exclusivity, a reverse hauteur just as rarified as Hollywood's glitter. "Becoming a member of the Actors Studio was more important than getting a job in Hollywood, even more important than getting good reviews on Broadway," said Ben Gazzara. "To get into the Actors Studio was the max. When Marilyn and people like that were invited in without the rigorous auditions that we youngsters had to go through we resented that, quite frankly." They wept when Lee announced Marilyn's impending arrival, worried that this was the beginning of the end. Was Lee—dazzled as he was by celebrity—about to sell out?

Marilyn was the first Hollywood crossover to descend the steps of Malin Studios, bringing with her an unwelcome breeze of balmy LA air. Twice a week she'd walk down Broadway and into an old theater building, the heavy door clanging behind her. She'd slip into a metal chair in the back row. Lee would be pacing, booming about conscious preparation or imaginary realities. There was Ellen Burstyn, with her tremulous voice that always seemed ready to break into tears. Patricia Neal with her elegant pageboy and lazy-moon eyes. Thirty-year-old Paul Newman sat and smoked in a white T-shirt and loafers, feet propped on his chair like a teenager, a look of intense engagement on his chiseled face.

With their casual clothes, intense looks, and deli coffee in white paper cups, the Studio crowd could be chilly and insular. They spoke almost in riddles, their banter strung with Leeisms and their own inside references. Their arcane language bewildered some but attracted Marilyn, who always favored the byzantine over the simple. But she was shy, in a class full of extroverts. Would they ever accept her?

Marilyn knew what it was like to be on the outs. Back in LA, she'd attempted to join Charles Laughton's Shakespeare group. She showed up twice, too paralyzed to participate, painfully insecure about her lack of education. But at twenty-eight, Marilyn was no longer the starlet-on-training-wheels in a too-tight halter lugging around a dictionary. Taking the leap into the Actors Studio was nothing. She'd already put everything on the line by fleeing Hollywood and breaking her contract with Fox. Marilyn would not languish—not in a marriage, not even in a book that was unfulfilling, and certainly not in her career. She'd sooner be in peril than a slump.

To take the focus off her looks, Marilyn dressed down in a loose men's crewneck, wore no makeup, and covered her hair in a white kerchief. Along with her purse, she carried a Thermos that looked like it had come from a child's lunch box.

Those first few weeks she barely spoke, sitting quietly in the back, camel coat slung round her shoulders. "She was so modest, so attentive," recalled one Studio member, "that she could have been some girl who had just come from a convent." Thanks to her humility, most of Lee's students liked her in spite of themselves. She even won over the skeptical Gazzara: "Everyone seemed to like her too—including me."

What would it really be like to work with Marilyn Monroe, who already had a reputation for being a diva? Her chronic lateness had been grudgingly accepted in LA, but Lee locked the doors at eleven sharp. And while Marilyn loved New York, she never would adapt to its frenzied pace. "Busy" for her meant maybe one meeting in the afternoon and a party later that night. She had to do everything at her own pace—and that usually meant spending hours priming for a meeting and the rest of the afternoon collapsed in recovery.

Luckily, Lee understood Marilyn's internal logic: "Darling, you don't have to be on time for anything. Be early." He enlisted the help of Studio actor Delos Smith, who happily became her male lady's maid. He'd arrive to find her inevitably in the bath, soaking in perfumed bath oil. (She'd had to bathe in dirty water as a child when she lived with her foster families, so Delos allowed her this luxury.) When she finally would emerge from the tub, she'd never dry off and dress—she'd wrap herself in a towel and lie in bed for at least thirty more minutes. After that, it was impossible to get her up. Eventually, Delos cracked the code of How to Get Marilyn Out of Bed. The key was to sneak into the bed while she was still bathing. So when she'd stagger from bath to bed, poised to fling herself under the covers, she'd see Delos lying in the sheets, shoes and all. That was usually enough incentive to keep her out of the bed—with no other choice than to get dressed and eventually go to Malin Studios.

It makes sense that Marilyn's first Studio friend was this bearded boho iconoclast. Delos saw past Marilyn's Hollywood varnish. "At home, she lost all that star glamour. Her clothes were unkempt, I don't know what the maid was doing all that time." He found her eccentricities endearing, beguiling as a child's. As tokens of friendship and gratitude, she'd give Delos crazy little gifts such as labels clipped from her Maximillian mink coat or thirty-five-cent makeup mirrors. Once she quietly slipped a pair of airplane booties in his pocket.

In the beginning, Marilyn was skittish as a hunted rabbit. Those first few weeks she stuck close to Delos, even pinching him when someone got too close or brushed up against her. (He didn't mind.)

Her first scene was from Clifford Odets's *Golden Boy* (Marilyn's choice) which she was scheduled to perform with dark-haired actor Phil Roth. Along with her initials, MM, Marilyn had penciled in PL10757, Phil's name and number, on the script. She went over her lines alone for days in her suite, wrapped in a bathrobe drinking coffee. Finally she worked up her courage to call Phil and picked up the telephone.

"Hi!" she said, in a soft, baby voice. "This is Marilyn."

"Marilyn who?" he joked.

"You know," she hesitated, worried that she'd dialed the wrong number. "Marilyn, that actress from class."

"Ohhhh, that Marilyn." Phil invited her over to practice. This would be the first time she'd met with any of them outside class.

By the time she'd climbed the stairs to his fifth-floor walk-up, Marilyn was out of breath. Looking around at his paper-strewn apartment, she said, "You need some woman to clean up this place." Before they started, she insisted on emptying ashtrays, sweeping the floor, and arranging Phil's papers in neat little stacks. (She never cleaned her own place, let alone a man's—housework was acceptable only as a novelty or game.) Perhaps she wanted to endear herself to him, or perhaps she needed to declutter before she could focus. Either way, Roth was charmed.

Despite Malin Studios' casual atmosphere, Marilyn prepared for her scenes as if they were MGM screen tests, carefully selecting her props and makeup. She once picked a scene to do with Delos from French playwright Eugène Brieux's *Damaged Goods*. (Marilyn was playing a 1920s prostitute with syphilis.) She wore a sheer silk sheath with no bra underneath—just "nipples, smiles and dimples . . ." She twirled a string of long costume pearls, causing Delos to swing instinctively around his stethoscope. The students laughed; Lee loved it—though Paula Strasberg, his wife, later claimed they looked like "two goddamn pinwheels." "Gone were the strained efforts of artificial behavior and clichés," remembered classmate Ed Easty. "She held nothing back. After the scene, Lee whirled around in his seat and demanded from the class, 'Well, was that scene excellent or not?' The crowd, not easy with praise, answered yes, yes it was."

As Marilyn tried new scenes in class, she discovered that she'd been preparing for the Studio all her life. Her work with Michael Chekhov had already familiarized her with Stanislavski's technique—drawing on personal experiences to channel dramatic emotions. She felt a kinship with these actors, her fellow class-mates who suffered through sleep deprivation, bread-and-water di-ets, and psychoanalysis just to get into character. These were her people—people who followed instinct instead of rules, intuition instead of doctrine. She began to see that there was some crazy magic happening here in Malin Studios and was willing to do any-thing to belong—even break through her crippling shyness.

"Marilyn came to the Actors Studio with her hat in her hand," wrote Shelley Winters. "She wanted so badly to connect to the theatre people, serious writers and performers." But they could be an impenetrable crew. The members themselves could be bois-terous and frank, yet as a whole they remained strangely sphinx-like. They socialized and worked and partied in their own magical world. She'd always been a bit of an outcast on the Hollywood circuit, and she didn't care—but these were people she admired. For her, the doors of the Elmo and Stork Club were flung wide open, but she needed to earn her right to bars like Jim Downey's, with whiskey shots for five cents apiece.

It's hard to imagine the world's most famous woman intimidated by cheap liquor and scrappy kids in undershirts. With their de-grees from the New School and Bolshie camaraderie, they had everything Marilyn didn't—sophistication, formal training, and re-spect. Most were years younger with far more professional confi-dence. Those nights taking classes at UCLA would never make up for her dismal education. How could she compete with these sharp ingenues when she felt like last year's washed-up starlet? Perhaps she should have stayed married, stayed in Hollywood, and faded into her thirties with dignity.

Lee recognized Marilyn's insecurity and fretted over his new protégée. He urged reluctant Studio members to welcome her into the fold. Like the parent of a shy child, he was always pushing other actors to include her. "We're her family now," Lee once said privately to Shelley Winters. "You can be a true-blue sister to Marilyn." Back in LA Marilyn really had looked up to the older Shelley as a big sister. In 1951, they shared men, minks, swimsuits, Sinatra records, and a rent-controlled apartment in West Hollywood. Marilyn had to borrow a bed from Twentieth's prop department; the only furniture she'd owned was a white piano. Both were obsessively ambitious, hypersensitive, and preferred work to holidays. To stave off Sunday hangovers they played classical records on Shelley's Capehart while reading aloud from the album notes. At 12:01 sharp, they'd switch to Nat King Cole and Frank Sinatra—enough art for one day.

Shelley had the same sensual, animal intelligence that beguiled and infuriated Hollywood's directors. Over pastrami on rye at Greenblatt's Deli, they'd practiced the parted lip smile that became Marilyn's trademark. Fragile and prone to hysterics, Shelley wept in bathrooms over married men, cried on Marlon Brando's shoulder, and lost a bottle of placebo Seconals in Elizabeth Taylor's camel coat. Shelley was sympathetic to Marilyn—she, too, had filled her prescriptions at Schwab's, walked across Sunset Boulevard to Victor's and chased benzos with triple gin martinis while terrified bartenders plied her with hors d'oeuvres. Now they were both in New York to perfect their craft.

Marlon Brando was the type to stick a bottle of Chianti in his back pocket, whisk you away on his motorcycle, and carry you up to his lair lit with pyramids of orange incense and candles stuck in Coca-Cola bottles. But underneath the swagger and brass was a man who loved kittens and cried while reading *The Little Engine That Could* to his nephew. He had a gentle, protective streak—especially with women. Back in Hollywood, he had come to the rescue of a wildly drunk Shelley Winters and sobered her up with onion soup and crackers. (She refused to eat anything unless he allowed her more drinks, so they compromised on wine spritzers.)

Marlon and Marilyn were an obvious match: Both shared an electrifying intensity and a compulsively perfectionist streak. Like Marilyn, he infuriated as often as he bewitched. Much to directors' chagrin, he was always chewing gum—he'd only pretend to take it out when it came time to film a scene—even a makeout scene. Like Marilyn, Marlon was a compulsive reader—Kant, Rousseau, Locke, Nietzsche, Melville, Faulkner, Tolstoy, Dostoyevsky, and his favorite, *Wuthering Heights*. They even shared the same breakfast drink: raw eggs whisked in a glass of hot milk.

More important, Marlon had what most celebrities lack: perspective. To prepare for his role as a wounded soldier, he ditched his suite at the Chateau Marmont to stay in a thirty-two-bed ward at a veterans' hospital in the San Fernando Valley. His refusal to accept special treatment won over the veterans, who included him in their pranks (pillow fights and hypodermic syringes as makeshift water pistols). Marilyn committed to her roles just as obsessively—you'd ask her what time it was and she'd answer in character.

She admired the way Marlon barreled around class pretending to be a chicken, or directing *Hedda Gabler* as if it were a futuristic Russian dystopia. "While he's playing a scene, he's always searching," Marilyn told *Pageant Magazine*. "You feel he's trying to find out about himself. He searches under everything . . . while he's talking to you." She'd call him in the middle of the night (he was usually awake) to discuss scenes from class. What did he think? What did he think Lee thought? Friends like Marlon encouraged her to trust her inner gifts. She knew he was on a similar quest, and his friendship gave her courage. Amy observed, "If Marlon turned up at the Actors Studio and said, 'Do you want to go to dinner,' fine. Now what they did after dinner . . . I don't think it was planned. If it happened it happened."

Tentatively, Marilyn started joining her classmates for lunch at Howard Johnson's, drinks at Jim Downey's, and of course, the Studio's notorious parties. Shelley Winters might be running around in Laurette Taylor's old nightgown or a wrinkled checked shirt thrown over a cocktail dress. Grand theater dame Cheryl Crawford would be there; so would Ben Gazzara, Anne Jackson and Eli Wallach, Julie Harris, and Maureen Stapleton. Even notorious recluse William Inge would be poking shyly around. At 2 a.m., they'd pile into Checker cabs—heaps of fur coats "ranging from squirrel to sable"—and taxi to Lee's apartment on Central Park West. Lee would bring out his records, and they'd sit on the floor listening to opera while his wife served up plates of borscht and pot roast.

This was a dramatic shift from the fizzy, urbane sort of socializing she'd been up to for the past three months with Milton Greene and the Rat Pack. Instead of the Elmo's red velvet ropes, there was Paul Newman taping up streamers and tossing confetti. Instead of late-night mambos with Capote to the sounds of Count Basie, there were tramp banjo bands (friends of a friend's) playing "loudly and badly." Instead of caviar cups and Dom Pérignon, they drank punch-bowl concoctions of cheap wine, vodka, and fruit juice—and all were expected to chip in.

These sorts of parties were new to Marilyn, but she loved them. She loved how all that passion at class spilled into parties. Hollywood parties were all about sex or, even worse, networking. She'd rather stay home with a bottle of wine than brave the glaring emptiness of Doheny Drive. Despite her modeling background and high-octane flash, Marilyn had more in common with these ramshackle bohemians than anyone in LA. But did her colleagues think so, too?

Months into her work at the Studio, Marilyn was still occasionally met with frosty reserve. This skepticism always sprang from her movie star glamour. Despite the black polo coat and newsboy cap, her beauty was undeniable. "Even with no makeup Marilyn looked terrific," said Ben Gazzara. "I'll never forget, Marilyn was sitting next to me, you know, during a class, and there was a scene being played called *The Cat* by Colette, and it's about a young couple waking up after their wedding night and rolling in bed naked and Marilyn turns to me and says, 'Ben, would you like to do that scene with me?' And I said, 'I don't think so, Marilyn.' I did refuse; I was a gentleman. You see, she scared me."

Her overwhelming sensuality intimidated many of the younger actors, men and women alike. Carroll Baker admitted to having been jealous and insecure in her presence. Baker wrote of their first meeting: "I was already hating her for flaunting her availability at Jack [Baker's husband] when she turned to say hello to me—and presented me with that same seductive quality of 'Come on'! I suddenly felt drawn to her and leaned in a bit closer than necessary to accept her outstretched hand. Her hand was lusciously warm and plump, and I found myself clinging to it that added moment. Maybe I imagined it, but I thought I smelled the fruity aroma of sex."

No wonder she never stopped worrying about being seen as the dumb blonde. She saw her classmates as colleagues—they saw her as a vampy pinup girl. Marilyn could have been the valedictorian of Vassar, and she'd still be ditzy until proven deep, bimbo until proven bookish. Had she fled the slick sexism of Hollywood only to be mired in a subtler sort of misogyny?

The sexism wasn't always subtle. Carroll Baker recalls playwright

Paddy Chayefsky stomping around the Studio with a smirk: "Oh, boy, would I like to fuck that!" When he was formally introduced to Marilyn at a Fire Island party he stared mutely at her chest: "Gee, I thought you'd be much fuller."

Even benign rejection tended to crush the hypersensitive Marilyn. She once phoned Louis Gossett Jr. and asked him if he wanted to do a love scene with her from *The Rose Tattoo*. Gossett turned down the opportunity, so starstruck by his classmate that he knew he'd be unable to utter a single line.

"She would walk into class with a man's shirt tied at her waist, her feet in flip-flops, the clean musky smell of Lifebuoy soap wafting after her," he remembered. "Her hair, pulled back with a rubber band, was always a little wet, as if she'd just stepped out of a shower. She took a liking to me. I'd come in the room and she'd be going, 'Where's Lou?' I couldn't do any scenes with her, she was just one of the sexiest, most wonderful women I've ever met. I almost had to quit class because of her. With that Lifebuoy soap and that woman sitting there in the flip-flops—I swear, I've never been affected so much by a woman in all my life."

Of course, Marilyn felt alienated after events like these. She had reached out—she who was new to the Studio, still a bit of an outsider. How was she to know that on her, flip-flops, rubber bands, and the scent of cheap soap were more potent than a cocktail of stilettos, red lipstick, and Chanel No 5?

But Marilyn was determined to stick it out. She'd spent years working with jaded directors who screamed "Cut!," stubbed out their cigarettes, then ran home to their air-conditioned penthouses and B-list models. The Actors Studio was her chance to cast off all that cheap sequined drudgery.

As she threw herself into her work, Marilyn found herself remarkably suited to Method acting. It matched her nature, exploratory and inward-focused. Years earlier, photographer Philippe

Halsman would get her into character by inventing situations: terrorized by a monster, or kissed by a lover, or drinking the most delicious mai tai. Lee dug even deeper, pushing her to excavate her own heavy past. She had plenty of dark matter to draw upon—foster mothers muttering doomsday prayers over breakfast, the orphanage with its cardboard birthday cakes full of dust. A born student, Marilyn took this very seriously, fearlessly conjuring bolts of memory, electric and terrifying.

She stuck to a grueling schedule—private classes with Lee on Wednesdays and Fridays, more classes Wednesdays and Thursdays, Malin Studios Tuesdays and Fridays, and psychoanalysis five days a week. She started arriving to class on time, relying less and less on Delos. The one time she was late (Dr. Hohenberg's session ran overtime), she ran into her classmate Fred Stewart on 44th Street near Fifth Avenue. The doors were locked, and Marilyn was distressed. "Can't we sneak in some way? I don't want to miss anything." Fred led her up an iron spiral staircase to a tiny little alcove above the stage. They huddled, hidden in shadows, Marilyn rapt and reverent.

Gradually, her dedication became obvious even to the most skeptical. Word quickly spread through New York's theater circles that Marilyn was "working like a Trojan," staying late at the Actors Studio, and skipping her rounds on the social circuit. "Must make much much more more more effort," she wrote in her journal. "Remember you can sit on top of the world . . . Remember there is nothing you lack—nothing to be self-conscious about—you have everything but the discipline and technique which you are learning and seeking on your own—after all nothing was or is being given to you—you have had none of this work thrown your way—you sought it—it didn't seek you."

Around this time, Marilyn revealed to Shelley Winters that all of this—New York, the Studio, the psychoanalysis, and MMP—

was a crusade. "That's how she put it," Shelley remembered, "a crusade to find the meaning of her own life that would give her the strength to succeed in being a 'true actress.' She said that—'true actress.' It was like she wanted to trade in who she had been and become something else."

For the first time, Marilyn began to believe in her own talent. She had dared to provoke the studio system; now all eyes were on her. "She wanted what she deserved," recalled her friend Ralph Roberts. "She was smart to refuse to do any more of their bidding. And if they fired her, she said they'd want her back but she'd only agree under her own terms."

Marilyn was right: In ten months, Fox would be begging for her. She was about to bring Hollywood to its knees.

Eight
The Strasbergs

"Being a most serious actress is not something
God has removed from my destiny. . . . It's
therefore my prerogative to make the dream of
creative fulfillment come true for me. That is
what I believe God is saying to me and is the
answer to my prayers."   MARILYN MONROE

*L*ee Strasberg became Marilyn's guru and god—prowling the
classroom in horn-rimmed glasses and rumpled-up garments
that vaguely resembled hospital scrubs. "Speak up!" he'd bellow.
"Try harder!" She'd watch, lips parted, smoke curling up from her

cigarette, light streaming on her face like a da Vinci Madonna. Very quickly, it became obvious that she was Lee's favorite.

This student-teacher bond extended far beyond class. Marilyn began dining at his home, often staying late into the evening. Lee and Paula took in actors as if they were stray kittens. Marilyn would soon become their favorite kitten.

A retired stage actress and Tallulah Bankhead's best friend, Paula Strasberg was steeped in old theater lore—stage makeup, hot lights, and heavy red curtains. In her youth she'd played the sloe-eyed coquette. Paula loved anything trimmed, beribboned, feathered, or sequined, and in those days she looked like she'd stepped straight out of the Moulin Rouge. She'd given that up to be den mother of the theater tribe, and while black snoods and kerchiefs replaced modish little veils, there was still something lushly sensual about her. She was easy to picture as an overripe Colette, with her rich throaty laughs, lace handkerchiefs, and Japanese fans scattered round the floor along with smelling salts, tarot cards, and Bally dance slippers.

By the time she met Marilyn, Paula had become the official Jewish Mother of New York's theater crowd. Her kitchen was legendary—the tiled floor in black and white checks, the fridge stocked with champagne, ice cream, and apple pies. Actors flocked to the kitchen every Sunday for brunch, piling their plates with bialys, lox, and cream cheese. Clifford Odets would be looming over the counter, drunkenly reciting poetry. Franchot Tone would barrel in bloodied up from a bar fight or howling over his latest girlfriend. At the Strasbergs' you were permitted—even encouraged—to be different. You didn't need to censor yourself, and "normal" was a four-letter word. EVERY EMOTION IS VALID said a sign Paula had pasted onto the kitchen wall. No wonder Marilyn felt so at home.

Paula was the perfect surrogate mother—always ready to coddle you with hugs or horoscopes or ice cream from Serendipity. Marilyn loved being mothered, especially by Paula, but she had much more in common with the prickly, cerebral Lee. She worshipped Lee's passion, his focus, even his bristly intellectualism. True, he could be pedantic (he loved both Bach and Beethoven, but Bach was better—no matter what). This could grate on people—especially his family—but Marilyn loved rigid, uncompromising men. She could listen to Lee for hours, kneeling by his feet in the library as he smoked his pipe and rhapsodized on German philosophy or Kabuki theater.

The Strasbergs ensconced Marilyn as one of their own—even more than did the charming, affable Greenes, with their gorgeous family and white Christmases in Connecticut. For a changeling like Marilyn, even the warmest nuclear families could feel chilly and insular. The Strasbergs were expansive, sprawling, and delightfully imperfect. Their sense of family expanded to include anyone like-minded—the only prerequisite was talent. For Lee and Paula, art ran thicker than blood. They weren't the kind of parents who'd blow you off for their daughter Susie's ballet recital or their son Johnny's rugby match.

This was fabulous for Marilyn, but Susie and Johnny found their father cold. Family closeness was entirely wrapped up in theater—the work. If Susie cried over a boy or a mishap at school, Lee would brush her off: "Darling, I'm really only concerned as this pertains to the work." Johnny had it even worse: He wanted to drive a convertible, hammer houses for the summer, and eventually study medicine. He had little interest in theater, and at the Strasbergs', theater was everything.

"Our door was open to many artists, but Marilyn was special," remembered Susie, who at sixteen was preparing to appear on Broadway in *The Diary of Anne Frank*. It was obvious to Susie that Marilyn and Lee shared some strange affinity. Lee had always been surrounded by striking, talented women—Carroll Baker, Julie Newmar, Anne Bancroft—but Marilyn was different. What was it about this strange, floaty woman that had her flinty father so enthralled?

Susie remembers the first day she met Marilyn—both chilly and warm, it was just barely spring. The scent of pot roast and onions mixed with smoke from Lee's pipe while Mozart's concertos played softly in the background. Paula flailed her arms to signal "Quiet upon entry—Daddy's coaching someone!" Lee never coached one on one—that was Paula's job. Even more surprising was the sound of gentle laughter. Suddenly, Lee flung open the doors of his study and stepped into the dining room with Marilyn Monroe.

This was Susie's vision of Marilyn—a sunbeam on her father's arm, cottony hair, eyes huge and blue and skin as bare and vaporous as a Fragonard milkmaid's. The hall was narrow and poky, and at dusk the light flickered against the red-flocked wallpaper, creating the chiaroscuro effect of smoky oil paintings. Marilyn stood out in powder pastels surrounded by a halo of light.

Susie watched, shocked. Her father—who never could stand being touched—cradled Marilyn's arm in his own.

"Hi, I'm Marilyn Monroe," she said. "You might not remember me, but we met in California."

As if she possibly could have forgotten meeting Marilyn Monroe.

Visiting LA the year before, Susie had been crashing the Fox lot with her friend Steffi Skolsky, when she'd stumbled on Cukor's *Show Business* set. She'd watched in awe as Marilyn danced and sang, "We're having a heat wave, a tropical heat wave. . . ." And it was hot, crushingly hot, no breeze, palm fronds sticky and unmoving—or, as Paul Newman might put it, "just another lousy day in paradise." Dozens of cameramen crowded the humid room.

DiMaggio stood stone-faced, wiping his brow with a spotless starched handkerchief. In her limp brown hair and sickly dull skin, Susie felt self-conscious and puny. Then Marilyn slipped on the slick floor. She looked embarrassed and lost—almost desperate. And though Marilyn was a megawatt star, Susie felt sorry for her.

Later, she wandered upstairs in a trance, straight into Marilyn's dressing room. "Come on, face, give me a break," Marilyn sang to herself in the mirror, wiping off lipstick and flesh-toned pancake. She glanced up at Susie. "Sorry, I look like shit," she said with a sigh, not at all angry at her little intruder. When she realized Susie was only a girl, she gasped, "Oops, sorry," covering her mouth with a manicured hand.

In platform heels and a Carmen Miranda headdress, Marilyn towered over little Susie, who was barely five-one. In full makeup, she seemed larger than life. But now she was touchable, smaller, and far more beautiful.

"It didn't seem possible," Susie recalled. "Was this vibrant, shimmering mermaid who somehow managed to undulate on her high heel—this clear-eyed, normal-size girl—the same overblown, sexy, exotic creature I'd met a little over a year ago in Hollywood?" It's as if this were the real Marilyn in her natural habitat, unleashed from Hollywood's gaudy zoo.

After dinner, Lee lit his pipe and put on a Vivaldi record. Paula started the dishes, Johnny slinked off to his room, and Susie joined Marilyn in the huge study, which looked out onto Central Park. She watched Marilyn browse the bookshelves in awe—books on science, psychology, art, anthropology, politics, music, dance, costume, customs. Books in French, German, and Italian (Lee taught himself all three as a child). He even had books in languages he couldn't read—such as Japanese—and translators who made house calls when he felt like learning them. "God, has he actually read all these?" Marilyn exclaimed, visibly impressed. "These damned books," Paula grimaced. "We'll have the greatest library in the world, and starve to death!"

Marilyn nestled on the floor next to the mirrored fireplace wall as Lee bombarded her with questions: Who was the actress she most admired? (Eleonora Duse.) Which poets did she love most? (Whitman, Dickinson.) Was she interested in psychology? (Yes!) He wanted to get to the white hot core of things, just like Marilyn did.

Susie followed Marilyn into the kitchen and found her scanning Paula's little shelf of books on tarot, diet, astrology, and Catholic metaphysics. Much to Susie's surprise, Marilyn asked about her acting career—what parts had she done since they'd met in California? Oh, and did Susie know they were both Geminis? Paula beamed from her station at the sink, silently plunging dishes into soapy water.

Just then, Susie remembered something Marilyn had told her the previous year in California. "I really admire your father," Marilyn whispered, her lips hot and close to Susie's ear. "I'm going to come to New York and study acting with him. It's what I want to do more than anything."

"Sure you are," Susie had thought as she walked away. "There's about as much chance of that as a snowstorm in July in Hollywood."

 They grew to know each other cautiously, making the first shy overtures in the kitchen as Paula stirred pots of red cabbage and brisket. Marilyn would lean statuesque against the wall, Susie perched on a stool, elbows propped on the counter. Still in her school uniform of V-neck sweater and Peter Pan collar, bobby socks, and white buck shoes, crinoline peeking out of her circle skirt. They'd trade beauty tips. Marilyn admired Susie's hair—she always wanted to have silky locks like that. Susie confessed she'd give anything for "two more inches of leg," and Marilyn passed on Amy's trick of matching her heels to her stockings—black with black, nude with nude. (Susie immediately went shopping.) Marilyn taught her how to lighten her hair with lemon and beer: "If it doesn't work, you can always drink it. Once you're legal of course," she added with a wink.

It wasn't just makeup tips. Even this early, Susie could sense that Marilyn took control of her own image, her own destiny, in ways that she hadn't seen before. Years later she would channel her own Marilyn moments—once shocking a photographer by demanding to go over proofs herself. "Well," Susie would say with a sniff, "Marilyn does it."

At sixteen, Susie longed to grow up and slip into Marilyn's stilettos. (Only Cuban heels allowed.) Like many teens, her concept of Marilyn was wrapped in poeticism. She fantasized about being Marilyn the way she imagined being Anna Karenina; Mary, Queen of Scots; or Queen Elizabeth. Yet for all her star power, Marilyn was oddly accessible. "She wasn't distant like Greta Garbo, haughty and pretentious like Joan Crawford, or foreign like Ingrid Bergman. I felt like she could be any friend of mine, or me."

Most women Marilyn's age would have taken a maternal attitude toward Susie. But Marilyn related to her as an equal. "She had this kind of innocence and fun," remembered Susie. The two were co-conspirators at Sunday brunches—two teenagers slipping away from the adult table. Those crisp afternoons they'd float through Lee's study, staring idly out the window at Central Park, all clear blue sky and budding trees. While lounging in Paula's room, they found a beat-up copy of the *Kama Sutra* and decided to "rehearse" on the floor in their skirts. Marilyn was the man: "Boy, this is a switch."

They leaped up on hearing Lee's footsteps. "Education Inter-ruptus," Marilyn said. But the major lesson was that even in this era of doomed femmes and cast-iron virgins, sex could be breezy—even fun.

Another Sunday a young student approached Marilyn—all shaky, as if he were meeting the queen or walking a plank. He presented her with a cocktail ring, which she held to her eye for inspection. Instead of a stone, it had a miniature portrait of her infamous nude calendar.

"Oh, Susie," she cried, "look what they've done."

Susie gave the student a black look—how dare he upset Marilyn?

"See," Marilyn moaned, "they've smudged my eye."

In the buttoned-up world of the fifties, Marilyn was fun and unfettered. Shopping with Marilyn was pure joy, and Susie loved to watch her scamper round the dressing rooms in underwear or less. Everyone has a version of "that time Marilyn got naked in the fitting room of Saks." But for Susie, it was a revelation: "Listen, in a day and age when we were wearing girdles, she talked about sex as if it were something natural and normal.

"She knew in the fifties when very few of us did that the an-swer to her happiness wasn't in furs or minks or fame, it was in-side. She was a gutsy, courageous lady. She made that journey inward, which is dangerous. She stood up before the women's move-ment did. She broke away from the Hollywood Studio. She stood up to the McCarthy committee. She risked a lot."

❦ Gradually, Marilyn became part of the Strasberg family, even spending the night in Johnny's room (he'd be banished to the couch). Both shy, they circled each other warily like teen alley cats.

"He was the only boy in America not happy to have Marilyn Monroe sleeping in his bed," Susie said of her disgruntled little brother.

Of course, they fell in love with Marilyn—not just her beauty and talent but her childlike naturalness, her easy grace in accepting favors, flattery, or a frozen hot chocolate from Serendipity. She was more fun to compliment than anyone in the world—she'd smile and say "Gee, thanks!" and look like you'd made her day. People who are good at taking compliments are generally good at giving them, and Marilyn tended to compliment Susie far more than Susie ever praised Marilyn. "I love your lipstick, Susie, where did you buy it?" she'd say, or "People respect you, Susie, that's so wonderful."

"Because she was so much needier than I was," said Susie, who envied the way her parents doted on Marilyn, "she got a certain kind of attention that of course I didn't get." But Marilyn was remarkably healthy in some ways, aware of her desires, interior and otherwise. Thanks to her keen emotional intelligence, she had the ability to communicate her needs, approaching directors for extra takes, or requesting help from her drama coaches when she needed it.

Marilyn tended to get what she wanted without really asking— an ice cream sundae, house calls from hairdressers, tailors at midnight, script changes, late passes, doctor's notes. This could be an infuriating quality to behold. It's easy to call her needy, princessy— but she gave as much as she got and more. Mikomoto pearls to Paula, a Thunderbird for Johnny, bags of clothes and attention for Susie, endless funding for the Actors Studio. On a smaller scale, she knew what you needed before you knew it yourself—a cigarette, a tête-à-tête in the powder room, a sweater, or simply to be left alone.

Ultimately, Susie did get to the bottom of why Marilyn fascinated her father and everyone else: "She permitted us to see her angels and demons without fear." It was this vulnerability that was so bewitching—and, of course, what made her a perfect match for Strasberg and the Method.

Hollywood was shocked by Marilyn's attachment to Lee—what was their precious pinup doing with the king of "mumbleschool" acting? "She is being taught acting by the kind of people who don't believe in underarm deodorants," ranted Billy Wilder. "These are the kind of people who believe in sitting on the floor when there are six comfortable chairs in the room. They are making her throw away everything she has and be ashamed of herself. Her success is she can't act. She's going through a whole evolution and if she takes it seriously it is the end of Monroe. She will lose her male audience. She will become a Julie Harris, and she will lose everything of her own and make herself ugly and lose the healthy admiration of the crowd in the bleachers. I don't know who to blame—Lee Strasberg or Milton Greene. Who is Milton Greene anyhow?"

The press didn't know what to make of it either. Soon enough, her nemesis Dorothy Kilgallen was snarking in her columns, hinting that Lee Strasberg was replacing Milton Greene.

"Milton Greene was not my Svengali," Marilyn snapped. "I'm nobody's slave and never have been. . . . Now they write that Lee Strasberg is my Svengali. But why shouldn't I have a coach? Why shouldn't I try to improve myself? I want to accomplish certain things. I am ambitious. Is it a crime to better yourself? It's good to study with different teachers and you'll find something to learn in each of them. I studied privately with Michael Chekhov as I am now studying with Lee Strasberg. And I am learning."

To the outside world, it often looked like Marilyn was being controlled, manipulated by Lee the hypnotic guru or Milton the lovable puppeteer. No one would acknowledge that at last, Marilyn was remarkably in control of her own life and making her usual informed, empowered decision to learn from the best.

"You see," she explained, "not only didn't I have any acting experience, but I worked in pictures where I was directed by directors who had never directed before. I had directors so stupid all they can do is repeat the lines of the script to me like they're reading a timetable. So I didn't get help from them. I had to find it elsewhere."

In the hands of talented, sensitive directors Marilyn flourished, but many were fussy tyrants who scrambled over angles and lights, squeezed in shots, and cut just before six o'clock to save money. Other than themselves, they were most impressed with lavish sets, prizing fancy light fixtures, and spray-painted lions over quality acting. When Marilyn committed to a role she insisted on getting each shot right—no matter what the director said. Her concerns were giving each shot her best, each day learning more about her craft. "I believe in learning and developing myself," she said firmly. Her pursuit of knowledge was one of the most touching things about her.

This yearning went beyond dedication to art. Marilyn sought out mentors first for guidance—then for love. It's undeniable that she blurred boundaries, with midnight phone calls, correspondence that read like love letters, and transatlantic flights.

But neediness and confidence are not mutually exclusive. Marilyn needed love—but she certainly didn't need anyone's approval. For the most part, she kept her own counsel, often going against expert advice. Marilyn trusted her own talent and intuition more than she ever trusted anyone else—not her husbands, not Milton Greene, not even Lee.

⌘ Whether it was her career, her love life, or a book she was reading, Marilyn made up her own rules as she went along. In class she was highly professional but always a little bit playful and flirtatious. Even Eli Wallach hesitated to do scenes with her, concerned that "people might talk." This puzzled Marilyn—an actor such as Eli fretting over gossip? She'd been shrugging off public opinion for years. When she reached out to Lou Gossett about doing that scene from *The Rose Tattoo,* he was stunned. "Do you realize you'd be crossing racial barriers and entering forbidden territory?" Marilyn dismissed his concerns. They never did the scene, but Lou never forgot Marilyn's courage.

Ultimately, the Studio respected her for pushing the limits. After all, theirs was an ethos based on rawness, risk, and emotional honesty. "Monty Clift, Kim Stanley, Gerry Page, Marlon, Jimmy Dean," wrote Susie Strasberg, "they were closer to crazy than sensible. None of them had a nodding acquaintance with sensible." Slowly, Marilyn began to realize this was exactly where she belonged.

Her way of seeing things was always startlingly original—and her classmates appreciated her quirky logic and quick mind. They began to listen and perk up when she spoke. "Wellllll," she'd sigh in her cheruby bird tones, answering tentatively but earnestly with a light flicker of her brow. At first she'd hesitate, worried she might embarrass herself or say the wrong thing. "In an early observation," wrote the actor Gary Vitacco-Robles, "Marilyn watched Eli Wallach and Maureen Stapleton perform and was moved to tears by their emoting until Strasberg delivered thirty minutes of sharp criticism. Marilyn panicked and second-guessed her own judgment about acting." But gradually she began speaking up, even daring to disagree with her friends. When newbie Earle Hyman performed his first scene at the Studio, Eli Wallach criticized his work for being unclear. The room went silent until Marilyn raised her hand.

"Well, I don't know, Lee, but it seems to me that life is sometimes unclear."

Before long, Marilyn was joining the crowd for after-class drinks at Jim Downey's. "I enjoy the people here," she told a reporter that spring. "They love their work, they listen, and they look you in the eye." Her new friends were touched by how happy she was to be included.

Marilyn had surprised them. Many found they could relax around her; she was so at ease with the complexities of human experience and its endless range of emotion. That's what made her such a compelling actress and such a delightful friend. They knew that underneath the sex goddess was a brilliant baby animal—alert, responsive, and eager to learn.

"I think we all respected the fact that the best-known woman in America wanted to learn more about her craft," wrote Ben Gazzara. "She committed herself to get better," said Lou Gossett. "She was rubbing elbows with Estelle Parsons, Peggy Feury, Lee Grant, Kim Stanley, Eva Marie Saint—people who raised the bar—and she was raising the bar with them."

Lou rated Marilyn the best actor in the class. "If she had stayed, she would've had Oscars and Tonys and everything else. That's how natural she was."

꿴 Their respect gave her confidence—more confidence than all the awards and Hollywood contracts in the world. Perhaps she really could be a great dramatic actress—America's Eleonora Duse with a back-lot past and candy fluff hair.

If Marilyn's hopes were high, Lee's were even higher. One day that spring Marilyn joined Lee, Michael V. Gazzo, and Ben Gazzara for lunch at a Ninth Avenue diner. They chattered over tables crammed with ketchup bottles and creamers, tuna on rye, and wax-paper cones of cold tap water cradled in stainless steel. Marilyn sipped coffee in her black polo coat while Lee chattered on about a future class project: *Macbeth*.

"You see," he explained, his sandwich untouched and cut neatly in two, "Lady Macbeth's control over her husband has never been made completely clear." Only Marilyn could do it believably—have a man like Macbeth so utterly in her thrall. He thought Ben would work well with Marilyn and threatened to cast him as the lead.

Marilyn beamed, but Ben nearly spat out his coffee. "Marilyn was delightful," he wrote years later. "She spoke in an adorable little whisper, which worked very well for the movies, but Lady Macbeth would be strutting her stuff on a large stage, and it was doubtful that Marilyn would ever be heard past the second row. That didn't deter Lee. He obviously had a mad, fatherly crush on Marilyn and thought he could help her do just about anything."

Could he?

Nine

In Bloom

"Life starts from NOW."   MARILYN MONROE

By now, Marilyn was living in a three-room suite at the Waldorf-Astoria, on Park Avenue. "You entered Marilyn's apartment directly into the living room," remembers James Haspiel, Marilyn's teenage admirer and friend, "on a bulletin board there on the right there were pages from foreign magazines; a portrait of Albert Einstein, and another picture of Einstein walking down a road, seen from behind. There was another page that appeared to me to be a picture of a cluster of hungry orphans all huddled together." A sketch of Marilyn by actor Zero Mostel was propped on a tiny table.

Then the bedroom: False lashes cut into wedges scattered everywhere. Squat jars of Erno Lazslo's Phelityl cream sealed with glossy black lids. Nightstands crammed with bottles of Jicky, Fracas, and Chanel; cigarette packs stacked by blue tins of Nivea cream. Heaps of Ferragamos tumbling from the closet. An unmade bed pushed to the wall and strewn with books—*The Little Prince,* Freud's *Psychopathology of Everyday Life,* and *Stanislavsky Directs.* A telephone faced the headboard to hide her number from the riffraff. And a portrait of Abraham Lincoln pasted overhead like a rock star.

This all came at a price. Milton subsidized everything for Marilyn—even her personal expenses. He mortgaged his home to pay for her sublets, lawyers, hairdressers, beauticians, clothes, makeup, psychiatrists—even medical bills. One thousand a week for her suite at the Towers, $125 a week for psychoanalysis, $500 a week for "beautification," and $50 a week for perfume. On top of that was a press agent and a private secretary who moonlighted as hairstylist when Caruso couldn't make house calls. "She liked convenience," Milton recalled. "She was a bit lazy. She liked to have people come over to do her hair, wax her legs. She'd pay someone to brush her hair, because she might not end up brushing it herself." (Like that of most other platinum blondes, Marilyn's hair was high-maintenance. Her natural texture was quite kinky and needed regular straightening permanents, and her roots needed retouching every four or five days. Her baby-fine hair tangled quickly, and she shampooed it each day—highly unusual by mid-century standards. Stylists maintained Marilyn's shade with a special concoction of silver bleach mixed with twenty-volume peroxide and a violet toner to strip out the yellow.)

The cost was justified for Marilyn and Milton, who wanted to show Fox what she was worth. Besides, Marilyn loved the suite's airy Frenchness, the high ceilings flooded with sunlight, "bright and fluffy in blue and gold and a bit of white." She kept her windows thrown open, buckets of white camellias in the bedroom, and Sinatra spinning on the phonograph. She lived in white ter-rycloth bathrobes, belt tied behind her like a sash. In solitary mo-ments, she'd glide out to the balcony and light a cigarette, gulping in smoke and balmy city air.

"Hotel life is no kind of life for a woman," Jane Russell warned her. But it suited Marilyn—the starchy white sheets and free flowing mimosas, the unmoored feeling so conducive to creative work. When she wasn't working or socializing, she'd lie in bed reading, listening to records, or talking on the phone—activities made for hotels. This was the kind of solitude she loved—like her twenty-sixth birthday—alone at the Bel-Air, French doors flung open to a terrace of oleander, honeysuckle, and palms. Steaks, bottles of champagne. Joe phoning from New York. Rooms stuffed with telegrams, flowers, and presents from Fox.

For Marilyn, hotels featured heavily in those magical stretches when life hung in the balance, when she didn't know if she would make it or not. Back in 1951 she leased an elegant suite at the Beverly Carlton. She spent her days driving to Mal-ibu, her evenings at UCLA studying Titian, Tintoretto, and Ra-phael. At night she'd toss a chop in the Roto-Broil and leaf through scripts while munching on raw carrots. She'd lie back on her triple-size bed—her first real piece of furniture, the walls painted burgundy red, oyster white, and dove gray, just the way she wanted them.

"Great conflict was going on inside her," wrote Sidney Skolsky, who accompanied Marilyn on her Pacific Coast joyrides. She'd blast down 101 at 80 miles per hour, past Laurel Canyon, then park somewhere along Malibu beach and drag Sidney on exhaust-ing walks. "I'd listen to her talk," wrote Sidney. "Mainly she talked career. . . . She'd say that she'd keep working and that nothing—do you hear?—nothing would stop her from becoming a movie star. Then in the next breath she'd doubt that she could ever make it."

After one of these drives, she bought a full-length mirror. She stuck it on the door of her coffin-size closet, which tumbled with sweaters, slips, and hangers nabbed from Fox's wardrobe departments. At the top of the mirror she scrawled NUNC in red lipstick. It's Latin for "now."

꽃 As much as she loved her suite at the Waldorf, Marilyn spent more time roaming the streets, basking in the glamour of her first Manhattan spring. You'd see her strolling down Broadway in a white tennis sweater, sleeves pushed up, camel coat in hand, stopping at Childs' for burgers and black coffee. Or leaving Jim Downey's with Eli Wallach, her hair pushed back by a white kerchief, skin makeup-free and coated with lanolin. She spent days with Sam Shaw combing through Third Avenue junk shops, or hitting a Central Park hot dog stand before plopping onto a bench for a long afternoon of people-watching. She was eager to explore everything about New York—so eager that she barely remembered to put on clothes. Once she threw on her mink right over her underwear, grabbed a pair of pumps and raced out the door to meet Sam for a walk down Fifth Avenue. Drunk from the city's haphazard beauty, she hardly noticed how hot she was in her coat, or its dark fur pressed against her bare skin.

Celebrity photographer and Brooklyn Heights native, Sam was Marilyn's ideal tour guide, and she quickly fell in love with his neighborhood haunts. "She'd walk the brick paved side streets of the Heights," he wrote, "examining the restored carriage houses along Love Lane, visiting the musty book stacks of the Long Island Historical Society, pondering the outstretched arm of the statue of Reverend Henry Ward Beecher in the churchyard of the ruins of Plymouth Church."

One morning, they crossed the Brooklyn Bridge—Marilyn in her camel coat, Sam with a Nikon slung round his neck. They were strolling the Promenade when it started to rain. Sam darted into a phone booth to ring a friend who lived nearby, asking if he could drop in with "a friend" to escape the sudden storm.

Norman Rosten—a poet and close friend of Arthur Miller's—had been given no warning of Marilyn's arrival. He first glimpsed her in the stairwell, sodden in her camel coat, no makeup, her wet hair piecey with silver glints from the rain. "I watched from above as she turned into the second floor," Rosten wrote. "She looked like a pretty high school kid on an errand." When they reached the door, Sam mumbled a name. Norman misheard it as "Marion." He still had no idea who she was.

Marilyn glanced up—"Pleased to meet you"—then curled into the nearest chair with a baby-deer smile. When Norman noticed her wet shoes she slipped them off, leaving her chilly feet bare and exposed. His wife, Hedda, put coffee on and found a pair of slippers. They chatted about the rain, the Brooklyn Botanic Garden. Marilyn barely spoke—just in breathless little cloudbursts.

She leaped up to scan the bookshelf. Marilyn, like all compulsive readers, always made an immediate dash to the bookshelf, a fast path to easy friendship. "Hey, I've read this too," she'd exclaim, eager to connect, eager to find out: Does this person's inner landscape match mine? She grabbed a skinny book from a nearby table: *Songs for Patricia* by Norman Rosten. When Norman said he wrote it for his daughter, her eyes widened. She opened the book and read quietly until Hedda returned with coffee and cake.

HEDDA: "Do you live around here?"

MARILYN: "No, I'm not from New York. I'm studying at the Actors Studio."

HEDDA: "That's wonderful. Then you must have been in theater. What plays have you been in?"

MARILYN: "No, I've never been on the stage. But I have done some movies."

HEDDA: "Oh? What was your movie name?"

MARILYN: "Marilyn Monroe."

That night, the Rostens planned to hit a party three blocks down. When they invited Marilyn to tag along, she lit up in delight. She knew she'd go unnoticed in that soggy camel coat. Norman introduced her: "I'd like you to meet a friend, Marilyn Monroe." Everyone laughed, drank, thinking it was a good joke. "Sure," said the host, "happy to meet any of your friends, even Greta Garbo."

Marilyn giggled, drank, and chatted—all the while passing for another milk-fed ingenue hoping to make it big. Even without her Monroe name, people were just as drawn to her. Norman watched in awe: "Was it her voice, the half-shy, half-curious way she looked at people, her sudden warmth, that quick, infectious laugh? It was like she'd stepped into the reality of her true self," he observed, in this Brooklyn Heights brownstone thousands of miles away.

When Marilyn returned to her suite, she sat down to write her new friend a note. She thanked him for the visit, for the party, and most of all for the book. (Norman sent her home with *Songs for Patricia*.) She mentioned that she used to write poetry, usually when she was depressed—she had once showed it to a friend who had cried upon reading it. "But it was an old friend," she concluded, "one I'd known for a long time." Scrawled in light pencil, Waldorf-Astoria letterhead, April 1955.

That spring, Marilyn took up poetry again—often inspired by the city itself—the Brooklyn Bridge, the Williamsburg Bridge, and Central Park. She took walks alone, or hailed a cab and asked the driver to take her over the bridge and drop her off near the Esplanade. Marilyn loved walking. In this way she was made for New

York. Back in Hollywood she startled everyone by hiking around
Beverly Hills in jeans and a sweatshirt. (No one ever walked in
Beverly Hills—not even to the newsstand—the police would stop
you.) In New York she could be like Baudelaire—a flâneur roaming the streets for rough patches of beauty. Everything inspired
her: flower vendors; the East River, "like Pepsi Cola"; even taxi
drivers. "Impatient taxi drivers," began one poem, "driving hot dusty
New York streets/ So they can save for a vacation driving hot dusty/
Highways. . . ." Another, called "The Towers," opened with this
line: "So many lights in the darkness. . . ."

🌱 As Marilyn's support system grew, so did her confidence.
She threw open her doors to the press, often inviting them into her
own suite. Holding court from her luxurious perch, she bantered
with journalists, flirting back, entertaining them with mimosas
and gossip.

"I arrived at her apartment at the Waldorf Towers at the ap-
pointed time, 9:30 a.m.," wrote Maurice Zolotow, who interviewed
Marilyn in the spring of 1955. "Frank Goodman, her New York
publicity man, was there. We waited. She was 'getting ready,'
Goodman told me. We waited. At ten past ten she emerged.

"Marilyn, judging by the flush on her skin—and I was able to
see a good deal of her skin—had recently bathed. The aroma of
Chanel No 5 pervaded the small living room. She wore a white
terry cloth robe with nothing underneath. No stockings and no
slippers. Her legs were slim and finely tapered, and sometimes,
when she flowed into a change of position in the armchair in which
she was curled, I glimpsed a vista of white thighs. Her thighs were
also beautifully tapered. I was struck by the fact that her toenails
were painted platinum-white, to harmonize with the shade of her
hair. Her hair was unkempt. I assumed she had not had time to

brush and comb it. Later I found out she doesn't like kempt hair. She wore no cosmetics on her lips cheeks or eyelashes. I wasn't sure about her eyebrows. She might have had eyebrow pencil on her eyebrows. She appeared sweet and guileless, though the mole on her left cheek imparted an eighteenth-century Madame du Barry touch, a dramatic contrast to her angelic features."

He noticed the books stacked on the end table—James Joyce, Emerson, the letters of George Sand—the English bicycle propped by the kitchen window. The tiny gray kitten batting a rolled-up sock. "Milton Greene and I have a lot in common," she said when asked about MMP. "We have parallel aims and ideas. I think he's very capable and talented and a lot of other people will see it too. It is ridiculous to think that he is using me or I am using him." When prodded about her financial arrangements, Marilyn bristled. "That's my business," she snapped, "how I'm living and supporting myself."

What struck Zolotow most was her total self-possession, how she spoke with none of her usual shyness. "It wasn't about money," Marilyn said of her break with Fox. "It was about my rights as an actress and as a human being. I know they didn't want to hurt me. They sincerely thought they were choosing the best for the Studio and for me. I feel it is up to me to show them that I am capable of interpreting roles with more depth, more feeling than they have ever seen me do. But I must have approval of the script and a good director," she insisted. "I want good stories—not just to be thrown into any old thing. I think I am a serious actress, and I want to prove it."

✑ Zolotow lingered, and Marilyn got up to concoct a milk punch spiked with chocolate syrup and shots of Marsala (a remnant of the DiMaggio days). Maurice mentioned *Ulysses* and Molly

Bloom's soliloquy, and Marilyn marveled that a man "would go into a woman's mind" like that. She showed him her latest junk-shop find, a reproduction bust of Nefertiti ("Do I look like her?"). They commiserated about anxiety and therapists, discussed psychoanalysis as a sort of religion.

"I believe more in Freud than in mysticism," she said with a laugh. "I do not think I will ever take the road of religion, and yet I still believe in many things that cannot be explained by science. I am still learning. I am still seeking. I believe human nature is a dynamic thing, and a person should never stop growing and changing. I am not afraid of change and growth. I believe in freedom and independence."

"I want to learn," she added after a pause. "I want to learn so badly. I read and study as much as I can, because I want to grow as a person."

Before Maurice left, Marilyn read him some of her cityscape poems. She told him that she'd "fallen in love" with Brooklyn, that she wanted to buy a little brownstone there and travel West only to make pictures. "New York is my home now," she said. "I love it here. I'll never live in Hollywood anymore."

When Zolotow asked if New York had changed her, she answered quickly and firmly: "Oh, yes. I have found freedom and independence, and I don't intend to let them slip away."

Marilyn was blossoming. Her hopes soared like the blurry spiked spires of St. Patrick's Cathedral. Lee had her constantly thinking, observing, and expanding. She studied the animals at the Central Park Zoo, their movements and gestures. The slow lope of the bison, the sun bear's hot claw—black matte as if it had been manicured. The thick, wet lashes of a giraffe; the sad little capuchin monkeys with their furrowed blonde brows. She liked the sea lions—they'd bark and splash and gaze up like puppies, beadlets of water glistening on their crested, canine heads. But it was a lioness named June who Marilyn grew attached to and seemed to tame within an hour. Every so often June would creep to the edge of her cage, swishing her tawny tail, and Marilyn would stick her hand through the iron bars and pet the dark tuft of fur at its tip.

A chill crept up, the sun dropped and glowed pink against the blackening gate. The zookeeper clanged a bell and called, "Closing in ten minutes." Marilyn lingered, clinging to the lion's cold cage. Something about June's weary glamour touched Marilyn. She hated to leave her. "She'll be all alone in the dark," she cried on the phone to Susie that night. "She'll be lonely."

Marilyn has often been compared to daffodils, hummingbirds, kittens, wrought-iron butterflies. But it was the writer Karen Blixen who saw Marilyn as one of the baby lion cubs she'd cuddled so many times in Kenya, exotic, adorable, and, she wrote, utterly terrifying: "I would not keep her."

Compelled to delve deep in her own traumatic past, Marilyn spent nights in her bathrobe smoking in bed, gouging her memory for clues. She scribbled stories—of switches, churches, and aprons—her frantic slant filling sheet after sheet of starchy white paper, pausing to flip through Freud's letters or Edith Hamilton's *Mythology*. Self-discovery and acting were two quests that defined Marilyn's life, and under the tutelage of Lee Strasberg, they became intertwined forever.

She first approached her therapist with wary self-consciousness. "I'm afraid to ever say anything," Marilyn wrote, "for fear she will think I am trying to flatter her." But she quickly began to trust Dr. Hohenberg and even examined her reasons for not having trusted in the past. With her customary bravery, Marilyn addressed the sexual abuse she'd suffered as a child, and the foster mother who hadn't believed her. "I will not be punished," she wrote, "or be whipped/ or be threatened/ or not be loved/ or sent to the hill to burn with bad people/ or ashamed/ exposed and known and seen/ or ashamed of my sensitive feelings/ SO WHAT/ they are reality. My body is my body, every part of it."

"It's much better to know reality," she wrote, urging herself to face things clearly, "and to have as few illusions as possible. I can and will help myself and work on things analytically no matter how painful." Her flaws, she discovered, were her greatest gifts. "My sensitivity is so strong—much deeper and stronger than that of Susie's. . . . Do not be afraid of my sensitivity. . . . I can and will channel it." She learned to embrace her quirkiest qualities, even the "crazy thoughts." Through therapy and work with Lee she explored her neuroses, owning them with confidence and authority. Gradually, she began to see herself for who she really was—an intelligent, ambitious, complicated woman on the verge of something great.

That spring, Strasberg hinted that she'd soon play a "tremendous part"—as long as she continued her path of relentless self-inquiry. "Remember," she wrote, "technical things can be done to deal with your sensitivity and turn it from fear into the proper channels— which is dealing with fear, not running away." Instead of fleeing from her fears she'd harness them through work and break free from the "constraints and shackles" of the past. She vowed to live in "The Present—whatever it may be—because that's how it is and it's so much better."

For now, this introspection only boosted her glow. She stopped covering her freckles with camouflage cake and looked years younger for it. She switched out the mink for a shimmery trench worn open over gauzy tops or cream-colored polos. She ditched heavy scarves for floppy black hats, her lashes left bare and blonde as a baby's.

As the days grew longer, she'd walk the forty blocks home from the Strasberg dinners, once in a sleeveless dress in brown and white stripes and a thick leather belt, a tawny shoulder bag dangling from her arm. She looped scarves of orange chiffon round her throat, daubed her mouth with coral, and unbuttoned her blouses to show off her tan.

In May, she had trunks shipped back from LA: a tangerine tube dress, Japanese tea gowns, blue velvet midis, and boleros in black faille. Taffeta petticoats and frocks trimmed in gold, Bermuda shorts with matching tops in biscuity silk. The black Danskins came out again, and she undulated in them like a gorgeous otter. She began playing with her image more, throwing together unusual outfits. She'd walk to class in stilettos worn with baggy sweaters and slacks, her rumpled hair topped with a gondolier's hat. She swanned around Broadway in leopard-print leotards paired with black pedal pushers, a man's white shirt knotted at her breast.

That spring, six teens attached themselves to Marilyn. They were a watchful little flock, standing guard by the Waldorf entrance on East 50th Street, picking her up from acting class, carrying her groceries, dropping off newspapers, fetching prescriptions from the pharmacy. Sometimes they acted as little couriers, running hand-written notes back and forth with Jane Russell, who was living down the block. They christened themselves the Monroe Six and were fiercely protective of their "Mazzie." At half Marilyn's age, they were acutely perceptive of her vulnerability and loved her all the more for it.

Jimmy Haspiel was a Bushwick runaway who roamed New York's streets and rooftops like some 1950s Artful Dodger. He never fit in with the Monroe Six, with their satchels of homework, hot suppers, and after-school jobs. "It frustrated and hurt me a lot. We all converged on Monroe at about the same time, yet I wasn't allowed *in*." Yet Marilyn—lover of wastrels and street urchins, sad tramps and "helpless little ones"—grew closest to Jimmy. In his vagabond background, she saw herself—the orphanage and those dark starlet days surviving on peanut butter and crackers, scrounging for pennies to buy a cake of soap.

Even Marilyn couldn't resist the hyperbolic worship of a lovestruck teen. She was equal-opportunity when it came to admirers, preferring a cabdriver's honest wolf whistle to smarmy flattery. Half foundling, half footman, Jimmy Haspiel would usher her to premieres, beating back the clawing crowd, casually looping his arm through hers: "I'll take you out to the car, Marilyn." This was just the sort of gallantry Marilyn liked—sweet, playful, and shot through with irony. She hated that red carpet pomp and banter—why not shock the crowd with a greaser escort, a dropout in leather jacket and jeans?

Like a medieval courtier, Haspiel kept watch on the church stoop across the street from the Towers, or crouched in the ledges of display windows at Saks. He often saw her assistant, Peter Leonardi, hauling piles of clothes down the street to the cleaners. Peter, very Hollywood in his chic haircut, black tees, black Wayfarers, and tight blazers. Always sunglasses, even inside. He did odd jobs—hairstylist, bodyguard, courier—in addition to showing Marilyn parts of New York she wouldn't have otherwise seen. On warm days they'd throw bikes into the back of his banged-up cherry convertible and head to Coney Island. She liked the Bowery, too, and often asked Pete to drive her there. They'd spend the day tramping down Rivington and Delancey, past blood-donor stations and battered saloons, occasionally handing out money to the homeless. "I think one of the pluses in it for her was that they were not looking back at 'Marilyn Monroe,'" wrote Jimmy Haspiel, who sometimes accompanied them on their trips downtown.

"She was able to do something very humane within the boundaries of anonymity, which wasn't going to be bragged about for the rest of the time by the people to whom it had happened. People-wise, it was just a one-on-one situation: 'Can I help you out a little bit?' So Pete would empty his pockets of all the money he had, then he would have to wait until the end of the week when she got her $40 a week spending money allowance."

On Sundays, Norman Rosten would be parked by the Waldorf, a trunkful of champagne packed on ice and one chilled bottle stashed in the glove compartment. Marilyn would run out in her striped capris, leap over the seat, and grab him for a kiss.

"With the roof down, visible as hell, she was a blinking buoy, a sweet-sounding siren, a magnetic field," Norman wrote. "People waved and shouted from passing cars as we crossed the 59th Street Bridge. 'Hi Marilyn!' 'Hello Marilyn!' 'Hey, good luck!' 'Is that you, Marilyn? Love you!' And she waved back sipping champagne from a paper cup."

"Cheer up," she said, laughing at Norman's grimace. "They won't hurt us."

In June, she bought a black Cadillac convertible. She loved her car, but she was what Jimmy called a California driver—pulling out into the wrong lane to swing around traffic, making wide turns at the busiest intersections. Whenever she hailed a cab, she'd point and say, "I'm going that way," never east, west, uptown, or downtown. At night she'd pile in friends and drive to Chez Vito or Gino's. She even drove herself down Broadway to catch *The Skin of Our Teeth* premiere. At dusk you might find her in the Waldorf garage, lounging in her car, feet propped on the dash, hair pulled back, face slathered in hormone cream.

Jimmy caught these moments with his five-dollar camera—jumping into Rosten's convertible while clutching a copy of *Confidential* magazine, or hair ruffled in a pompadour, laughing and begging him not to aim "right up her nose." That spring, Jimmy snapped a shot of her driving down Lexington past the Mayflower Coffee Shop: top down, shades on, laughing at the wheel. This soon became Marilyn's favorite; she demanded that he lend her the original color slide. "We argued for weeks until I got it back," Jimmy remembered. "I think that is why she liked this particular picture so much, because it defined her as a very real person."

Jimmy's snapshots capture a sense of joyous freedom unique to this time in Marilyn's life. That spring, she surged with energy—acting classes, Broadway plays, interviews, and therapy sessions. She woke up at seven—even on Sundays—and took early-morning bike rides alone in Central Park. When her energy flagged, she'd stop by Dr. Max Jacobson's Upper East Side office for "miracle tissue regenerator" shots: amphetamines, animal hormones, bone marrow, B-vitamins, and human placenta.

The camera adored her like never before—during midnight walks in the park with Sam Shaw, dashing to the Stork Club for a quick drink with Joe, or stalking down the aisle of St. Patrick's Cathedral, half an hour late for Constance Collier's funeral, dressed like a vampy abbess. Her black dress hung suspiciously loose—Capote thought it looked borrowed—her blonde head was covered by a black chiffon scarf. She wore silk stockings, pumps, and saucer-size sunglasses. ("Are false lashes funeral appropriate?") The black enhanced what Capote called her "vanilla-pallor." Never before had she looked this starkly sexy.

"Oh, baby," she told Truman, squeezing into the back row. "I'm so sorry."

With the *Seven Year Itch* premiere right around the corner, publicity cranked at full blast. Her white-halter image went up on 46th and Lexington, right across from the Howard Johnson's where she lunched with Eli. They'd get burgers and watch workmen hoist a gargantuan Marilyn over the Trans-Lux Theatre. She went up in pieces—the forty-foot cutout was too heavy to move at once—and at first all you saw were slingbacks and legs under a flutter of white skirt. Marilyn gazed out the window, observing the workmen lower her cutout torso onto an expanse of hip and thigh. "That's the way they think of me," she mused in her matter-of-fact way. "With my skirt over my head. I told Twentieth Century Fox that I want to play Grushenka in *The Brothers Karamazov*," she confided, her mind drifting back to winter when she'd been the butt of so many jokes. "They all laughed, but none of them have read the book. I call them 19th Century Fox."

"Marilyn knew a great deal more about the Dostoyevsky masterpiece than people who were joshing her about becoming a longhair," Earl Wilson wrote, once again leaping to her defense. He reported that she was winning over highly esteemed directors, playwrights, and actors, including Clifton Webb, who saw Marilyn out and about on Broadway: "She likes to talk about the theater, and the kind of thing that makes people tick. She is intense and completely straightforward. She reads all the time. She is in complete control of her career."

"Marilyn should have a show written just for her," declared playwright George Abbott. "With that personality, she's entitled to it." She even charmed the reclusive William Motter Inge, who wrote *A Loss of Roses* specifically for her. "Every word the character speaks," he explained, "I've composed as coming from Marilyn's lips."

"I was present at an Actors Studio party," Earl wrote, "where she stole the show completely. And I witnessed something that shows she is respected as an actress around Broadway. 'Could I get your autograph?' asked Lawrence Langner of the Theatre Guild, who has directed and employed the greatest stars, including Katharine Hepburn and Helen Hayes. I transmitted the message to Marilyn. She inscribed a card, 'Love and Kisses,' and then her name, and when I mentioned who he was, she said 'I should get his autograph!' And he gave her one of the most glowing messages I've ever seen. It said: 'Dear Marilyn: We need you for our Shakespeare Theater. Yours admiringly, Lawrence Langer. PS-For 'A Midsummer Night's Dream.'" Later, Wilson asked Langner when he'd last asked for an actress's autograph. It had been forty-seven years ago: from Zena Dare in London, 1908.

With heavyweight dramatists backing Marilyn up, it grew harder and harder to make her into a joke. She thought of Fox, Zanuck, and all the other men who'd cut her down. This time, the joke would be on them.

That spring, Marilyn wrote this on the Waldorf's crispy white stationery: "Not a scared little girl anymore."

Ten

Shangri-la

But will he look like this when he is dead oh
unbearable fact inevitable yet sooner would I
rather his love die than/ or him?   MARILYN MONROE

January 1951. Thirty-six-year-old Arthur Miller was still basking in the glow of his newly won Pulitzer. *Death of a Salesman* took
him to Hollywood for the first time, where he and Elia Kazan were
house-sitting for Charlie Feldman. Beverly Hills was miles away
from Miller's humble writer's life in Brooklyn Heights, full of clank-
ing typewriters and chain-linked fences, with his progressive, be-
spectacled wife Mary Slattery and three children cozily installed

in the Little Red Schoolhouse. Now he was plopped in a Spanish Colonial mansion surrounded by swimming pools, Renoirs, Vuillards, Bonnards, Modiglianis, and streams of ingénues trailing clouds of money and Arpège.

Arthur set his Corona by Feldman's pool—officially he was here to work. The plan was to edit his screenplay *The Hook*, then shop it around the studios with Kazan. Their first stop was Twentieth Century Fox, where Kazan hoped to run into one of his girlfriends. They dropped in on the set of *As Young As You Feel*, where a young blonde actress was rehearsing a scene. "That's Marilyn Monroe," Kazan whispered, nudging Arthur. "Fair game and easy prey," he grinned, staring straight ahead. As if to confirm, Marilyn shot him a look, eyes brimming with tears. Maybe it was her honest tears, or the way she swayed in her dress of black openwork lace, but something struck Arthur, triggering a protective response that would last for a decade.

Of course she recognized Arthur Miller—the literary Lincoln and working man's Hemingway. He fished; he hunted; he even boxed. He certainly looked the part, with his corncob pipe, lumberjack plaids, and Brandoesque tees. Arthur's quiet reserve and lanky grace appealed to Marilyn, who preferred the congressman to the dandy, the simple tie and jacket to the chichi dinner suit. Instead of swooning over Tony Curtis, she liked her sixty-something acting coach or Jawaharlal Nehru. Her ideal man had the soul of Thomas Wolfe and the heart of Abraham Lincoln, masculine without bravado. No wonder she was lonely and dateless. There weren't many Wolfes and Lincolns in this town of flashy cads and clammy bullies.

The next day, Feldman threw a party in absentia for Miller, with an orchestra, lavish buffet tables, and a fully stocked bar in each room. "I asked Art to cover for me," wrote Kazan, who was working late that night and unable to pick up Marilyn. "When he called to tell her he'd pick her up she said no, she'd take a taxi and meet us at Feldman's. Art wouldn't allow it—he'd come and pick her up. Again she demurred. I said don't worry about it, she's used to that, but Art insisted. And the first thing that impressed Marilyn about her future husband was that he refused to let her come to the party in a taxi. How little these glamour girls expect out of life."

Within minutes, they were dancing together. Arthur rarely flirted with women and usually required a few stiff drinks before he could force out a greeting, much less a fox-trot. But the orchestra and the moonlit pool, the heady scent of perfume mixed with amaryllis—even the dizzying proximity to celebrity—disarmed him. Best of all was this dazzlingly warm-blooded creature, fresh and alive in his arms. He shivered, thrilled to know that he could in fact "lose himself in sensuality."

By the time Kazan showed up, the spark was obvious. "When I arrived, I could see that need had met need, and the lovely light of desire was in their eyes. I watched them dance. Art was a good dancer—and how happy she was in his arms."

Not everyone was so pleased. Catty observations abounded from men and women alike. "She looks like the prow of a ship," snarked one, nodding at Marilyn's cleavage. "In this roomful of actresses and wives of sybaritic men," wrote Arthur, "all striving to dress and behave with an emphatically ladylike reserve, Marilyn Monroe seemed almost ludicrously provocative, a strange bird in the aviary, if only because her dress was so blatantly tight, declaring rather than insinuating that she had brought her body along with her and it was the best body in the room. The female resentment that surrounded her at Feldman's approached the consistency of acrid smoke." He watched her dance with another man, transfixed by her intoxicating mix of boldness and vulnerability. Clutching her drink, eyes half shut, he was suddenly struck by how fragile she was. Actress Evelyn Keyes seemed to read his mind. "They'll eat her alive," she said softly and took another sip of scotch.

Perhaps that's why Marilyn avoided these parties. She rarely danced and usually hid in the kitchen for an hour or two before slipping out early to chat on the phone with Sidney Skolsky. But tonight she stayed late, curled up on the couch, legs folded under her dress. Arthur slowly began to caress her foot, and held her little toe. She was touched by the gesture's tender audacity. All her life she wanted to be protected, not seduced.

She also wanted to be understood. Maybe it was the toe-holding, or the way he'd insisted on picking her up for the party, but Marilyn trusted Arthur. She found herself talking, mostly about Hollywood, its daily brutalities and exploitation. The cigarette girls and sinister men and garish laughter settling out in a haze of cigars and liquor around Calabasas pools. The humiliating "dates" she forced herself to endure because she'd spent her last dime on acting lessons and couldn't afford dinner. Arthur listened for hours without revulsion or judgment, washing all those ugly little acts clean away. He simply nodded and squeezed her toe tighter. After all, even he knew that "to survive in this velvet jungle of Hollywood, one had to reckon with wolves."

❧ They spent the next few days teaming around as a threesome—Miller, Monroe, and Kazan—browsing Hollywood's secondhand shops, driving around the Canyons, picnicking on Malibu beach, strolling the Santa Monica Pier. Marilyn even crashed their business meeting with the tyrannical Harry Cohn. With cat eyeglasses and a stenographer's pad, she passed unrecognized as their personal secretary. (This was her secret revenge on the lecherous Cohn, who'd promised Columbia's good roles if only she'd join him in bed.) Cohn rejected *The Hook,* but they had a good laugh at his expense.

Driving through the Canyons, head flung back, sandwiched between those two talented men, Marilyn's affections began to transfer to Arthur. She wasn't that crazy about Kazan anyway. It was one of those breezy little flings so common in Hollywood—more like a friendly favor—kind of like taking someone to lunch with your agent or passing along an important phone number. But Marilyn was Hollywood's ultimate freak of nature—a romantic—who'd somehow emerged from years of abuse with her ideals unscathed.

"Her romantic innocence was something you did not usually run across in the picture business," wrote Maurice Zolotow. "The goings on behind the walls of some Hollywood homes are like scenes that may be observed in the violent wards of psychiatric institutions. You have the Don Juans and the nymphomaniacs who bounce like ping pong balls. . . ." Men still ruled the business, from moguls such as Zanuck to the talent scouts who promised bit parts in musicals or electrolysis and rhinoplasty in exchange for sex. But Arthur had grown up simply, worked as a dishwasher, and barely mentioned his Pulitzer. He had looked into her eyes and held her toe, and that impressed Marilyn more than all the yachts in Malibu, all the Cadillacs in Beverly Hills.

For Arthur, this had been an out-of-body experience, like he'd been plucked from Brooklyn Heights and dropped straight into Candyland. The past three days had hardly seemed real.

Their goodbye had all the trappings of a film noir romance, including a dramatic airport farewell witnessed by Kazan. Marilyn wore a straight camel skirt and white silk blouse, her blonde hair brushed over her left brow. Panic set in as Arthur waited to board, and he felt fated to protect this angelic creature with her "radioactive core." Grimly determined to stay faithful to his wife, he kissed Marilyn's forehead and flew to New York, the scent of her Nivea cream on his hands.

❧ For the entire ten years that Arthur knew Marilyn, he was running—away from her, toward her, but always running, and running for his life. When he returned to his life back on 155 Willow Street, he wrote to Kazan of his desire for Marilyn, and his "situation at home," which seemed to grow worse and worse. In one particularly theatrical plea, Arthur begged Kazan to take "one last look at her." (Kazan was more than happy to oblige.) Two days later he wrote Kazan again—this time for Marilyn's address.

Their correspondence was exploratory, confessional, and on Miller's part, fraught with guilt. When she wrote of her need for a role model, Arthur suggested Lincoln, and recommended Carl Sandburg's recent biography. Marilyn dashed to Martindale's books and lugged back six volumes, with a copy of Miller's *Focus* thrown in for good measure. Eventually his letters dwindled, but she kept them in a stack on her nightstand, right next to her portrait of Abraham Lincoln.

❧ Years passed. Arthur threw away Marilyn's letters. But his dreams of her crept back, as much as he tried to keep them at bay. Marilyn surfaced in his work, his reading habits, his correspondence with friends. He couldn't shake her, this "whirling light" that never left him. Not even four years later, in the spring of 1955, when he spotted her at a New York party, standing alone sipping vodka and orange juice.

He approached her tentatively, gingerly, asked about her work at the Studio, told her a little about his new play. Much had changed. In three years Marilyn had gone from starlet on the verge to full-blown movie star. She'd married the ultimate celebrity athlete and was now newly separated. As usual, her life was moving at warp speed.

Meanwhile, Arthur's life had been trudging along laboriously. In the four years since they'd parted he looked like he'd aged ten. Writer's block, marital strife, political censorship, and the HUAC had strained his mouth into a grim line bracketed by two deep Lincolnesque grooves. But Marilyn loved all this. To her they were signs of wisdom and maturity. Best of all, he wore glasses now— horn-rimmed ones.

Arthur didn't kiss Marilyn that night, and he didn't take her home. He stewed for two weeks, then picked up the phone and called Paula Strasberg. Paula—thrilled to involve herself in any taboo romance—gave him Marilyn's number. This time there was no hesitation. Arthur fell in love "completely, seriously, with the ardor of a man released."

From the very beginning, the tenor of their relationship was irresistibly fugitive—stolen moments of tenderness crossed by silence. They'd hole up in her suite at the Waldorf and order filet mignon, tiny French peas, and (Marilyn's favorite) vanilla ice cream. After dinner they'd drift to the balcony for hours of smoking and talking.

Confessional by nature but extremely self-aware, Marilyn fought conflicting urges to shut down and open up. She tended to be evasive about her past—and for good reason. Journalists and even friends accused her of embellishing the truth and outright lying. "I've never told all about my life," Marilyn once admitted in an interview with Elsa Maxwell, one of the few press members she trusted. "No one would believe it all could have happened. They would say I was talking for publicity. It was pretty terrible. . . ."

But Arthur was different. He listened to her. Holding her gaze and lighting her cigarettes, he was just as tender and protective as she'd remembered him. Unlike the slavering skirt-chasers and gossipy press hounds, this man wanted to see her soul—even the deep black pang of her childhood.

Shyly at first but with growing confidence, Marilyn began to talk. She talked about the casting agents who told her to smile while lifting up her sweater for inspection ("Look, her tits tilt straight up!"). About the man who took her to Santa Monica beach, offered her an ice cream, then dug his fingers into the flesh of her thigh, hissing in her ear about her "admirable bones." About how one night, weak from months of living off crackers, she'd been lured to a Bel Air mansion with the promise of a home-cooked meal. How she was presented with a rubbery omelet, pounced upon, then flung out into the dark clutching her shoes and a handful of aspirin. She told Arthur about the early years: the orphanages, the scratchy frocks, the foster homes full of bellowing Bibles and sexual abuse. Her foster mother hissing under her breath: "I can't stand the way that kid looks at me. . . . We've got to just get rid of her." She told him about the death of Aunt Ana, how she slept next to her dead body, how the gravediggers held a ladder for her to climb into Aunt Ana's grave, and how she lay there gazing skyward, the cold earth black against her back while the gravediggers leaned on their shovels and smoked. It was stories like these that would stun Miller into silence, bury him alive with desire to save her. He called her "the saddest girl in the world," which she accurately interpreted as a statement of love.

Before she met Arthur, Marilyn thought men wanted "happy girls." How liberating to be loved for her demons and even her own weaknesses. To meet a man who didn't flinch at the first hint of darkness, recoil from the spiked thorns under this smooth vanilla sex angel. They fell in love on that balcony, talking past sunrise, urban dawn sounds floating up from the streets—delivery trucks, bakeries, and flower stalls. He could listen to her for hours, this package of beauty and pathos who used to sneak into her foster home's aviary and put out watermelon rinds to feed the flies. "They would have starved to death if I hadn't," she said.

Later, he would find these qualities babyish—even irritating—but right now they were intoxicating, exotic, and completely foreign. His current wife didn't need him—she had been the one to support him, she had done the cooking, the budgeting and the bookkeeping, kept the icebox stocked and bills paid while he wrote. Like many men, Arthur would ricochet from thin-lipped pragmatism to voluptuous need and back again. "I was alternately soaring and anxious," he wrote, "that I might be slipping into a new life not my own."

Journalists pounced on the poetic frisson of the match, which begged to be plied with Freudian issues. Marilyn did refer to Arthur as "her Abraham Lincoln," and she had a habit of telling strangers that Lincoln (or Clark Gable, depending on the day) was her father. There is a long tradition of pathologizing Marilyn's passions, diagnosing her choices and curiosities as symptoms of an underlying desperation rooted in her fractured childhood. When applied to her relationship with Arthur, this psychologizing misses the mark. Though Marilyn deeply admired Miller (she'd never involve herself with a man she couldn't respect), he was not and never would be her mentor. He was her lover.

Besides, Arthur and Marilyn shared many qualities: self-protectiveness mixed with startling candor, stubborn streaks that often got them in trouble. Both were naive idealists with intellectual and working-class sympathies. Both were introspective and obsessively honest. Marilyn's "bracing candor" had been a major attraction to Arthur, who, in his own quiet way, could be shockingly confessional. Most of all, they shared a need to go gently against the grain—"It was the very inappropriateness," wrote Arthur, "that made me know it was appropriate." An odd statement—quixotic, defiant, and utterly Marilynesque.

At its core, their relationship was progressive and thoroughly modern. So what if she lost checkbooks and burned steaks? Arthur didn't want her in the kitchen, sweating over a pot of Bolognese. (To be fair, neither did Joe. He knew Marilyn struggled with cooking and would rather force down a plate of burned spaghetti than hurt her feelings.) Arthur knew that Marilyn belonged on the stage, just like her beloved Eleonora Duse.

Equally bold were his permissive views on sexuality. Marilyn was far more experienced than he—after all, he'd married his college sweetheart and he was shy with women regardless. But for Arthur there were no double standards, and he didn't split women into virgins and whores. "I've known social workers," he said, "who have had a more checkered history than she has." He admired how she challenged the hypocrisy so common in post-war American sexual politics. "America was still a virgin," he added, "still denying her illicit dreams."

Unlike Joe DiMaggio, Arthur didn't flinch at Marilyn's plunging necklines and skintight skirts. Why shouldn't she wear them? Besides, he knew that image was vital to her career, and her career was as vital to her as writing was to him. A fellow artist, he respected her work and her opinion. They read aloud to each other and talked late into the night about Ibsen, Dostoyevsky, and her current obsession, James Joyce. After the silence and space of her DiMaggio marriage, this was the romance of Marilyn's dreams.

Between their high profiles and the shadow of adultery, Arthur and Marilyn kept their romance a secret, even from some of their closest friends. "I knew somehow it was Arthur," Amy Greene admitted years later, "because he was married, and it was all so secretive. I figured if she was dating Irving Dishman I'd know about it. Milton, of course, knew that they were seeing each other. She needed a confidant, and he was the one she turned to at that time. He never told me, because Milton is such a sphinx. If somebody says 'This is our secret,' you can put him on the rack and you're never going to get it out of him. All he would say to me is 'Marilyn is keeping company,' which I think is so sweet. But one day we were driving back from New York, and having been suckled by a Cuban witch many years ago, a bolt of lightning came through the car and I said, 'It's Arthur Miller.' Milton almost went off the road. Then he looked at me and said, 'Yes, it is.' The next day, obviously Milton told her, because she seemed to be relieved, and she said that it was Arthur she was secretly seeing. From that moment on, she would just say Arthur, or Art, or she'd be really cute and say AM. She was sharing a confidence, and she enjoyed that kind of thing. She'd talk about him to anyone that would listen. My impression was that they were having a wonderful time in bed and he was going home to his wife."

A few weeks after the big reveal, Marilyn announced that Arthur was coming to Weston for Sunday lunch. "She started in on preparations, and Kitty had to do this, and Clyde had to do that. We had a wonderful ham, and we had chicken and cornflakes, which is another thing Kitty made that was absolutely marvelous, and we had salads, and another thing that Marilyn loved—Kitty's carrots with sugar. We had a wonderful sweet potato pie. Marilyn loved Kitty's sweet potato pies—she was so proud of them—it's like she'd discovered them herself. So she insisted that Kitty make one of those, and another deep-dish apple pie. She was a typical Jewish yenta, giving the man she was involved with wonderful things to eat. We were all on our best behavior because Arthur was coming. We brought out the good wine, and the house was shiny, and the flowers were wonderful, and I have never been so bored with a human being in my entire life."

Empathetic, Marilyn could not help but sense Amy's disappointment. "She would start trying to bring in other conversations—things like 'Oh, Amy loved *Death of a Salesman*.' Then I told the story of the night I saw it. No one clapped at the end, because we were all so moved that it was like a sacrilege to destroy whatever it was that sat with us inside the theater—us meaning the entire audience—by clapping. Well, he loved that. And then he said it was a very common occurrence. Then we got up, and we went into the living room. We had coffee—he was a big coffee drinker. He talked about everything. He talked about the theater, he talked about movies, he talked about films he was going to make and who he wanted to star in them. Marilyn of course loved it, sitting there at his feet. He stayed an entire afternoon. When he's on, you literally have to sit there and worship at the shrine, and nobody can get a word in edgewise. I will say that he was probably nervous because he was meeting us. I give him credit for making an effort—going into a strange house, especially considering that Milton and I knew he was sleeping with Marilyn. This was the mid-fifties—it wasn't '65 when no one cared what you did."

Despite their awkward first lunch, Amy was touched when Arthur reached out weeks later. "He invited us for dinner in New York," she said, "and it was a very touchy situation, because there we are with the blonde bombshell, and he's married, and where could we go where the two of them wouldn't be recognized? We went to a restaurant called Jimmy's La Grange—it was in a brownstone and the backroom was quite dark, with candles and smoky partitions. Milton and I had been taking her for some time, and everyone was very cool about it—there was a lovely piano player there. Milton, Marilyn, and I arrived early, and Arthur slipped in later. At this point we were still on our best behavior. This second meeting was better. He was more relaxed, we were more relaxed, and it was sort of Marilyn's evening. She was the Charming Child.

She was wonderful—you could eat her with a spoon. She eased all the factions. Arthur kept quiet—maybe she said to him, 'Let somebody else talk.' Arthur asked Milton very pertinent business questions, and he was charming the second time around. It was a lovely evening. That was our best evening out in public, but there were more good evenings to come. One night we had a lovely dinner party in Marilyn's suite at the Towers. When you were with Marilyn and Arthur at that time, you could feel the passion sparks. There was something there between the two of them, and you could certainly feel it, so it wasn't phony."

Gradually, Marilyn and Arthur emerged from the Waldorf and were seen around town together. When *A View From the Bridge* rehearsals began at New Amsterdam Theatre, he'd walk to Childs' Restaurant on 46th and Broadway to meet Marilyn for lunch. She'd be waiting for him in a scarf and dark glasses, fresh out of acting class and eager to chat about what she'd learned. The rare actress who never dated actors, Marilyn could finally bond with a lover over the experience of shared work. Arthur talked about his latest project, a screenplay about Brooklyn's juvenile gangs. The New York City Youth Board had already granted him funding as well as access to local social workers who led him nightly through back alleys of Gowanus and Red Hook. He'd listen in on secret meetings, then cab it back to Manhattan, slipping through the Waldorf's private entrance and into Marilyn's bed. "From life on the streets," he remembered, "to Marilyn high in the Waldorf Tower was a cosmic leap, but not such discontinuity as it would seem."

The DiMaggio courtship had centered on dates—dinners at La Scala and Romanoff's, drinks at the Stork Club. But with Arthur, Marilyn explored New York even further. They went to coffee shops in the Village, boating on City Island, and took his dog for walks in Prospect Park. He bought her an English gearshift bicycle, and together they'd ride through Central Park or down Ocean

Parkway all the way to Coney Island. They took long, lazy walks through the Heights, past Italianate brownstones and row houses of red brick. The neighborhood's quiet history was the polar opposite of Hollywood flash.

As she fell in love with Arthur, she fell more deeply in love with New York. They discovered a mutual love of bridges, especially the Brooklyn Bridge, which loomed heavily over Arthur's imagination and work. Sometimes they'd walk over the bridge down toward the waterfront, where longshoremen did their scrapwork and the dockers heaved loads of heavy cargo. He led her past walls of graffiti, pointing out the chalk-scrawled DOVE PETE PANTO, which had triggered his screenplay *The Hook*. With Arthur as her guide, Marilyn's world grew larger each day. For her, Brooklyn was more than a neighborhood, it was her Shangri-la. "Brooklyn became Nirvana to her," wrote Sam Shaw, "a magical place, her true home."

"It's my favorite place in the world," she raved. "I haven't traveled much, but I don't think I'll find a place that can ever replace Brooklyn. I just like walking around. The view is better from Brooklyn. You can look back over and see Manhattan—that's the best view. It's the people and the streets and the atmosphere. I just love it."

Everything seemed poised for a magical summer. Hand in hand with Arthur, gazing at her beloved East River, Hollywood was the last thing on her mind.

On June 1—Marilyn's twenty-ninth birthday—*The Seven Year Itch* premiered to blockbuster reviews and dazzling box office receipts. Everyone was thrilled but Marilyn, who shrank under the crush of flashing bulbs, surrounded by reporters with their thrusting pens. Her hair was stiff and overstyled, her face powdered dull, her red lipstick layered red and thick, giving her a sad-clown look. The Van Cleef earrings hung heavy, drooping down toward her shoulders. "I hope it's the last of those kinds of parts I'll have to play," she moaned. "If I thought I had to keep on wiggling in crummy movies, I wouldn't want to work in movies anymore. I could go back to working in a factory if I had to."

DiMaggio escorted her, sparking more reconciliation rumors. "They look just like lovebirds," *Photoplay* reported. Not really—Joe beamed for the pack, but Marilyn looked distracted and distant. Later that evening she stormed out of the birthday party he'd planned for her at Toot's Shor. Perhaps she couldn't handle one more man laying claim to her.

The morning after *The Seven Year Itch* premiere, Marilyn received two letters. The first from Billy Wilder, his tone urgent and pleading:

Marilyn, I've been reading about your desire to do Cordelia, to do The Brothers Karamazov. Stay with what you are doing now. You've got a feeling for film comedy which no one else has. You're creating a very interesting character, and if you stay with it, you won't fall by the wayside as many actors and actresses do. The older you get, the better you'll get. There will be parts for you if you continue to create this character. You'll have a chance to become another Mae West. And as Mae West continued over the years, you can continue your career.

The second was from Cheryl Crawford:

I want to tell you that when you and Lee feel you are ready to do a show I want very much to be your producer. I think I have a deep and sympathetic understanding of your career. I am not interested in exploiting your fame, but in helping you bring your true dream into being in the finest possible way. When

you finish I'd like to tell you about my ideas, and I'm also hav-
ing another play written, which could very much be for you.
I would also give Lee an interest from my share for his invalu-
able assistance, and surround you with the kind of actors in
the studio who would truly help you and protect you. There is
no rush. I just want to go on record and I'd like to know how
you feel about it. I don't want to see you do any of this 'dumb
blonde' mishmash, but really present the truth of yourself which
I admire.

When would Marilyn present her personal truth? And what would it look like when she finally did?

❧ That afternoon, Marilyn called Milton and backed out of a trip to Tuscany she'd planned to take with his family. Even amid all the chaos of the previous night, the scene with Joe and the emotional fallout, she recognized this moment as a turning point. *Itch* had made her the hottest star in the world, and she was be-coming aware of her power on both coasts. The press, Fox, and all of Hollywood had finally snapped to attention. Soon they'd make her an offer. And as usual, she would be ready.

Eleven
Fire Island

"Marilyn changed my family's life, and we changed hers. And nothing was ever the same again."

SUSAN STRASBERG

*B*y then, the Strasbergs were replacing the Greenes as Marilyn's surrogate family. She spent weekends at their beach house on Fire Island, roaming the rickety boardwalks for funnel cakes and hot dogs, sketching in the cattails with Susie, or drenching herself in jasmine-y Ambre Solaire. No cars were allowed on the island—just a Jeep taxi cruising up and down the beach in the evenings. They'd walk to Ocean Beach in a little caravan, pulling red wagons strung with bells, packed with books and snacks. Marilyn in the short robe she wore as a cover-up,

Johnny sulking in Breton stripes, Susie in a babyish one-piece she hated, Lee in his baseball cap and glasses, and Paula draped in black smocks and wide-brimmed sunhats, hovering over Susie with a parasol.

"There were a lot of theater people at that part of the island," Susie wrote years later. "They were sophisticates, which meant they stared at Marilyn Monroe from a distance instead of staring up close." In Ocean Beach Marilyn enjoyed relative anonymity. She'd throw down her towel and sink into *Ulysses* or wander toward the water's edge to chat with Lee. "Love Is a Many-Splendored Thing" would be playing on a nearby radio. Susie would be lying on her stomach, a copy of *Photoplay* hidden between the pages of *War and Peace* or *Remembrance of Things Past*. Paula would be rooting through baskets laden with fans and scarves, fussing like a round owl, rubbing sunscreen on Susie's shoulders. Susie hated this— everyone was looking at her—and besides, she wanted to get tan. "What do you care," Paula said with a huff. "You're an actress; this is for your part; you have to stay pale. Anne Frank didn't go outside for two years."

This was Marilyn's first family vacation and her first summer on an East Coast beach. She'd frolicked on Catalina Island and skipped around on Santa Monica, but this was her first blast of salty driftwood and North Atlantic ozone. She'd play in shallow surf, wading out past her knees, maybe to her waist but never over her head. Susie would show off, running deep into the high surf, diving like a dolphin, glancing back in hopes that Marilyn was watching. "Come on in," she'd taunt, secretly pleased to have one-upped her rival. But Marilyn would wave, kick up some sand and foam, and continue talking to Lee, who rarely went in past his ankles. He'd stand at the ocean's edge, shirt buttoned to chin in the searing heat. Susie once asked him why he never went further. "Because, darling," he said staring straight into the sea, "I don't want to get involved."

࿇ On Fire Island, Marilyn indulged in happy sunny family things, the things she never really had. She shared a bedroom with Susie, ran around barefoot, went days without makeup, and played with the neighbor's kids. There were barbecues, picnics, radios blasting "Sugarbush, I love you so . . ." Lee manned the grill in his baseball hat, boxers, and farmer's tan: "Who wants hot dogs and who wants chicken?"

That summer Marilyn and Susie lived as sisters. Their room faced east, windows flung open, overlooking the dunes. Lulled by waves and salt breeze, they'd lounge on their twin beds, whispering late into the night about Hollywood and boyfriends. Marilyn's perfume hung heavy in the air, mixing with the ocean's marshy, quartzy scent. They'd quote poetry from their beds, usually Whitman—he was a Gemini, just like they were. On nights like these, Marilyn seemed to shed her glamour, a school chum with wet hair and a sunburned nose.

Neither one slept much on Fire Island. Their little room steeped in a dreamy fever. For Susie, this was the happy kind of insomnia—sleepovers and secrets and dreams that come true after Labor Day. She soon realized Marilyn was dealing with a darker sort of restlessness. She'd doze off, then wake to see Marilyn whiling away the hours with beauty rituals—shaving her legs, bleaching her hair, rubbing Vaseline into her cheeks, or simply staring out the window.

Once Marilyn stood naked in the moonlight, brushing her hair in long, sensuous strokes. Susie stared, transfixed by the peachy gleam of her skin. "It had a resiliency and buoyancy, like a child's." Open jars of face cream, razors, vials of cuticle oil strewn on the bed, bottles of pills and perfume stacked on the nightstand—tokens of some magical world of sex and glamour.

"I wish I was like you," Susie whispered. Marilyn, of course, protested. "Oh, no, Susie. I wish I were like you! You're about to play a great part on Broadway—Anne Frank—and people have respect for you. No, no—I have none of those things."

New York entertainers flocked to Ocean Beach, and the Strasbergs' cottage was their unofficial summer headquarters. A steady stream of guests breezed through their doors that summer— including Anne Bancroft, who lived next door. Lee "hired" ex-boxer and Studio actor Marty Fried for random duties—setting up the beach umbrella, babysitting Marilyn—but mostly, he just clung to Lee all day, listening to him rhapsodize on Stanislavski or his opinions on Japanese Noh.

"Lee would barbecue steaks," remembers Studio member Jack Garfein, "and Marilyn would be running around barefoot drinking champagne. Other stars would come out to Fire Island to kiss ass with Lee—Shelley Winters, Anne Bancroft. Lee was getting famous because of his association with Marilyn." On Sundays Paula held her legendary brunches, and bustled about serving bagels and hot coffee before collapsing on a sofa with a battery fan. After brunch, Lee would make his famous ice cream sodas, with extra cherries for Marilyn and lashings of whipped cream. "Everybody came for Lee's blessing," wrote Shelley Winters. "We would tell him our problems, we would ask for his help with a script or love affair." Lee would sit guru-like, nodding and shrugging.

Paula's summertime feasts were as much of a lure as Lee's blessing. Bloody Marys at brunch, champagne at night, salads, buttered corn on the cob, caviar blini, and baked potatoes with sour cream and chives. She kept her famous "Jewish icebox" stocked with Zabar's salamis, triple-cream Brie, honey cakes from fancy Midtown bakeries, and even the occasional Sacher torte.

Marilyn's orphanage days were long over, but this kind of opulence was new to her. Alone she ate simply, starkly—breakfasts of black coffee and broiled grapefruit, dinners of Roto-Broiled liver with a raw carrot on the side. Thanks to her surrogate families, Marilyn relished home-cooked meals for the first time—new potatoes and peas with the Greenes, pot roasts and pies with the Strasbergs. She shucked clams with the Rostens, grilled hot dogs with Lee. At night she'd pad around the Strasbergs' kitchen in one of Arthur's shirts, poking around the refrigerator for leftover chicken or vanilla ice cream.

The only person who didn't appreciate Paula's cooking was Johnny. "I'm trying to lose weight," he'd screech, pushing away a stack of Danish. "It's just baby fat" was Paula's humiliating consolation. "I don't think you're fat, Johnny," Marilyn offered. Johnny flushed red and fled.

One evening, Marilyn decided to cook everyone dinner— chicken au champagne. Beach-salty and glowing, she tied an apron over her swimsuit and disappeared into the kitchen, leaving the Strasbergs to read the paper and sip tea on the porch. They heard a bottle pop, some fizzy murmuring, and a bit of rustling cutlery. Then came the scream. Everyone raced to the kitchen. Marilyn wasn't known for her cooking—what if she'd cut herself? Instead, they found her screaming at the chicken. It was a whole chicken— it still had eyes, black beady eyes peering up in reproach. Marilyn trembled, crying that the chicken looked like a bird, and she couldn't cook it while it still looked like a bird because the poor bird was once alive and now it's dead and think of the bird's parents.

Lee praised her sensitivity and took over, leaving Marilyn to collapse on the porch with the leftover bottle. Meanwhile, Lee "chopped the hell out of that chicken till it looked like nothing that had a mother."

❧ On rainy days, Susie would spread the porch with newspapers and drag out her brushes and paints. Within minutes she felt two wistful eyes boring into her back. Marilyn wanted to paint, too. This was the classic Strasberg dynamic—preteen Susie acting as the older sibling, forced to share toys with baby Marilyn. Susie dutifully set her up with a brush and offered the use of her rainbow palette. (Marilyn: "I like black and white.")

Holding her brush as if it were a pen, Marilyn quickly sketched two figures. The first was a child with one sock falling down. One eye black, one clear. Solar and pale. A bleached-out negative of herself. Ragged frock bored into her memory like a sunspot. Sad little halogen bonnet. She titled it *Lonely*. The other was a feline woman in bold, sexy strokes. "That one should say, 'Life is wonderful, so what the hell,'" Marilyn said with a laugh. She wondered aloud if they were self-portraits, a Rorschach test in reverse.

By now the parents were hovering over Marilyn. Paula was hugging her; Lee was beaming and nodding and saying "Yes, darling" like he always did. "We must buy Marilyn her own set of paints!" When Susie asked if she'd like to keep her work, Marilyn demurred. "Oh, no, Susie, they're yours; you're the artist. Thanks for helping me," she added sweetly. Jealousy spiked with a pang of guilt.

"Whatever I'd experienced so far in my life," Susie wrote years later, "she'd experienced more intensely. There was a song in *Annie Get Your Gun* that went, 'Anything you can do, I can do better. . . .' She liked painting, we both wrote poetry, we read a lot of the same books, both skipping the parts that bored us, we bought our clothes at the same store."

Their jealousy cut both ways. Marilyn adored Susie but envied her perfect childhood. Pink birthday frocks from Tallulah Bankhead. Midnight dance lessons from Charlie Chaplin. *Swan Lake* on the record player, the beautiful Oona O'Neill passed out on the couch, smiling in her sleep. A Jewish mother, a genius father, and an adorable baby brother you could play jacks with and teach to spell. What did Susie know about loneliness?

Plenty. Marilyn never knew her father, but Susie's rejected her constantly, even as a baby. Lee pushed Susie away when she tried to crawl into his lap, his neck stiffening when she tugged on his sleeve to play. In fact, Lee rejected Susie before she was even born—he'd avoided the hospital while Paula was in labor. What if Susie was an ugly baby, he reasoned later. He knew that babies were born red and bald and wrinkled, and what if Susie looked like that and he didn't love her? That's the kind of man Lee was.

Sometimes the rivalry pulled them closer. It was part of the sister relationship Marilyn never had, the languid, easy banter and conspiratorial vibe. But Susie didn't understand how girls bonded— she'd never had a sister either, or even any close girlfriends. Marilyn overwhelmed Susie with her questions: Where did she get her makeup? What kind was it? Where did she buy her clothes, where did she go for facials, what music did she listen to? In her insecurity and paranoia, Susie mistook friendliness for competitiveness. She wanted to seal shut like an oyster—she didn't want to tell Marilyn that she used Revlon mascara and Johnson & Johnson's baby powder. Or she'd swing in the other direction, racked by guilt, awkwardly rattling off torrents of trivia Marilyn didn't even want. "Gee, thanks, Susie," chirped Marilyn with her wide-eyed stare. Could this blonde child-woman read her mind? Susie felt even worse.

Paula would try to soothe Susie, stroking her hair, telling her imitation was the sincerest form of flattery. But why would Marilyn

Monroe—the most famous woman in the world—try to imitate a
scrawny sixteen-year-old who had barely even been kissed?

❧ One evening before dinner, Paula did astrological charts for
Susie, Marilyn, and Anne Frank. Paula threw up her hands in
delight—Marilyn, Susie, and Anne were all Geminis with Leo
rising and Pluto in the twelfth house. She knew it. There were no
accidents. It was *bashert*—God's will. Lee grimaced, stomped outside, and fired up the grill.

On cloudy days, Marilyn lounged in the bedroom with Paula—
hushed voices, veiled references to a mysterious "Arturo." Lee was
still oblivious, but Paula reveled in the scandal. Why shouldn't
Marilyn attach herself to a Pulitzer Prize–winning playwright?
Though Paula fervently believed in Marilyn's talent, deep down she
thought that the "most glorious achievement of a woman was to
be a partner to an extraordinary man." In this way Paula was
Marilyn's polar opposite. Marilyn knew what her greatest achievement would be—she was working on it now, every second, every
day, engaged in the battle of her life.

At night, they'd all drink champagne, turn on the radio, and
dance—or rather, they'd watch Marilyn dance. Like many girls
who've been trained in ballet, Susie could only dance formally—
she was in awe of how Marilyn danced spontaneously, like a child.
"She followed her feet and didn't look at them the way I did," Susie
said. Besides, when Marilyn danced you couldn't look at anything
else: her sinuous movements, her jingle-bell laugh, her frantic
energy warming up the room.

What was Paula thinking when Lee sat there, glowing with pleasure behind his newspaper? There's no indication that Paula was
jealous—she adored Marilyn. She'd been a modern dancer herself,

but her "I gain if I look at lettuce" figure embarrassed her, and there was no way she was dancing, especially next to Marilyn Monroe. "Johnny," Paula would order, "you dance with Marilyn." Mortified, Johnny would dash out the backdoor. And Marilyn would dance alone on those bubbly summer nights.

⌒ Despite all that family closeness and balmy calm, some black anxiety unleashed itself that summer. Marilyn was sometimes near tears in the evenings—fretting over her Fox contract or something Arthur had said. Paula would do her best, padding around the porch with the teapot and chilled bottles of Dom Pérignon. "The Geminis are restless tonight," she'd say, urging Marilyn to alternate champagne with sips of milky tea.

During their moonlit chats, Susie would encourage Marilyn, talk about how much Lee loved her, how he thought she was a better actress than Joan Crawford and Gloria Swanson. But Marilyn would change the subject, sighing with her cast-down wounded-fawn eyes. "It's hard when you grow up an orphan," she'd say. "It gets so you don't expect anything good. . . ." Whenever Susie brought up the future, Marilyn would return to her past.

After months of heavy psychoanalysis, Marilyn had started to obsess over her childhood: the foster homes, the orphanage, the mother strapped down and stuck in an insane asylum. Tangled in memory's toxic net, she'd obsess over flashbacks late at night. She'd lie in her twin bed, listening to the surf, the moonlight spilling on the dark floorboards of stained wood. Then she'd start talking about her foster homes and how rough they'd been. She'd go on for a while then catch herself. "Maybe it wasn't all that bad," she'd say, trailing off. Of course, it really had been that bad.

Susie was only half-listening. With her Broadway debut only

months away, she was desperately trying to focus, to submerge herself in Anne Frank's story and spirit. But how could she concentrate with this dazzling, vulnerable woman lying three feet away?

~ Marilyn was one of them by now, and the Strasbergs grew
used to her disheveled night terrors—wrapped in a ratty bathrobe, face glazed in coats of Vaseline and lanolin.

One night close to four, Susie woke to a whimpering. She crept
down the hallway and saw her father holding Marilyn, rocking her
gently and singing a Brahms lullaby—the same song he sang to her
as a baby. Hit by a wave of jealousy, a lump rose in Susie's throat: "I
can't sleep; he's not holding me and singing to me."

Yet, here he is with Marilyn—a grown, gorgeous woman with
the world at her feet—rocking her to sleep as if she were his own
flesh. Before long, Susie's envy softened into compassion. Even at
sixteen, she could see that Marilyn's "need was so great."

The catbirds meowed in the early pink chill. It was six in the
morning before Marilyn fell asleep.

~ Despite her support system and her love of New York,
Marilyn was starting to take more pills than ever. Her suite at the
Waldorf cost Milton $1,000 a week, and their negotiations with
Fox were going nowhere. She wasn't even an official member of
the Actors Studio. On a personal level, she had alienated Joe—her
knight and protector—for good. She had embarrassed him and
(somewhat brattily) rejected him, and he wasn't coming back. Her
connection with Arthur was tentative at best—he was still married, with no plans at this point to get a divorce.

Seeds of insecurity had taken root, and she began to question
all her relationships—even with the Greenes. Amy intimidated

Marilyn—so cool and slim in her sleek sheaths from Anne Klein. She barely even drank. But everyone else took downers: Doctors up and down Manhattan were doling out Miltowns like lollipops at a bank. Milton took as many pills as Marilyn did. He had them stockpiled, thanks to his physician brother—yet somehow he functioned when she could not. And why weren't things coming together? Perhaps the press was right. Maybe she had been arrogant, foolish to leave Hollywood. Marilyn was beginning to realize that she was extremely vulnerable.

In March, everything had been pink elephants, pillow fights, and cocktails at the Copa. The initial buzz of her Great Escape, her defiance of Hollywood and her fresh start in New York hadn't yet worn off. Marilyn had leaped into the abyss, intoxicated by the giddy, glamorous unknown, only to realize she was in free fall.

Still, what was the alternative? Numbing out in LA by the pool at Chateau Marmont? Now she was living authentically—with a shot at freedom, success, respect, creative fulfillment, even the promise of love. All these riches come at a price. If Hollywood was death by pancake makeup, New York was a daily date with the magnifying mirror. Marilyn wouldn't have it any other way.

Twelve

In the Bulrushes

"I'm trying to become an artist, and to be true,
and sometimes feel I'm on the verge of craziness.
I'm just trying to get the truest part of myself out,
and it's very hard."   MARILYN MONROE

*F*irmly ensconced with the Strasbergs, Marilyn was seeing less
and less of the Greenes. "Now she comes out from New York only
occasionally. I do believe Josh misses Marilyn," Amy admitted in
an interview for *Photoplay.* "I miss it, too."

When Milton and Amy returned from Italy, Marilyn caught up
with them in Richard Rodgers's Connecticut pool. Almost tom-
boyish, her hair cropped shorter than ever before, she posed for
Milton—toasting the camera with her clear plastic cup, playing

with a red-and-white inner tube, hugging an inflatable yellow pony, cradling a black puppy, kissing its nose, caressing its tiny white paws.

Sun cream. Pool toys. Chlorine on warm skin. Plastic tumblers of whiskey and ginger ale, the steady thrum of midsummer wasps. Dark foliage in the background, trees hemlock black against the blaze-pink lowering sun. Milton and Marilyn splashed with childlike glee. That sad, fluttery choke in the throat when you should be fizzy with light. Their friendship was about to change, and they both knew it.

Thanks to Arthur Miller, Marilyn's relationship with Milton was already under strain. He dismissed the Greenes as fashionable socialites; they found him pedantic and humorless. When Milton made efforts to connect over drinks, Arthur would respond in contemptuous monosyllables or, even worse, lecture him on social theory. Milton was exasperated with Miller's ego and "dreary long-hairiness."

"I believe in gloomy things, not pink tights," Arthur wrote to Marilyn, as if that were a good thing. Marilyn believed in pink tights. She believed in the Copa and pink elephants and the circus and Dean Martin at the Friars Club and dancing at the Elmo with Truman Capote. But she couldn't have that giddy fun with Arthur. Their relationship was heavier, missing the natural joy she shared with Milton—giggling like teenagers, speeding down the highway with a backseat piled with boas and bras. Would Arthur get drunk and put a barrette on Sammy Davis Jr.'s dog? No, he wouldn't.

When they would bike together through Brooklyn Heights, it wasn't with a child's gleeful abandon. There was always something weighty, a gravity to it. After all, Arthur had called her "the saddest girl in the world" and meant it as a compliment. "I thought she was a very serious girl—that's because I loved her," he said.

Being a "serious girl" was key to keeping Arthur's love. No wonder she rarely laughed around him.

"We used to play out in the country," said Milton, recalling happier times. "Her laugh—it was happy; it was like a little girl's. But when she got involved with Miller—that was a whole other story. Then you had to act differently. You had to be different, you know?"

Amy noticed with alarm how close they were getting. She couldn't imagine Marilyn marrying a snob who proudly announced that he "believed in gloomy things" and didn't own a suit. She watched with increasing alarm as Marilyn began to defer to Arthur as some sage or teacher. "Every time that they would meet, Arthur would come in with one or two books that he wanted Marilyn to read. She would say 'What did you bring me, Arthur?' There was a lot of Dostoyevsky going around—*Crime and Punishment*. There was a lot of Karl Marx, and a lot of Arthur's own work. There was a lot of Saroyan, too. Then all of the sudden we started having these big deep discussions about communism. And being a naturalized citizen. To me this whole country is bigger than John Wayne—I love it. And Arthur immediately started attacking it, which put me on the defensive. I was also younger, and let's say after reading one book on Marx I realized that what they wanted was total fantasy, it was completely nonsensical, so why are we devoting so much time to it? That was my first resentment of him. And also I found that he was force-feeding her, and she could not back away from it and say, 'Just a minute, what is it that you are telling me?' Arthur would keep looking at Marilyn, like 'What is this dummy doing?' I was beginning to see that God had clay feet."

Amy bristled when she heard Marilyn parroting Arthur's ideas as if they were her own: "Two days later she would mouth something Arthur said two nights before. I'd say, 'What was that? Why are you saying that?' She'd say, 'Arthur said it.' I finally had to tell her I don't give a shit what Arthur says. Then I all of the sudden was becoming very patriotic, and I was giving her the Bill of Rights." Even the perpetually good-natured Milton was ruffled by Arthur's disruptive presence. "It wasn't easy," he said with a sigh, "because Marilyn was sort of matching him—matching Arthur Miller."

Milton knew firsthand what it was like to live with Marilyn's chaos. Back in Connecticut she'd reined herself in, but her suite at the Waldorf was an explosion. "It was always a mess," he groaned. "Even if you cleaned up after her, five minutes later it was a mess." A soggy copy of *Swann's Way* under the tub, slick with bath oil, uncapped bottles of Lustre-Creme shampoo spilling out on the tiles like yellow cake batter. She was a glittering tornado, clothes cascading from the closet, suitcases never fully unpacked, bed unmade, and sheets balled on the floor. "It's the way she takes her clothes off," Milton rationalized. "Instead of hanging them up and letting them air out or putting them in the hamper, she'd throw them on the floor. The makeup table was the same way—powder everywhere."

Milton wasn't fazed by this in the least, and even the tidy Amy could take it in stride. But could Arthur handle a life with Marilyn—the phone ringing and lawyers calling and burning dinner then throwing it out and ordering in ("Oh, what the heck") then dinner at Gino's and drinks with Sinatra at the Subway Inn then frantic phone calls at 4 a.m. because she'd lost a script or plane ticket or was nervous about her shoot tomorrow.

Arthur was protective, which Marilyn always loved in a man. But he always had that solemn sense of destiny—he was there to rescue her. From what, the horror of Hollywood? She'd already freed herself from that. She was studying, improving; she was happy. What dark shape did he see in her future?

He thought he knew the "real" Marilyn, and he would whisk her away from this toxic glut of glitz. Arthur was blind. This may have been the only year in Marilyn's life when she didn't need to be saved.

❧ That summer, Marilyn relaxed into an oasis of sheltering friendships and relative calm. When she wasn't with the Strasbergs, she spent weekends with the Rostens, who offered another safe, gentle space with their breezy beach house in Port Jefferson.

"As a summer weekend house guest," wrote Norman Rosten, "she fit in well with the family." She loved her little guest room ("Make it dark and give me air."); she loved their enormous library and its cool mildew scent. The Rostens understood Marilyn's need for space and left her alone for hours, content to read, stretched on a window seat nuzzling Bam-Moo the beagle. She'd sleep in, whip some eggs in hot milk, then take a late-morning stroll with Candy the cat.

At night, she helped cook: shucking clams, rinsing spaghetti, always leaping up to wash the dishes. She held clean glasses up to the light for inspection, then filled them with Dom Pérignon. "Champagne and caviar were the opposite of waifdom," wrote Norman. "Each popping cork proclaimed: Look at me, this is no abandoned child, no orphan!" He kept the fridge stocked with pink cartons of cottage cheese—Marilyn's favorite late-night snack.

Beach days with the Rostens were lively. The whole family would pile into the car—umbrellas, blankets, picnic baskets stuffed with crackers, cheese, and olives, and the trunk packed with champagne and beer on dry ice. They'd set up shop on the beach: striped umbrellas wedged in the sand, blankets and towels strewn with books and Dixie cups. Hedda would be wearing her pink bandeau and matching shawl, rooting through her straw bag for a lighter and pack of Chesterfields; Marilyn, a boater's hat and one of Arthur's shirts, rereading the Molly Bloom chapter from *Ulysses*. She'd stride through the sand munching green apples, tightening her halter with its white drawstring cord. Sometimes she'd climb into Norman's little speedboat or grab the hand of his twelve-year-old daughter, Patricia, and run laughing through the surf.

By the end of the summer, Marilyn had grown extremely close to the Rostens, particularly Norman. Snapshots show them cavorting on the beach, Marilyn in white terry shorts and a harlequin halter, Norman in pinstriped swimming trunks and a rumpled gray polo shirt. She's posed in the sand, one hand on her hip, the other perched on his shoulder as he cracks open a beer.

Marilyn rarely talked to Norman about acting or Hollywood. He'd escort her to the occasional concert or premiere, but he felt most comfortable with the stripped-down, summer Marilyn— barefoot on the beach in clam diggers and a blouse or splashing through the waves in her silly white bathing cap.

Like all good friends, they had their own language. With Milton it was renegade dress-up and glamour, with Sam Shaw it was urban high jinks and art, and with Norman it was pet names and poetry. She called him Claude-Claude; she was Noodle, Clump, Sugar Finny, Pussy, or Max. "She gave herself pretty names," Norman wrote. "An identity name, the little funny imp. That was an appealing part of her character. She had a great sense of humor."

Together they were Normalyn, a nickname she coined and signed on the very first letter she wrote him. They called each other daily but wrote letters even more, a practice they'd continue for the rest of her life. (For the most part, Marilyn was an erratic correspondent—she treasured her letters from friends but often left them unanswered for months, even years.) With Norman it was easy—the way they communicated in playful fragments and bolts came naturally to her. In Norman Marilyn found the empathy she so desperately sought. She knew he wasn't judging her— not even on the worst days when she had to type her letters because her hands were shaking so much. He bucked her up, bolstered her ego. Now, in the summer of 1955, Marilyn wrote the most touching words she'd ever say to a friend, or anyone: "I'm so glad you were born and I'm living at the same time as you."

૭~ "My wife believed I loved Marilyn," wrote Norman, "but so did she. If love is that force or presence, we both did." Hedda had been Mary Slattery's roommate in Ann Arbor, but she had more in common with Marilyn. In fact, Arthur had pursued Hedda first—drawn to her doe-eyed gaze and "terrific body," the way she dashed around campus in crispy white blouses, pausing to wave at someone or light one of her seemingly endless cigarettes. Now, at forty-one, she'd developed a rattling smoker's cough but was still girlish in shirtwaists and the kittenish slippers she'd favored since college.

Like Marilyn, Hedda was neurotic, giggly, brainy, and a touch naive. They bonded deeply that summer, cooking together or driving to Sag Harbor to check out the sales racks at Saks. Sometimes they'd pick out clothes for Norman: well-tailored shirts and black cashmere pullovers. One afternoon Marilyn realized she needed more sundresses—she'd been wearing the same eyelet blue for weeks. She grabbed six dresses (same style, different colors) and dashed into the fitting room, the starstruck assistant hot at her heels. The salesgirl unzipped Marilyn, who stood naked and calm as "Venus rising from that famous half shell." Marilyn proceeded to try on each dress, all the while happily chatting with the shocked shopgirl about the weather and the season's styles. Was it against Saks policy to try on dresses naked? It didn't matter. Marilyn bought all six.

They took early evening walks—Marilyn clutching Hedda's hand, hair pushed under a red patterned kerchief, in white terry slippers and sleeveless blouse of black Irish linen, buttoned up the front in mother-of-pearl. Hedda was a curvy little bird in cat-eye glasses and ballet flats, Patricia sandy and barefoot.

At night, they played badminton, Marilyn giggling over the birdie. The children loved her. "She was fun to be with," recalled Patricia Rosten, "because she broke the rules, and children love being around grown-ups who can get away with that. When Marilyn touched me or hugged me I felt a warmth and softness (dare I use the word maternal in relation to her?) that was very reassuring. It was not unlike falling into that champagne-colored quilt that graced her bed."

Marilyn traveled light, wearing the same knit halter for weeks, pairing it with shorts for the beach and capris for jaunts in town. She lugged around her entire makeup kit—a huge metal tackle box stuffed with hundreds of tiny bottles—but left most of the makeup untouched, sticking to sun cream and a few drops of Chanel.

"Once when she was visiting us," wrote Patricia years later, "I became bored with the adult conversation and found myself wandering through the other empty rooms. As I passed Marilyn's bedroom a large box on a table by the window caught my eye. It looked like a huge metal tackle box. In a moment of curiosity and bad manners I lifted the lid and peered inside. It was filled with cosmetics—lipstick, eyeliners, mascara, brushes, sticks of stage pancake makeup. I was so fascinated by hundreds of little jars bottles and compacts that I didn't hear the sound of footsteps coming down the carpeted hallway. Marilyn discovered me deep in her makeup box. She acted like it was the most natural thing in the world to find me there. Before I could even feel embarrassed, she said that since I was so intrigued by the art of makeup she would show me how to do the job right. The next twenty minutes or so I was in a kind of dream as I watched her skillful hands transform my child's face into something that even I might have called glamorous. My eyelids glimmered, my cheekbones were highlighted, my mouth was rosy with color. I thought I could pass for seventeen. Not content with doing a partial makeover she also did my hair, which I usually wore stringy around my shoulders. She put it in an elegant French twist. She'd been so proud of her handiwork that she happily took me by the hand into the living room and showed me off to the grownups."

Blighted by poverty and neglect, Marilyn's childhood offered little chances for merriment or play. Yet she treasured moments she did have, whether romping outside in her foster neighborhoods, playing make-believe games with girls at the orphanage, or simply dreaming and doodling in a room by herself. She never shook that feeling of childlike otherness, adrift and unheard in the world of adults. "When you grow up," she'd say with a sigh to Patricia, "they make playing very difficult for you."

℘ That summer, Marilyn met the photojournalist Eve Arnold. They met by chance, while walking the beach in Port Jefferson. "I saw Norman Rosten approaching with a blond girl in the dusk with the light behind her," Eve wrote years later. She barely recognized Marilyn, who looked "small and remote" stripped bare of her satin and makeup, her hair a mess of salt and candy-floss quartz. To Eve's surprise, Marilyn suggested they all meet the next day for a swim. "There seemed to be an understanding that this was going to be a social gathering," Eve remembered.

Eve was right. She arrived to find the Rostens unloading crates of champagne from their car. A small group of friends were spreading out blankets. As usual, Marilyn was nowhere to be seen.

"I felt a stir all along the crowded beach," Eve wrote. "People were turning to look at Marilyn moving slowly down a cliff side from the meadow above our heads. She was wearing a bikini—tight shorts of white balloon cloth and a bifurcated bra, each section barely covered a breast and supported by a narrow band at the base. There were string shoulder straps to hold it up, and on her head she wore a huge hat of straw. For shoes she was wearing a pair of government issue army boots."

It was a blistering weekend, and the public beach teemed with people. For a while, all seemed calm. They sunned themselves and drank champagne. Marilyn played softball with Eve's five-year-old son. Norman's friends stood knee-deep in water, smoking cigarettes. A photographer from the *Port Jefferson Times* wandered by, a speed graphic camera flung over his shoulder. He paused, squinted, and shuffled away muttering, "That ain't Marilyn Monroe."

Two teenage boys paddled by, spotted Marilyn and sped away with the news. Within minutes teens swarmed by the dozen, the girls screeching, the boys crazed, the babies waving rocks and bits of charcoal for Marilyn's signature.

"Marilyn, you look terrific!"
"Marilyn, how about a kiss?"
"Marilyn, you're my favorite!"
"Marilyn, I see all your movies!"

She laughed with the crowd, and signed rocks for the little ones. They touched her arms and waist, screamed and pleaded, circled her tighter as she backed toward the water. She gave a fearful little wave and broke into a swim, with dozens of young fans wading in behind her.

Norman swam after Marilyn as the teens closed in on her like sharks. "Several of our group swam after her," he wrote later, "trying to cut them off. They kept clamoring for Marilyn; she was surrounded." He seized her by the arm with one hand, batted away boys with another: "Beat it!" Gradually they drifted into colder, deeper, water, and Marilyn stopped moving.

"You go back and let me die," she said weakly.

A motorboat swooped in, with a kid in a crew cut at the wheel. Norman climbed in first, then hauled Marilyn—who was deadweight at this point—over the side. "I looked at her as she lay exhausted, her legs curled up, her pink toes gleaming in the sun," Norman remembered. "The boy-pilot also regarded her with an adolescent's transfixed stare, forgetting the wheel and executing two tight circles before I realized what was happening." Norman began to shout at the boy, but Marilyn stopped him: "Don't be nervous; it's a wonderful weekend!"

❧ The day's chaos cemented Marilyn's trust in Eve, who had stood back rather than insisting on pictures. She agreed to a photo shoot and scheduled it for Labor Day weekend. Once again she'd be at the Rostens, and Eve was worried about finding a sliver of pure beach. Shooting at dawn would work, but she knew better than to force wake-up calls on Marilyn. Eventually, Eve decided on an abandoned playground in the marshland town of Mount Sinai.

All weekend, Marilyn was impossible to pin down. Every time Eve called she brushed her off with a vague "tomorrow," and it was Labor Day before Marilyn agreed to work. Eve arrived at the Rostens to find Marilyn still at lunch, toying with a plate of cottage cheese, deep in conversation with Hedda. Then came the panic over hair, makeup, which accessories she'd need, and which bathing suits to take. Clutching her copy of *Ulysses*, Marilyn jumped into Eve's car.

It was five by the time they reached Mount Sinai—just in time for the magic hour. They worked quickly, seizing the slippery golden light. Playground; swing set; pink, pearly toenails. Just the slightest, shell-pink sunburn on her nose. Perched on the monkey bars absorbed in *Ulysses*, or chin propped on the book gazing straight at the camera, Marilyn looked a bit like Molly Bloom herself. In the same diamond halter she'd lived in all summer, she sat cross-legged with the book in her lap, black flats tossed aside, hair cropped shorter than ever before. She flipped the book open to the last lines of the last page, mouthing the words to herself in a low whisper: ". . . and his heart beating and I said yes yes I will Yes."

Crouched in Eve's car, Marilyn stripped off her swimsuit and slipped into a leopard-print maillot. She loved the idea of a leopard in the bulrushes. The marshes were sludgy and swampy, but she splashed through the mud, playing like a tawny baby. She giggled, creeping through the reeds, beckoning to the camera as Eve clicked away, struggling to keep her Nikon dry.

"It was amusing to watch and follow where she led," recalled Eve, bewitched by her subject's irreverent humor and sexy sense of play. As usual, Marilyn directed herself. "She was in control, setting the style and pace, and I would follow, just praying my reflexes would be fast enough to accommodate her antics." She crawled through the swamp as if she were stalking her prey, while the sun sank lower, casting hemlock shadows on the murky reeds. By sunset she was coated in mud, giggling and exhilarated.

They returned to the Rostens' for one final summer feast, though Marilyn claimed she was dieting and stuck to cottage cheese. That night everyone skinny-dipped in the moonlight. Marilyn was the only one who kept her bathing suit on.

‿᠊᠊᠊ A few days later, Marilyn called Eve at four in the morning. In six hours she'd be flying to Illinois for an event honoring Abraham Lincoln—would Eve like to come? Eve, half asleep but intrigued, said yes. Who could say no to Marilyn?

The itinerary was grueling: plane to Chicago, two-hour lay-over, plane to Champaign, car cavalcade to Bement, all in fifteen hours. Why put herself through this for such a small-town affair? Marilyn saw it quite differently. Her compassion for everyday Americans was as sincere as her love of Lincoln himself. Didn't the people of Bement have a right to art and culture? Civilization wasn't the province of Manhattan's upper class. For Marilyn, this was a nobler cause than glittery publicity tours, and well worth the effort.

They arrived at LaGuardia just before dawn. Eve was exhausted, but Marilyn giggled and joked with Jimmy Haspiel and the MM6, who'd subwayed to the airport to see her off. In her blue eyelet frock and white Ferragamos, hair freshly feathered by Pete Leon-ardi, she frolicked for the benefit of the paparazzi, skipping around and chatting. Aside from her gigantic makeup box, she carried no luggage—just an oversize children's book, *Lincoln: A Picture Story of His Life*. (A spoof on her own ditzy image—bringing a kids' book instead of the double volume Sandburg she was actually reading.) Just before they took off, Pete gave Jimmy a lock snipped from Marilyn's platinum head.

On the first flight, Marilyn wrote her Lincoln speech while Pete back-combed her hair. Then she unlocked the seat's folding table, pulled out her beauty box, and pushed back the window's red curtains to make use of the natural light. Elbows propped on the table, she peered into her magnifying mirror, lining her lower lids to create the illusion of shadow, her cheap costume clip-on pearls glinting in the sun. She combed her lashes and stroked them with mascara, all the while rehearsing her speech in whispers with Eve. "'Our Late Beloved President,'" Eve marveled later. "It sounded as though Eisenhower, not Lincoln, had just died."

"She rode it all with aplomb," wrote Eve, "but when we got to Bement she was frazzled." Local press, radio, and television had been alerted, and the paparazzi slavered at each stop. Eve stood guard at the airport toilets. Marilyn had been taking diuretic tablets for kidney issues, but in her excitement she'd left the pills in New York. Now her ankles and feet were swollen from the flights. By the time she reached Bryant Cottage, the historic home where Lincoln had debated Stephen Douglas, Marilyn was exhausted. She asked for a basin of water for soaking, kicked off her mules, and collapsed.

Peter passed out—slumped on the floor, sunglasses on, head resting on the edge of Marilyn's bed. Someone procured the water basin and Marilyn rallied, soaking her feet and snacking on white grapes (natural diuretics). Sufficiently refreshed, she stripped off her dress so Eve could iron it, touched up her makeup, and brushed up on her speech. Her hair was matted beyond repair, but she let Peter nap, pulled on a pair of wrist-length black gloves, and, as Eve put it later, "went forth valiantly to 'bring art to the masses.'"

Despite Eve's cynicism, Marilyn enjoyed herself. She gave her speech, judged a beard-growing contest, and browsed wheat shafts, river maps, and taxidermy bears. She flirted with sailors, shook hands with the mayor, bantered with the local press, and winked at some farmers. Shortly after nightfall, it was time to leave.

By now, the prairie winds had picked up. Their tiny plane in Champaign couldn't fly above the storm, and they'd have to spend the night in Bement. Marilyn looked frantic. She was exhausted: swollen ankles, no luggage, no tubs of Laszlo creams, no razors, not even a single bottle of Chanel No 5. "She looked so crushed that I stepped in," recalled Eve. "Surely planes were flying out of Chicago, and we were only eighty miles away." Couldn't a car take them to the airport? But it was past nine—were there even any flights still bound for New York?

Marilyn shivered in her summer lace dress. Eve slipped off her cardigan, draping it round her bare shoulders. Pete took charge of logistics, called Chicago, and found a New York–bound plane that agreed to hold seats. The governor lent them his official car and crew, and off they went, flanked by motorcycles, speeding down the highway to Chicago.

By the time they reached the airport, the plane was waiting on the tarmac. It was past eleven, the lights were off, and the passengers were asleep. Marilyn stumbled aboard, a bedraggled cat in rumpled eyelet, her skin puffy and parched from planes and lack of sleep. "Nobody recognized her," Eve remembered years later. "Her hair was tangled; she was just a tired, ordinary girl."

It was two in the morning when they landed in New York. Before parting, Marilyn flung her arms round Eve and thanked her for bringing her home.

e̸ Between the Strasbergs and the Rostens, Marilyn spent the summer surrounded by puppies, cookouts, boat rides, and bike rides. But sometimes Norman caught her looking wistful, playing on the porch with the beagle one moment and staring through the mesh screen the next, or leaning listlessly against a sand pine, absently swinging her badminton racket, frowning at some invisible demon. At moments like these he'd say whatever he could to make her laugh, and she'd join him inside for a drink with Hedda.

Why this retreat inward, why this anxiety? Why this slow summer shift toward melancholy, this deepening gravitas? After months of uncertainty, her future was finally starting to look more secure. Thanks to *The Seven Year Itch,* she now had bargaining power. There was a fresh buzz around MMP, and Milton was fielding exciting new offers. After years of degradation, Marilyn just might be winning the upper hand. Wasn't this everything she had been working for?

Her position at the Studio was no longer precarious. Weekdays in town were filled with parties—drinking screwdrivers out of Dixie cups and sharing chicken wings with Mike Gazzo. When she could, she'd pop by the Martin Beck Theatre to see Eli in *Teahouse* and romp around with him backstage. They'd go to Jim Downey's for dinner and drinks, occasionally joined by Arthur Miller. Marilyn—always at ease more with friends than lovers—would be laughing and dancing with Eli while Arthur would watch silently, "swiveling a cigarette from tooth to tooth like a gun." Sometimes she dragged him to the Strasbergs' brunches, where he'd lurk on the sidelines, a pipe clenched between his teeth. He hated to see Marilyn sitting at Lee's feet, Lee stroking her hair murmuring, "Yes, darling," and "Of course, darling."

Arthur was stressed. Paparazzi had already started to follow him everywhere—even biking down the cobblestones in Brooklyn Heights or the streets of Sheepshead Bay. *A View From the Bridge* was in production, but Marilyn left him completely distracted.

The stakes were high. Nearly forty, saddled with a stale marriage and stalled career, Arthur needed a change. Marilyn promised new happiness, maybe even a burst of creativity. But leaving his wife wouldn't resolve Arthur's issues, and neither would their subsequent divorce. Throughout his six-year relationship with Marilyn, Arthur would struggle with his work, suffer long dry spells, and would often be simply unable to write.

If Arthur expected Marilyn to be a muse, he was mistaken. She would never fit the Wife of the Great Man role—those beleaguered, understanding artists' wives, with their loving smiles and dinner reminders and home-cooked stews. She herself was an artist—and as with many other artists, the people closest to her often fell into caretaking roles. She was not the type of woman to inspire a man, cook a three-course meal, and put the children to bed. She didn't use alarm clocks. She cooked pasta with her hair dryer. It was her show, and it always would be.

Thirteen

Sutton Place

"New York is my home now."   MARILYN MONROE

*I*n September, Marilyn moved into an eighth-floor walk-up on
Sutton Place. Her luxury suite had been draining MMP's finances,
and Marilyn was happy to downsize. She redid her bedroom to
look just like the Waldorf: white walls, white chairs, pink taffeta
counterpane, with Abraham Lincoln looming over the bed. She
stacked books on the nightstand with a framed photo of Albert
Einstein perched on top as if he were her overseas boyfriend. She
hung paintings on the wall—one by director Jean Negulesco and
another simple drawing she'd done herself. Records were strewn
round the living room floor: Sinatra, Bing Crosby (Arthur's), and
Marilyn's own recordings, such as "Love Me or Leave Me," on 78

rpms with home-typed labels. The window looked out on her "Pepsi-Cola" East River and the floaty 59th Street Bridge.

With its fancy florists, sleek boutiques, and elegant brownstones full of Morgans and Rothschilds, Sutton Place was known as the Silk Stocking District and quickly became Marilyn's world. She filled her prescriptions at Whelan's Drug Store, ate coffee-cognac ice cream at Maxfield's, and shopped at corner grocers stocked with caviar, white truffles, and quail eggs. You might spot her strolling across 50th Street with a trench slung round her shoulders, munching popcorn given to her by one of the Monroe Six, or leaning out her window in a baby-blue bathrobe, gazing toward the East River in the early morning light.

No longer living out of hotels, Marilyn was beginning to feel like a real New Yorker. She spent hours admiring Picassos at the Modern, or lingering over vanilla sundaes with friends from acting class. Marilyn's constant crackles of fear were outweighed by a sense of joy, and for the first time in her life, belonging. Contented and secure in her private life, public opinion mattered less and less. "I learned early on to bring her the gossip-free *New York Times* if I brought her a newspaper," wrote Jimmy Haspiel. "When in the past I had offered Marilyn a newspaper and said, 'You are in Earl Wilson's column today,' her hand went right up between us, her palm facing me, her fingers pointed skywards, and she said, 'I'm not interested, Jimmy.' What Marilyn was doing was getting on with her life."

Those little digs that hurt her so much in the past had ceased to bother her. When Judy Holliday parodied her on the radio, Marilyn was secure enough to let it roll off. "I hear you did an impression of me," she teased when she caught Judy weeks later strolling down Fifth Avenue. Charmed, Judy asked her to tea the next day at her penthouse in the Dakota.

Judy spent the next morning tearing through her closet, yanking out dresses, ripping them off, and hurling them across the room in agony. "I look faaaaat," she wailed, twisting and grimacing in the mirror. Marilyn arrived one hour late, in an old sleeveless blouse, ballet flats, and a wrinkled cotton skirt stained by splotches of black grease. Her roots showed, her bare legs were mottled by mosquito bites and scabs. Somehow, she'd forgotten to shave her armpits. But the skin on her face glowed, and her heat-fatigued sigh sounded like marshmallows. She was heartbreakingly, ravishingly beautiful.

Judy gasped. Two weeks after her radio caricature, the "real thing" stood before her in all her scruffy beauty. Judy felt suddenly dowdy, despite her WASP waist dress and salon-coiffed hair. "I thought I was a real woman," she admitted later, "until Marilyn Monroe came over to my house for tea."

☙ By fall 1955, Sam Shaw, Norman Rosten, and Eli Wallach had emerged as her closest confidants—or, as Marilyn called them, Sam Spade, Claude-Claude, and Teacake. (Somehow her pet names always fit. Marlon Brando was Carlo. Paula was Black Bart. Lee was the Great White Father. Teenage Susie was miffed that she never got one.) But unlike Marilyn's masculine, silent husbands, her "brothers" were warm, communicative men who packed picnic baskets and read poetry. They understood her—especially her empathy, which extended to inanimate objects. (Sam Shaw: "If you were browsing through an antique shop and didn't like a lamp, she'd say she liked it and buy the poor lamp because no one else wanted it.") They humored her odd behavior, such as ordering plates of asparagus and bacon from the fanciest restaurants in town or calling at three in the morning to complain about her cat.

"You never know when she'd phone in the middle of the night without identifying herself," wrote Norman Rosten, "her voice low, breathless, impossible to disguise." "Hello, it's me," she'd chirp into the phone. "What's everybody doing?" Or "I thought we could stir up some mischief."

"You had to be on her time," Norman added. "She never got the time thing straightened out: it was a built in psychic time. Marilyn time. Possibly Einstein time."

Eli Wallach shared Marilyn's nutty sense of humor. When Shelley Winters told him about Marilyn's crush on Albert Einstein, Eli bought a picture and signed it "To my dear Marilyn, Love Albert." She giggled, had it framed in silver, and placed it on her beloved baby grand.

Their friendship ran deeper than simple jokes. Eli recognized Marilyn's intelligence and admired her courage. "This is no dumb blonde," he told *Coronet* magazine. "She's got guts. Marilyn is not any one thing; she's multidimensional." They both worried over being typecast—Marilyn as the ditsy blonde, Eli as the Italian hothead. In class he stuck up for her like a big brother. "She's smart," he said to Maureen Stapleton during Marilyn's timid first days at Malin Studios. "I know she's smart," Maureen had assured him.

In fact, Eli was so impressed by Marilyn's professionalism that he asked her to help him rewrite a contract. "I remember her putting on her little Ben Franklin spectacles to read the contract. 'All right,' she told me. 'Take out clauses three and four. And make sure they clarify your billing.'"

He loved that about Marilyn, how she shot lightness and play into serious moments. They were clowning around together—Wallach in a Sigmund Freud costume—when Marilyn suddenly looked up and whispered, "Eli, you're going to be working all your life."

In class they'd sit in each other's laps or jump up during a break and dance the Lindy. Sometimes he took her dancing on Swing

Street. "One time Marilyn and I were cavorting on the dance floor," Eli remembered. "I looked up to the balcony, where I noticed Milton Berle, Frank Sinatra, and Joe DiMaggio. I gulped and said that I didn't feel like dancing anymore. She looked up at them and smiled. 'The hell with them—let's keep going!'"

Soon enough their names appeared in gossip columns all over the country. "Please, Annie," Eli explained to his wife, Anne Jackson. "Think of Marilyn like my sister. I'm the beard for Arthur."

The beard worked a little too well, arousing suspicion even among some colleagues. "I followed her up Broadway," wrote Studio actor Stefan Gierasch, "while she was walking with Eli Wallach. She had grease on her face and was dressed down, but everyone still recognized her. Everyone always wondered if she was secretly dating Eli, but they never knew for sure."

"Fortunately, I wasn't famous," wrote Norman Rosten, who also escorted Marilyn to concerts and premieres. "I was a safe, non-recognizable, non-gossip companion. It sounds glamorous; it also was hard work. There we were one night, seated in Carnegie Hall, she in her devastating dress, I in my assembly-line suit, waiting for the great pianist Emil Gilels to enter on stage and be seated at the piano. 'Relax,' she whispered with that little laugh of hers. 'They don't know who you are.' I don't know if word of her presence got backstage, but Gilels played like a man inspired. At intermission, a Carnegie official approached and informed us that Mrs. Gilels was seated in a box across from our part of the dress circle and asked to meet her. Marilyn took my hand (she was worried I'd back out) and with half the hall watching, we crossed over to the box where Mrs. Gilels was chatting with a short, intense man. It was Gilels himself. Marilyn introduced me as 'my poet friend' and I tried my best to look poetic. He said to her 'You must visit Russia one day. Everyone would like to see you.' She answered, 'I would love to, and someday I will. Right now I'm reading Dostoevsky.'

Then she turned to Mrs. Gilels, who didn't seem to know more than a dozen words of English. 'He's a great man, your husband, you must be so proud of him.' Mrs. G. smiled sweetly. It was a high moment in international relations."

The next day's gossip column: MARILYN MONROE COOING POETRY WITH NORMAN ROSTEN. Norman groaned. Hedda laughed: "It's certainly better than 'wooing.'"

Far from a devious femme fatale, Marilyn befriended entire families. She was a regular guest at the Wallachs' home—eating bagels and gefilte fish, chatting with Anne over coffee in the kitchen, or babysitting their son Peter. She shared a birthday with Sam Shaw's preteen daughter, Edie, and surprised her one year with tickets to the circus. "Marilyn was so excited," Sam recalled years later. "She wore a skirt, a loose blouse, no make-up, a wig wrapped in a babushka like a scarf around her head. Edie I remember with lace trimmed bobby-socks, her hair tied in a bun and white dainty gloves. Both girls, a big sister and a kid sister."

"Three Gemini children fated to meet and play," wrote Norman Rosten of Marilyn, Edie Shaw, and his daughter, Patricia, whose birthday was right before theirs. "Edie and Patricia barely teenage, and Marilyn in her mid-twenties and ageless." Marilyn was always giving Patty little gifts and trinkets, including an adorable dog named Cindy. Marilyn had found the dog roaming the streets, half starved, barely able to walk. With the help of a vet, she nursed Cindy back to health and presented her as a birthday gift to Patty. "The playful spirit of the child lurked in her eyes, her walk, her psyche, particularly her laugh," wrote Norman Rosten. "That inner child stayed with her to the end."

Marilyn doted on her own pets with childlike intensity. That fall she adopted a russet striped cat who mysteriously got pregnant under her care. Marilyn obsessed over prenatal cat care, fed it caviar, and lined a box with a blanket. She called Norman and

Hedda with daily updates: "Cat looked fine, cat seemed to be breathing hard, cat didn't eat much, cat looked listless, cat looked crazy." Norman threatened to get an unlisted number if the kittens didn't arrive soon. Marilyn coached her pet through labor alone and rang Norman at midnight: "They're coming, the kittens! Hurry, take a cab!"

Marilyn always treated animals with empathy and care, just as she treated people. Years later she adopted a basset hound named Hugo and fretted over his moods. When Marilyn convinced herself that Hugo was depressed, it was Norman who helped feed the dog teaspoons of whiskey. "In those years people, friends were closer," mused Norman. "There was more meaning to friendship."

Throughout her life, Marilyn would refer to Norman Rosten as her "closest friend." They discussed dreams, poetry, and art. "I had mentioned the Rodin section at the Metropolitan Museum of Art," wrote Norman, "knowing it would delight her and for months she promised to see it. One day the phone rang: 'I'm ready, Claude, if you are!' It was the perfect Monroe sentence—directionless, timeless."

The Rodin wing was empty that afternoon, and there was something hushed and holy in the rooms. She wandered around the airy vault, the cool marble matching her own skimmed-milk pallor. She paused by *Pygmalion* but it was *The Hand of God* that stopped her cold: a vision of obsessive love coaxed out of stone. She tiptoed round it, slipping off her sunglasses, eyes as solemn and rapt as a child's. "This was a different dream, of love and happiness and culmination—a dream denied her," Norman wrote. "She stood before this vision transfixed, finger at her lips."

Ever the paradox, Marilyn was equally captivated by Francisco Goya. Back in May she'd rushed to the Met for its monthlong exhibit of his etchings and drawings—this time with Sam Shaw. She roamed, unrecognized, pausing to gape at his witches and ghouls, then suddenly turned to Sam: "I know this man well. We have the same dreams. I've had these dreams since I was a child."

Eager to learn more, Marilyn immediately bought Goya's biography. But she was bitterly disappointed—the book had none of the psychological insight she'd hoped for. Norman and Sam understood her frustration. They knew how personally she responded to art, instantly considering Goya a kindred spirit. They marveled at her complexity. Rodin's eros and Goya's demons coexisting in one angelic being.

"It isn't simple with Marilyn," mused Sam years after Marilyn's death. "Nothing ever is."

"She chose us because we were family men," said Sam Shaw, referring to Norman, Eli, and himself. "She felt safe with us—there was no threat or sexual tension." But Marilyn simply couldn't turn off the flirt, telling Norman she loved him, sitting in Eli Wallach's lap, making Sam girlish scrapbooks with crayon-drawn hearts ("I'd rather be dancing with *you*, Sam," she scrawled on one page). She pushed boundaries—she couldn't help herself. One weekend Marilyn ran into Eli at Idlewild Airport before a weekend flight to LA. He was waiting for a plane to San Francisco. She asked if he was flying alone and said, "If you had asked me I would have gone with you."

"That was one of the few times I thought she was cruel," claimed a mutual friend, who thought Marilyn was toying with Eli for sport. "She would never have gone to San Francisco with him."

But it's just as likely that Marilyn was compelled by her desire for closeness and warmth, her hatred of boredom, and the fact that she'd always been attracted to Eli. After all, he'd been on that list of "desirable men" she'd made years ago with Shelley Winters. Marilyn's interactions with men were always light and whimsical, infused with her sense of fun and play. Studio classmate Jack Garfein remembered one afternoon in particular:

"She called me and said that Strasberg said that I was very good at choosing women's clothes, and would I go shopping with her? And I said, 'Sure, why not?' So I met her, and we started to walk and talk, and I sensed that she liked me. At one point she said to me, 'Take my hand, Jack.' I said, 'Marilyn, if I take your hand tomorrow we're on the front pages of all the newspapers.' She said, 'Jack, don't be silly—you think people are occupied with me, with my life? Come on, they have their own lives they're living. . . . You want me to get their attention? Watch—I'll walk up on these steps here at Carnegie Hall; I'll stand a certain way and people will stop and say, "Oh, hi, Marilyn Monroe!" ' I said, 'Well, Marilyn, you're very modest and you're very nice, but I'm sorry, I don't think that that's what will happen if I take your hand.' She said 'Ok, let's go into a coffee shop. We'll sit at the counter; we'll order coffee—Jack, if nobody recognizes me at the coffee shop, will you stop being stupid and take my hand?' So we walked into the coffee shop, we sit right there, and the guy gives us coffee. Nobody recognized her—even the guy opposite her serving the coffee. So then we went and I took her hand, we went shopping, and of course, she had a great sense of humor. I said to her, 'Marilyn, it's just a year I've been married; I'm not looking for trouble, you know,' and she laughed. So we went into the store, and every time she was trying on a dress she would say to me 'Jack, I need to be zipped up' or 'Jack, I need to be buttoned' but laughing, knowing what it did to me. In no way was it directly seductive—it was enjoying life, like, 'Have some fun, Jack; see what joy or pleasure you could have.' I was trembling much of the time, but the irony of that is that she walked me home after that. . . . And I had a sense that if I wanted to invite her upstairs she probably would have come. I don't know what would have happened— you never know—that's the wonderful thing about women, women who are honest, who aren't racked by guilt: 'Oh, I misled this man; oh, how terrible, I made him feel that he could have me' instead of knowing there's fun in life, it's fun to have that feeling and that sense. So I sensed that she would have but I stopped and said, 'OK, Marilyn, I live here, I've got to go upstairs.' She laughed, because she knew that there was a conflict, and she was enjoying it. So she said, 'Get me a taxi,' and I said okay and got her a taxi, and she kissed me very lightly and she left. . . . She loved that mystery between a man and a woman."

Perhaps the constant flirtation was Marilyn's way of protecting herself, of scattering her heart in pieces instead of trusting it to one person alone. "One evening at our house with friends," remembered Norman Rosten, "someone suggested an impromptu poetry reading. The idea was to pass around a copy of Whitman and Yeats, each to open a page at random and read. At Marilyn's turn, she opened the Yeats and the poem could only have been presented to her, again, by fate. It was 'Never Give All the Heart.' She read the title, paused, and began the poem. She read it slowly, discovering it, letting the lines strike her, surprised, hanging on, winning by absolute simplicity and truth."

For everything that's lovely is/ But a brief, dreamy, kind delight/ O never give the heart outright . . .

"When she finished," Norman noted, "there was a hush. She stared into space."

༄ Away from the illicit atmosphere of hotels, Marilyn and Arthur relaxed into domesticity. They went to the Rostens' for low-key dinners or spent quiet evenings at home together. Jimmy Haspiel was shocked to spot Marilyn toting grocery bags stuffed with spinach, carrots, and celery stalks, loaves of sourdough and thick chunks of Parmesan. For Marilyn, these weren't just required ingredients for Sunday dinner—the parsley and celery and wedges of cheese were infused with all the hope and magic of a budding relationship. Marilyn's kitchen attempts usually ended in chaos. But she tried—clipping recipes from magazines, bookmarking pages in *Fannie Farmer,* stuffing typed shopping lists into *Joy of Cooking.* She called Norman and Hedda to test her concoctions: strange stews, wild omelets, bowls of sauce with meat tossed in as an afterthought. Bizarre salads: iceberg lettuce with olive oil and no vinegar or sometimes plain vinegar with shredded lettuce. Sometimes she'd throw together something simple such as peas and carrots—half starlet, half nursery food. If a dish was too spicy, she'd grab her hair dryer and point it at the pot, injecting a bit of whimsy into the impossibly mundane. As with many other artists, it pained Marilyn to pull herself from dream life into reality. That's why she struggled with the basics yet managed to whip up a stunning bouillabaisse.

That fall, Marilyn threw her first dinner party. She fussed for days, scrawling recipes and shopping lists on receipts, hotel stationery, and promotional notepads from City Title Insurance. She simmered mushrooms in butter, trussed up a pheasant, chopped walnuts with parsley, soaked French bread in cold water for stuffing. She ordered flowers from Judith Garden, a birthday cake from

Greenberg's, and rushed off to Bloomingdale's for flatware, crystal, and two dozen ramekins. "She did nothing else for two days," recalled a bemused Arthur Miller, who watched Marilyn desperately measure out cups of grated cheese and teaspoons of oregano. "I never saw anyone so worried about a simple meal. Actually the whole thing was overdone, too formal, too meticulous, too manicured."

The cooking, the quiet dinners, the scaling back on late nights at the Copa, even the russet cat—Marilyn was attempting domesticity. She wanted it to work. She'd tried it before with Joe. As usual, she'd wished hard and dreamed big—incapable of having realistic aspirations. She wasn't going to be a housewife—she'd be Demeter, a domestic goddess. She'd learn all of Arthur's favorite recipes, starch his shirts, fill bowls with fresh cut flowers—even take flower arranging classes! She'd light the table with candles in antique candlesticks, serve French wine. "I'll treat him like a king," she vowed. A life of infinite courtship, castles in the air.

It never worked. Domesticity didn't suit Marilyn. Her career provided structure—not housekeeping. The everyday realities of a live-in relationship either numbed her mind or cramped it into anxiety. As she gypsied from the Greenes to the Gladstone to the Waldorf to that cozy little sublet on Sutton Place, Marilyn found herself uneasy with permanence, more confident amid chaos. But she never stopped trying to make a home for herself, and came closer than she ever would that year in New York.

❧ In late September, Arthur's wife kicked him out of their Willow Street brownstone and into the Chelsea Hotel. The two grew even closer: Marilyn opening up more than ever, Arthur remaining an engaged and highly imaginative listener. Like Marilyn, Arthur had a soft spot for underdogs. He began to identify with her, especially her status as victim of a hostile, puritan society. He himself struggled daily with censorship, HUAC, and the slippery kinks of public opinion. At that moment, Arthur and Marilyn were very much the same—idols and outcasts in a culture driven by fear.

Marilyn's best friends responded to her vulnerability with compassion, but above all respected her strength. Milton, Norman, Eli, and Sam never viewed her as a victim. "At the beginning, maybe you could use that word, low pay, all kinds of hours, industry exploitation," wrote Sam Shaw. "But Marilyn fought back." Instead of focusing on Marilyn's strengths, Arthur fetishized her weaknesses, obsessing over the sordid, darkest details of her Hollywood exploitation. "It is your suffering in the past," he wrote to her in an early letter, "that I respect and even bow down to."

Old wounds are seductive—and the memory of old wounds is more seductive still. Arthur obsessed over Marilyn's lovers and the concept of sin, which he referenced repeatedly in their correspondence. "I have sinned, Marilyn," he wrote. "I am no better than you in any way. I can hate every man you were ever with, but I can't hate you."

For Arthur, promiscuity was linked to vulnerability—and vulnerability was the ultimate aphrodisiac.

Like many other writers, Arthur was a bit morbid. A whiff of death lured him in like the sexy haze of Shalimar. When he met a young war widow on a train to DC, he felt a mystical attraction to her: "The brush with death had made her sensually attached to life, to sex, and had given her a taste for the catastrophic." She'd confessed to him that she was sleeping with random soldiers on the docks. To his credit, Arthur wasn't judgmental—he was excited by her "dangerous sex and her desperation." Instead of recoiling at her sexual past, he relished in the vicarious thrill of decadence, passion, transgression—all the things he never had. Arthur obsessed over having sex with her, then promptly reported this fantasy—to his wife.

For all his sensitivity, Arthur could be remarkably dense in his understanding of women. Arthur was actually shocked that this blithe announcement had damaged his wife's trust in him.

Arthur vacillated between idealizing women and recoiling when they dared to violate his expectations. Just as Marilyn was expected to be his high-minded flesh goddess, Mary Slattery was his unflappable pillar of strength. He'd expected his "cool wife" to brush off the incident as "one more male inanity." Even worse, Mary's "silly and overblown" reaction had weakened his "mindless" faith in her.

Surely a prizewinning playwright is allowed his "male inanity," yet Arthur's jealousy of Milton Greene knew no bounds. And while he never begrudged Marilyn her sexy clothes or career, he grew alarmingly jealous of Milton. Within two years Miller would break up Marilyn and Milton, destroying the most vital friendship of her short life.

Of all the men in Marilyn's blonde orbit, Milton was the one who never intimidated her, who always listened, who never bossed her around and most importantly never underestimated her. Years later, Lee Strasberg would talk her out of roles she wanted: *Rain,* even *The Brothers Karamazov.* He never thought Marilyn was ready. And Marilyn—who could spend three hours applying and reapplying lipstick—would readily agree.

It's unclear whether Arthur thought Marilyn and Milton were lovers. Regardless, the more Marilyn saw of Miller, the less she saw of her supporter and friend.

Joe had never felt threatened by Milton Greene—or any of Marilyn's friends. Despite his reputation for chaining her to a pot of spaghetti, Joe had been remarkably lax with Marilyn's time. If anything, he had been grateful for men like Sid Skolsky and Sam

Shaw—men he trusted, who genuinely cared about Marilyn and could keep her happily out of his hair for a while. He'd encouraged Sam to take Marilyn antiquing. God knows he didn't want to. He never complained about the hours she spent at Schwab's with Sidney trading gossip and pills. (Joe affectionately referred to the two of them as "pill-pals.") DiMaggio had old-fashioned ideas about marriage. He wanted to know his girl was happy, busy, and safe while he watched baseball, bet on horses, or played cards. Joe's love—no matter how crudely literal—was unconditional. He could be scowling in his chair watching baseball, the television drowning out Marilyn's disappointed pleas—but he simply loved her because he had decided to love her, and he'd continue to love her no matter what.

But now Joe was in Sicily with the Shaws—drinking thick black espresso (having cut down on bourbon) and exploring his family roots. He made occasional dates with curvy blondes who looked vaguely like Marilyn, but focused primarily on self-improvement, though it wasn't called that back then. Still hoping for a reconciliation, he wrote notes to himself on his failings with Marilyn, how to be a better man and how to win her back. "Forget ego and pride," he scribbled on the back cover of *Sports Illustrated*. "Be warm, affectionate and love. Be patient no matter what. Remember," he warned, "this is not your wife. She is a fine girl and remember how unhappy you made her. Happiness is what you strive for—for HER. Don't forget how lonesome and unhappy you are—especially without her."

ᕁ On September 29, Marilyn emerged from 2 Sutton Place in a gray blouse, a gray skirt with matching belt, gray pumps, and pale pink lipstick, her hair swirled in a buttery chignon. She looked oddly schoolmarmish. This wasn't really her style, but to Jimmy

Haspiel, who happened to be lurking close by, "She was unspeakably beautiful, just unspeakably."

That night, she met Arthur Miller's parents, Augusta and Isidore, at the Coronet Theatre for the *View From the Bridge* premiere. They adored Marilyn and immediately invited her to lunch at their Brooklyn home. Ever the old soul, Marilyn immediately bonded with Isidore. "She loved Arthur's father very much," remembered Amy. "She was crazy about Isidore. Her enthusiasm brought his out. She always loved my mother-in-law, Celia. She sort of venerated old age."

Marilyn always clicked easily with in-laws, grandparents, stepchildren, and pets—it was daily intimacy that she couldn't quite handle. But here was Arthur, pushing things ahead at an alarming speed. Dressed in a black blouse and gray skirt, Marilyn was sitting in the kitchen over a bowl of borscht when she overheard Arthur announce to his father, "This is the girl I'm going to marry."

Fourteen

Baby Doll

On the screen of pitch blackness comes/
reappears the shapes of monsters my most
steadfast companions . . . and the world is
sleeping ah peace I need you—even a peaceful
monster.   MARILYN MONROE

Autumn, Greenwich Village, 1955. A Checker cab containing
one driver, two actors, one bottle of Dom Pérignon, a pack of Dixie
cups and a mystery woman inched down Macdougal Street. The
woman in the rumpled slacks, fern-green raincoat, and Saks loafers
(no socks) was Marilyn Monroe, but the driver didn't recognize
her under the black scarf and matte-black sunglasses. To her right
was the journalist John Gilmore, to her left Ray Myers—one of
the Studio's youngest students and Marilyn's babysitter for today,

per Lee's instructions. He often "hired" his youngest actors to trail Marilyn, keep her happy, (relatively) healthy, and out of trouble.

Marilyn whispered something to Ray, who leaned forward and tapped on the glass: "The lady wants to walk barefoot on the grass in Washington Square."

It started to rain—lightly, almost a mist. The driver flipped on the windshield wipers.

"Which side of the park?"

Marilyn slipped off her loafers and passed them to Ray. John carried the champagne. Flanked by both men she walked, head bowed, hands in pockets, her bare feet in the wet grass. She chose a bench, and John popped the bottle. Ray fumbled with the Dixie cups in his coat pocket. Marilyn wished they were listening to Vivaldi.

She said that Arthur once sneered at her—what could she possibly know about Vivaldi? "I know about Vivaldi, for God's sake," she muttered today, fists balled up in her pockets. Tears spilled out from her sunglasses. John fought to light a Chesterfield in the rain, and Ray wrapped his arm around Marilyn's shoulder, advising her to take deep breaths. (Method training?) "I know how to breathe," she said with a sigh, shrugging off Ray's hand and reaching for a cup.

The rain beat down harder, soaking their skin and their cigarettes, but they went on refilling their Dixie cups, chasing Seconals with champagne, breaking open the capsules, little beads swallowed straight to the brain.

Ray wanted to get out of the rain. Why don't they run across the street to Rienzi's? But Marilyn refused—someone might steal the bench—and besides, what if Rienzi's was full?

She brought up Joe and the *Seven Year Itch* fiasco—how he wanted a good Catholic wife, not some starlet "showing her damn-near-bared crotch to half of New York." Her face blanched: "I had no way to love him, because he didn't want me to be who I have to be."

Marilyn leaned forward, about to be sick. ("I don't want to throw up—what if someone steps in it!") Ray leaped up to get paper towels from Rienzi's—finally an excuse to go to Rienzi's!—and John sat there, drenched in his Brooks Brothers jacket, thinking that he'd fling himself under a taxi right then and there, if only Marilyn wanted him to.

❧ Despite her general glow, Marilyn's life in New York was still peppered by doubts, particularly involving Miller. By sleeping with a married man, she was at war with herself. "Her least favorite word was 'homewrecker,'" remembered Amy Greene, who witnessed Marilyn's inner torment.

Increasingly burdened by guilt, Marilyn was in need of a confidant. But who? Thanks to Arthur, the Greenes had already begun to fade from her life. Lee Strasberg was wholly uninterested in relationship talk, and Susie was only a teenager. Paula thrilled at the chance to discuss Arthur for hours, but her horoscopes and glassy-eyed talk of "fated love" left little room for substance. And Marilyn's "brothers"—Eli Wallach, Sam Shaw, and Norman Rosten—were all married. Particularly Norman—not only had he known Arthur's wife for years, he had a wife of his own who spoke French, cooked beef bourguignon, and hosted chic poetry readings. How could he relate to this sordid affair, safe in his warm little penumbra of Brooklyn Heights domesticity?

One night that fall, Marilyn found herself walking alone along the East River. The Monroe Six trailed her, solemn and silent as a pack of baby wolves. She stopped to look across the murky water toward Queens and its industrial skyline. A lone policeman spotted her—an incandescent kitten lost in the urban jungle. "Are you all right?" he asked. "Do you mind if I talk to you for a while?" she peeped, glancing up. The policeman kept her company for more than an hour, side by side on a bench, discussing, according to Jimmy, "life and what it all meant and why people did things."

As the finalization of the DiMaggio divorce drew near, Marilyn wondered if she was making a mistake, if a relationship with Miller really would lead to happiness. Yes, Arthur loved the "special warmth" Marilyn felt toward his father, which would continue long after their divorce. He loved how "she was able to walk into a crowded room and spot anyone there who had lost parents as a child or had spent time in orphanages." If he did acquire some of Marilyn's empathy, it was only a sliver. For Miller, a level of frosty detachment was vital "for the sake of getting on with life." Joe's red temper had sent Marilyn running, but did Arthur's ruthless cool pose an even greater threat?

Amy Greene disliked Arthur from the beginning, though she held her tongue for Marilyn's sake. She worried Arthur triggered Marilyn's deepest insecurity—her lack of formal education. Sometimes she'd call Amy or Norman with a dictionary in her hand, panicked over mispronouncing or misusing a word. Even this early into their love affair, she sensed that Arthur might be ashamed of her.

Marilyn's unruly intelligence threatened Arthur, as did all strong emotion and chaos. He admired what he called her "perceptive naïveté." He marveled at her ability to toss aside any book that didn't stimulate her—but something in him winced at it, too. Arthur noticed and remembered each intellectual "flaw"—her refusal to read a book the "proper" linear way, her inability to "suspend her disbelief towards fiction." It rattled him when Marilyn slammed a book shut, angered by a plot twist or sentence. He was even unnerved by Marilyn's outrage toward a blasé, almost campy depiction of rape in a novel. Inexplicably, her inability to "accept literary irony about a humiliation she had once experienced" baffled Arthur. Marilyn began to see the cracks in her Abraham Lincoln, and it chilled her to the bone.

On October 27, Marilyn's divorce from Joe DiMaggio became final. It had been exactly one year since she'd been crying on the steps of a courthouse in Santa Monica, and now she had a totally new life in New York. It was irrevocably over now. All of it: That Christmas he surprised her at the Beverly Hills Hotel, stocking her fridge with champagne and stringing her suite with twinkling lights. Joe was gone—his sweet Vermouth and Bay Rum cologne, his love of ice cream and quiet warmth with children. "He loved her beyond anyone's comprehension," remembered Sam Shaw. "He felt, but he didn't tell."

❧ Another source of stress was the House Un-American Activities Committee, which had been investigating Arthur since January. In October, they started a file on Marilyn herself. Actress Diana Herbert recalls spotting her swathed in scarves and sunglasses by a subway entrance on 58th Street. They ducked into a dim little Greek bistro for coffee and cakes. Marilyn was taut-nerved and tense. She kept peering twitchily out the window, and eventually admitted she was scanning for federal agents. Diana was alarmed. Was her friend unraveling? (In fact, Marilyn was correct—the FBI had been tracking her.) Hoping to distract Marilyn, Diana changed the subject to her new diet—she was eight months pregnant and sticking to baby-nourishing food. This triggered more tears from Marilyn, who'd also spent the summer with Park Avenue gynecologists—for flare-ups of agonizing endometriosis. Racked with pain, she agonized over medical texts, imagining uterine tissue ransacking her body until her organs fused together like some gruesome horror film. What's more, she doubted her ability to sustain a pregnancy—another blight on her precarious relationship with Arthur. Even if he divorced his wife, even if he wasn't imprisoned or deported, even if he chose to marry Marilyn (there were so many ifs), what if he wanted more children?

Marilyn lit up around children like she did around cameras, melting into an even softer, prettier version of herself. "She metamorphosed," remembers one friend. "The head tilted easily back, the eyelids closed down, she licked her lips, became that myth and smiled full into the child's face and sighed, 'Hi-iiiiiiiiii.'" That Christmas she told Kitty Owens of her dream to adopt orphans—as many as possible, from around the world.

But Marilyn was ambivalent about childbirth. She feared the loss of bodily control—sagging breasts and bulging waistlines. Endometriosis complicated pregnancies, and she'd had more than her share of harrowing surgeries. Above all, she lived under the shadow of her mother's mental illness, an illness that she knew had genetic roots.

Physical pain and shaky relationships weren't new to Marilyn. Vulnerability and sangfroid often coexist, and she had plenty of both in spades. She could handle anything if she felt secure in the thing that mattered most to her: her acting career. Tennessee Williams had been eyeing her for his new screenplay, *Baby Doll*— the story of a nineteen-year-old virgin bride who sucks her thumb, sleeps in a crib, and wields an intoxicating hold on the men around her. Marilyn was counting on the lead. She was the perfect child-woman, Persephone meets Playmate meets shantytown shepherdess.

But there were other factors at play. Director Elia Kazan had final choice, and he was still feuding with Arthur Miller. Even worse, Elia's wife had just discovered the fling he'd had with Marilyn back in 1951. Now he was dashing off mea culpa letters nightly, frantically downplaying the affair. He couldn't turn around and cast his former mistress in the film. Despite Marilyn's hopes and Tennessee's pleas, the role went to Carroll Baker.

"You're too old for the role," spat Kazan when he passed *Baby Doll* from Marilyn to Carroll. Too old—or too fat. Tennessee had wanted a curvier actress, but Kazan loudly insisted on casting "somebody who looks normal." Carroll crowed over her victory, cruelly and not too subtly slamming Marilyn's weight: "Tennessee Williams was there and he had to approve me. He said I wasn't fat enough!"

After the loss of *Baby Doll,* Marilyn spiraled into insecurity. She developed a habit of cupping her hands and coughing whenever she stepped out of a building. Her summery tan had faded, and she looked pale, puffy, and worn. Despite the mild weather she wore a fleecy coat of black wool paired with white bobby socks, polka-dot headscarves, and black patent pocketbooks—giving her a forlorn, frumpy look that was oddly babyish at the same time. Sometimes Jimmy saw her wandering through Saks wearing sunglasses and baggy black slacks, her face slathered with hormone cream. Without makeup, her nose looked as red and rabbity as a raw baby animal's. Or he'd find her at Whelan's slumped over a stool, coat thrown over whatever slip she woke up in, staring listlessly into her coffee. She'd be spotted leaving Dr. Hohenberg's, hailing a cab on the corner of 93rd and Lex, or ducking into the liquor store to write a $40 check for a $10 bottle of wine. (She was still subsisting on Milton's allowance of $40 dollars a week and needed spending money.)

She wore the wool coat on rainy days, drifting through midtown like a sodden black lamb. "One evening she trekked twenty-eight blocks in the rain," wrote Jimmy Haspiel, "and she was wearing that same woolen coat. By the time she arrived home, coat dragging along the sparkling sidewalk, under the weight of its water-logged wool; and Marilyn was all but drenched through to her alabaster skin, the back of her woolen coat looking not unlike the train of an ominous wedding dress."

Jimmy once caught her on the corner of Lexington and East 53rd, dragging plastic grocery bags, tired and pasty in her "teddy bear" coat and black pumps. A packed city bus happened to pass by, the whole crowd gaping down at her. The next day he cornered her at Whelan's: How dare that busload of gawkers stare her down. And besides, she looked "really terrible yesterday." "Well, Jimmy, don't let it bother you!" cried an exasperated Marilyn, flinging the copy of the *Times* he'd brought her.

But it did bother her. Milton used to catch her staring in the mirror for hours, slowly turning around, examining her jawline, her eyelids, her hips, and chin. "I never did ask her 'What do you see, what are you looking for, what are you worried about?' Only once did I ask her, 'What could happen in five years?'" Marilyn looked stricken. "You shouldn't think that way," she cried, whirling around. "That's not the way to think!" Milton cursed himself for being so stupid. "Hollywood used to figure once a woman is really in, they've got five years. Five years if they really take care of themselves. Those were her five years."

Like most mid-century American actresses, Marilyn fretted over aging. After forty, the only respectful options were to retire or become a character actress. Witchy spinsters, stately matrons, and deluded Miss Havisham types. Either feared like Joan Crawford or pitied like Blanche DuBois. Marlene Dietrich and Katharine Hepburn were permitted to hold on to their looks. Their tough talk and angular scaffolding seemed built to last decades, but Marilyn's ripe skin and glistening lips were frighteningly youth-dependent. As of now her value was still straight-up sex appeal—it always had been. Sexy Marilyn had pulled little Norma Jean out of poverty and won the love of millions of fans, the only love she truly trusted. They wanted the icon they knew and loved, not some pseudo-intellectual bumming around in Levi's. They wanted their hologram goddess, and Marilyn felt she owed it to them.

So she arched her back and waved, turning on what Capote called the inner light of true celebrity. "Want to see me be her?" she'd say to Susie Strasberg, walking down Ninth Avenue in sneakers and jeans. "Want to see me be her?" she'd say to Amy Greene, whipping off her headscarf on Broadway. Or she'd do the opposite. "No, I'm Sheree North," she might say, shaking her head when strangers stopped her on the way walking back from the Strasbergs. Or "No, I'm Mamie Van Doren." Jimmy—who'd often be hot on her heels—hated this. "Don't you realize that these people will go around for the rest of their lives saying, 'I saw Mamie Van Doren in person—and she's got Marilyn Monroe beat by a mile!'"

Truman Capote once spent a boozy afternoon with Marilyn at their favorite Chinese spot on Second Avenue. As usual, there was little food on the table—just bottles of unchilled Mumm's wine and water glasses stacked with ice. Marilyn looked sickly. She was drinking more than usual. Panic flickered across her pale face.

If Marilyn looked frazzled, she had good reason to be. Along with the stress of MMP, she was juggling too many identities: angelic lover for Arthur, star pupil for Lee, creative renegade for Milton, pinup goddess for her fans, and respected actress to the press and brutes back at Fox. Where was there room for Marilyn the avid learner, reader, caring friend, and committed artist?

Truman was ordering their third bottle of Mumm's when Marilyn retreated to the powder room—face powder, compact, lipstick in hand. She locked herself in the tiny room and stood still, staring into the dingy mirror.

"Marilyn," cried Truman when she emerged an hour later. "Where have you been?"

"Looking at her," she replied, smile slick with Max Factor Ruby Red.

❧ Back on Central Park West, closeness thickened into claustrophobia. The Strasbergs were cracking under the pressure of their own rigorous intimacy, lashing out with each of their own dysfunctional reflexes. Johnny swore under his breath, stormed off to his room, and blasted the radio. Paula threatened suicide or—even worse—to write a tell-all book revealing the family's twisted secrets. Lee bottled up his tension, slamming doors and exploding in rage-induced nosebleeds. Paula was worried he'd have a heart attack. Like Lee, Susie turned her anger inward. When things were unbearable, she'd lock herself in her closet and rip up nightgowns with her teeth. Even Sweetie Pie, the most neurotic cat in America, was agoraphobic—cowering in the coat closet for hours, hoping someone would take pity and throw him a lamb chop.

Paula eavesdropped. She started with Lee, considering it as a necessary evil since he never told her anything. Then she started spying on everyone: Susie, Johnny, probably even Marilyn, but in her case just to get the juicy scoop on Arthur.

With Susie's Broadway premiere closing in, Paula eavesdropped even more. Desperate for her daughter to succeed where she'd failed, Paula mourned the loss of her acting career, which she'd sacrificed for family. She blamed the children for the loss of her dream—and her figure. Taped to the fridge next to her EVERY EMOTION IS VALID sign was the Mayo Clinic diet: egg whites, steak, and grapefruit. Marilyn had simple tastes and actually enjoyed diet food, but it was a hardship for Paula, who lived for heavy Jewish casseroles and densely buttered breads.

"I don't have time to think myself into despair," Paula would lament, though sadly this wasn't the case. She lived for drama, seizing any event as an excuse for hysterics. Susie's ballet lessons, Johnny's threats to go to medical school, getting blacklisted, chronic foot pain, Lee's book- and record-buying sprees. She'd take to her bed for days, wailing on the phone draped in black, propped up in bed like a "little Buddha." "She was a frustrated actress," Amy Greene wrote years later. "She was a frustrated mother. She was a frustrated everything. This was one unhappy lady."

Milton admitted, "Marilyn thought Paula was marvelous, but I called her a witch. . . . To me, she looked just like a witch's tail."

Certainly Paula provided less stability than Amy's brisk, no-nonsense approach. But Marilyn relied on the Strasbergs, and they were happy to support her. "She was welcomed into our home even at five in the morning," wrote Susie. "There was a bed for her and arms to hold her."

Like many other actors of her era, Marilyn had a little pill habit by 1955. Just like Shelley Winters, she filled her prescriptions at Schwab's, casually grabbing a malted on her way out. By the early fifties barbiturate use was fairly standard, at least in the film industry. "We were all on those things," wrote her friend John Eula. "Blackbirds, up-birds, bluebirds, over-the-rainbow birds. Everybody carried them around in your briefcase like you do aspirin." Bowls of them were laid out at parties—pink Seconals and mint green Nembutals offered like jelly beans. But Marilyn wasn't a party girl—her sedative habit had little in common with the swanky pillheads of Doheny Drive, dipping their manicured hands in crystal dishes of barbiturates and benzodiazepines. Marilyn took her drugs alone, at night.

Part of the problem was the rigor of Hollywood set production. Marilyn's energy levels were too sensitive and erratic for strict studio schedules. "She doesn't eat on time, and she often sits up half the night reading or studying her scripts," Billy Wilder complained. "Then she hates to get up in the morning." Dawn call times require the discipline to force yourself to bed unspeakably early—no easy task for an obsessive perfectionist and chronic insomniac. Sometimes she put off sleep for hours, kicking around scripts, desperately calling friends to see who was awake, lining her eyes in swipes of lavish black, then rubbing it all off with Kleenex and cold cream. Then came the worry loop. Everyone else had been sleeping for hours; she'd look like death and miss her lines. By 4 a.m. she was facing another white night or knocking herself out with a Seconal—and either way she'd wake up bleary-eyed and groggy. Pills made her "womby and tomby," easing her way into peaceful sleep.

In New York, Marilyn had seemed to ease up on the pills, at least for a little while. Milton took diet pills and the occasional tranquilizer, but no more than anyone else in the business. The Greenes seemed to be a healthy, sobering influence on Marilyn, who wanted to keep it together, keep it chic. "When she lived with us," remembers Amy, "she was not zonked out at all." James Haspiel claimed that out of all the times he saw Marilyn that year, she was never drunk or even tipsy. But Milton saw a different side. "I think something in Marilyn was building up. She was drinking more and more," recalled Milton, who tried to keep her in check during public appearances. "I'd say to her, 'Learn to be smart. You have to be in front of a camera, you have to look a certain way. I'm behind the camera. So you let me drink, and I'll drink enough for the both of us.' She liked that; she got a kick out of that."

Something switched that fall, unleashing ugly rogue thoughts she'd worked so hard to pack down. In the orphanage days she'd dreamed of colors, fairy-tale shades of crimson and gold, purple-swathed kings, glinting knights, and pearly baby princesses. But by late 1955, Marilyn's nightmares resembled scenes from Bruegel and Bosch.

In journals she wrote down her nightmares and terrors, and the city's landscape that darkened around her. Her beloved East River grew eerily silent, save for "distant drums," "piercing screams," and "the thunderous rumbling of things unknown." She wrote of "sharp souls" taunting her nights, "ominous whispers" keeping her from sleep. Her dreams were fraught with moans "beyond sadness," "the cry of things too young to be known," and "the sobs of life itself." Despite her successes, she felt "sub-human," "surreal," and paralyzed by Imposter Syndrome. "I have a feeling things are not really happening," she wrote, "but I'm playing a part for which I feel guilty."

She dreamt of lying in a hospital cube, preparing to be cut open by "the Finest Surgeon Lee Strasberg." In the dream Dr. Hohenberg pumped her with anesthesia while Arthur fretted alone in the waiting room. Hedda called the hospital hourly, while Norman stopped by repeatedly "but mostly to comfort Art." Most vivid in her dream was Milton Greene, affably detached in a sumptuous penthouse suite, calling to check in from his elegant desk, "very worried" yet somehow relaxed, playing records, taking business calls, and snapping photos of "great paintings."

But when Lee cut her open he found no organs, just "finely cut sawdust—like a Raggedy Ann doll." "Strasberg is deeply disappointed," she wrote, "academically amazed that he had made such a mistake. He thought there was going to be so much more than he had ever dreamed possible in almost anyone, but instead there was absolutely nothing, devoid of every human living feeling." It was the ultimate nightmare—Strasberg's hopes for Marilyn are shattered; Dr. Hohenberg gives up her quest for a "permanent psychiatric cure." Even Arthur is let down—not just for Marilyn's sake but "for his play and for himself indirectly." Overwhelmed by insecurity, Marilyn was beginning to see herself as a grotesque experiment.

Sometimes she'd forget how many pills she'd taken and panic, terrified she'd slip into death while she slept. Back at the Greenes', Amy had counted them for her, but Arthur knew little of the sedatives and barbiturates, or the heavy painkillers she took for endometriosis. Besides, he fell asleep hours before Marilyn, leaving her alone with her worries and meds.

On nights like these, she'd take a cab to the Strasbergs', hoping for relief or at least someone to sit with her through the night. Three, four, five in the morning in a Juel Park nightgown, ringing the door-bell with a wild look in her eye. One of those nights, Johnny woke to the sound of her scratching the walls in a stupor, crawling the floors in her crumpled thin slip. Blue bruises bloomed from her forearms—she'd bitten herself in her dreams. "Johnny, I can't sleep," she slurred, stumbling toward the couch where he'd been dozing. She leaned on him for support, bare arm pressed against his shoul-der, her hot skin smelling like Orris butter cut with the bitter scent of phenobarbital.

"I think it's probably too late to wake them up, don't you?" she whispered. (It was never too late to wake up Lee and Paula where Marilyn was concerned.) "Do you mind if we just sit here for a while?"

Johnny tensed up. Should he wake the parents? Would they be angrier if he woke them up or more angry if he didn't? They sat in silence, air thick with adrenaline and drugs. "The situation that millions of men fantasized about terrified me. . . . At that moment she was so doped up that I wasn't sure she knew where she was." When Marilyn finally staggered back to bed, Johnny exhaled, sinking into queasy relief.

Marilyn and Johnny shared a special bond: their shyness, their outsider status and rebellion, the T-Bird she'd given him on his fifteenth birthday. Sadly, Johnny remembered her the way so many men remember Marilyn Monroe: "beautiful, drugged, and helpless."

ᕲ On October 5, 1955, *The Diary of Anne Frank* premiered on Broadway. Paula assigned Delos Smith and Marty Fried with the task of taking Marilyn to Cort Theatre. This was Susie's big day, no mishaps allowed. "I'll kill her if she's late," Paula hissed, for once entertaining the possibility of being annoyed with Marilyn. "Delos, it's up to you."

They arrived at Sutton Place prepared to find Marilyn lolling in the bath. To their shock, she was ready to go, dressed simply in black. In fact, they arrived so early at the theater that the staff were still taking dustcovers off the seats. Paula had put them up in the balcony—she wasn't taking any chances. She knew a typical Monroe entrance would hijack the audience and derail the entire production. But Marilyn kept herself subdued, unsequinned. "When she wanted to," remembers Delos, "she could get attention from anyone. She'd just do that walk and they'd become like pigs in heat and she'd shine. I thought she must use fluorescent makeup, the way she'd shine. . . . But she muted her light that night." In fact, Marilyn was so determined not to eclipse Susie that she didn't even break for intermission, staying hidden in the balcony with Marty and Delos. She wept profusely throughout the play and flung her arms around Susie after curtain call.

There was the typical postshow dressing-room whirl: flashing cameras and clothing racks crammed with belts, petticoats, ostrich boas, and woolen waistcoats. "Marilyn was very quiet," wrote Susie, "taking pictures with me for the *Life* photographer but staying in the background as much as she could." Photos show the two hugging like sisters—both in black—Marilyn in one of her scoop-necked slips and Susie in a crew-necked frock of velvet. Marilyn's smile was big-sister proud, Susie's lit up in giddy release.

Marilyn kept a low profile at the Sardi's after-party. She didn't even sit at the Strasbergs' table. Susie plopped down by her father, propped up her elbows and plowed through ham sandwiches, pizza, ice cream, and fruit salad. Suddenly Marilyn rushed up, placing her hands on Susie's slim shoulders. "Wasn't Susie wonderful?" she gushed to a stony Lee. "You must be so excited."

"No," Lee replied. "Relieved."

Fifteen

Cherie

"Personally, if I can realize certain things in my
work, I come the closest to being happy."

MARILYN MONROE

*E*ver since her escape from LA, Marilyn had been assembling
a support network, surrounding herself with people who believed
in her talent, her intelligence, and her depth. To the Rostens, the
Strasbergs, the Greenes, her friends at the Studio—she was more
than the sum of her candy-curvy blondeness. Marilyn had won
over New York, yet Hollywood lagged behind, unconvinced.

All of this was about to change. After the success of *The Seven
Year Itch*, Fox could no longer deny Marilyn's value—they wanted

her back, but at what price? For Marilyn, that meant creative control, director approval, and most important, respect.

Then agent Audrey Wood called with an offer: "I have a project in mind for your partner," she whispered, refusing to speak Marilyn's name in case the phones were bugged. A film adaptation of William Inge's *Bus Stop*. The story intrigued them: an innocent cowboy, a broken-down chanteuse on the run from her past. With her Hollywood dreams and childhood wounds, Cherie was the perfect role for the "new" Marilyn—even better than sexy, campy *Baby Doll*. For the first time she could play a real woman—not the cutout bimbos and adorable airheads from *Gentlemen* and *Itch*. Cherie's appeal was dusty honey and grit, and only Marilyn could get it right. This time, Fox was offering $8 million. She'd spent 1955 completely unemployed, so there wasn't much to think about. Milton was ready to accept right away.

Bus Stop was currently on Broadway at the Music Box Theatre, with Kim Stanley as the lead. Eager to dive into her new role, Marilyn called up the Greenes and bought three tickets. She loved how Kim attacked the role with such brutal intensity and watched, transfixed, as she transformed herself onstage. But very quickly, panic took over. "She thought she couldn't do it because Kim Stanley was doing such a good job," remembered Amy. "I mean, the insecurity absolutely loomed."

Milton dragged her back to the Music Box three more times. "They went back three times to see it," said Amy. "And each time Marilyn was more confident, and saw things she could do that Kim wasn't doing. At one point, Milton turned to Marilyn and said, 'You're Cherie.'" This time, she believed him.

Gradually, Marilyn realized she had it in her. The Method would allow her to become her own Cherie—less brassy and more vulnerable than Kim's. She practiced Cherie's Ozark twang and found that she had an ear for dialect. She connected to the character, run-down but full of dumb, desperate hope. It could have easily been Marilyn singing in that tawdry nightclub, batting her eyes at bombed-out cowboys who had fallen asleep in their whiskeys and beers. Marilyn's commitment manifested itself in whimsical ways, too. On an afternoon coffee break at Whelan's with Jimmy, she cried out when the waitress moved to refill his cup. "No, no. Please give him milk, he's a growing boy!" she said. "It would be a full quarter of a century before I would realize that that was a line from *Bus Stop,*" Jimmy mused years later.

Milton, thrilled to be back in his creative element, did a Cherie-inspired photo shoot later referred to as *The Black Sitting*. They kept it informal: Milton set the tone with jazz records and several bottles of red wine. It was cold out, so he'd brought Marilyn special fishnets with warm fabric hidden in the toes—he knew how numb her feet got in the studio. For the backdrop, he swathed the place in fabrics until it resembled a "black velvet womb." "They must have cornered the black velvet market on Seventh Avenue," Amy joked. "And they had strobe lights—remember strobe lights? There's something about black velvet that's very sensuous and very rich. Look at me, I'm a street kid, but here I am in black velvet—wow!"

"Originally we were going to do it in the morning," mused Milton years later, "but as usual she kept pushing it back and back. She had a dinner date with Arthur later in the evening. So she came in, and we had a drink. First it was vodka, then after the vodka we opened a bottle of champagne, and things just started to happen."

Five hours and twenty-eight rolls of film later, Marilyn became Cherie. She captured the character's faded sensuality without a trace of sadness. In her black bowler hat, mesh leotard and cane, Marilyn was half Marlene Dietrich and half burlesque Chaplin. Back to the camera in nothing but fishnets, or cabaret chic in a black feather boa, a tumbler of whiskey balanced on one knee, *The Black Sitting* had all the glamour, humor, and dress-up-box openness of MMP's early days.

Between her work with Lee and tension with Arthur, Marilyn hadn't spent much time with Milton these past few months. But this was just like the old days, running around pantsless in a sweater or an unzipped ballet tutu. "Nothing that day was planned," recalled Milton, who considered *The Black Sitting* his best work ever. "As things started to move and she started to get into it, she forgot about everything, where she had to be, what she had to do, she was having such a good time. The shoot went on until eleven at night—she even missed her date with Arthur. She called him from the studio—I think she was a little drunk. He was annoyed, but that didn't bother me, naturally."

The results were warm, alive, and cinematic. "Marilyn couldn't believe them, she loved them so much. We gave some shots to Josh Logan, who thought they were the greatest things I'd ever done. We gave some to Arthur—even his mother and father loved them. But he didn't see them all. We just gave him the close-ups of her face. If he saw the rest—well, who knows."

That fall, she met with Jimmy at Whelan's drugstore. She had the contact sheet for her *Black Sitting* stuffed in a manila envelope. Determined to protect him from the racier images, she made him look away, then said, "OK, you can look now, Jimmy." He remembered, "I turned around to an unexpected vision of Marilyn sitting there with a contact sheet of perhaps ten photo-images before her, the item pinned to the counter by her elbow covering up one image, her thumb masking another, and even a paper napkin hiding another! . . . She was in her special way being a caring and responsible person, only allowing me to see the 'tamer' ones."

Brimming with excitement and joy, *The Black Sitting* was a celebration of their recent success. The outside world always faded away when Milton and Marilyn got together. It was their creativity, their delight in the work, that counted, like two kittens tumbling with a ball of yarn. They'd just snagged a winning role, saved their reputations, and turned the tables on Fox, but deep down they were just two "kids playing in a playpen."

Throughout all this, Marilyn remained wrapped in Malin Studios and grew even closer to her classmates. Kim Stanley invited her to dinner parties; Maureen Stapleton hung on her every word. "It was easy to be intimidated by Marilyn, and I was," wrote Maureen. "She was so goddamned beautiful. Luscious. Sweet. But the intimidation disappeared fast because she was so committed and so ready to get better. I bitch about my upbringing, and my sad mother and sad aunts and no men around and nothing but dead ends all around, but I had love and food and the space and the silence to dream. Marilyn didn't have that. She told me once that she just wanted her own bedroom, her own bed, and a door she could close. And grass. Grass to run in. Trees to hug and flowers to pick. This was a girl who had nothing but the great gem that she was, and everyone got to hold and fondle that gem, and then put it back when they were done with it."

Marilyn tended to bond with dominant women—from the brassy, unflappable Elsa Maxwell to pert, sassy Amy Greene. With their gruff manners and husky voices, the Studio's self-described "tough broads" attracted her right away. Marilyn liked to be mothered, and Stapleton was often referred to as the Studio's "earth mother." Maureen knew Marilyn deserved better than ditsy-blonde roles. The way she saw it, she was a prisoner of her own good looks. "I never had that problem," Maureen chuckled years later. "People looked at me onstage and said, 'Jesus, that broad better be able to act!'"

In late fall, Lee judged Marilyn ready for her "debut"—a short private performance for Studio members. She chose a scene from

Anna Christie and picked Maureen as her partner. "Marilyn showed tremendous bravery by taking on *Anna Christie,*" Maureen marveled years later. "She could have chosen a role that wasn't too well known, so that her performance could have been criticized only on its own merit. But to do *Anna Christie,* something that's been done by a dozen wonderful people—Garbo included!" Instead of coasting by on beauty alone, Marilyn chose to challenge herself, a move that caught Maureen's attention and won her respect.

In fact, Marilyn was petrified by what she'd taken on. In her signature mix of ambition and fear, she insisted on rehearsing with Maureen four times a week. They'd stay late after class, work past dinner, then share a cab uptown. "Turn around," she'd tell the driver, blocks away from Maureen's. "We've got to go back and do it again." She practiced with Norman, Eli, and Arthur, with random late-night rehearsals in the park with Sam Shaw. "She worked to the point of a migraine," remembered Maureen, "and I would tell her to lighten up, go easy on yourself, but she couldn't: She wanted to be taken seriously; she wanted to get it right."

At home, she'd curl up with the script for hours—studying not just her lines but Anna's character. There was little information in O'Neill's description or dialogue—just a beautiful, broken woman prowling the docks. Who was Anna? Marilyn loved this kind of work. She'd talk to Arthur about it and ask him questions: Was it an end to life Anna desired? Was it death? Arthur was struck by Marilyn's innate grasp of the character: "She had a real tragic sense of what that girl was like." For the first time he saw her ambition in action. Underneath that angel-cake face was an artist of infinite discipline, laser-focused on the work in her lap. At night she'd sit by the window while he helped with her lines. Arthur read the part of old Chris, though he claimed he sounded like "a Southern cracker with a Scandinavian accent."

While preparing for the role of Anna Christie, Marilyn still managed to keep a public profile. She did publicity shots for the soon-to-premiere film of *The Rose Tattoo,* posing sexily with Marlon Brando in a black sheath and cape. Along with boosting sales for the upcoming show, the photos proved to the public that smart and sexy weren't mutually exclusive—that despite her work at the Studio, she wasn't schlepping around in sloppy sweaters and stringy hair.

On December 12, *The Rose Tattoo* premiered at the Astor Theatre. Marilyn stepped out of her limo in skintight black and clouds of Chanel, glowing in the arms of Marlon Brando. Tossing around her white ermine, she flirted with the pack of cameras, blowing kisses from a mouth coated in Vaseline rimmed in toffee-colored lip liner. A pair of clip-ons dangled from her ears, five swishing lines of baguette-cut rhinestones that brushed her shoulders and clavicle whenever she smiled at Marlon, her glamorous-lamb look set off by his slightly thuggish beauty. Coupled up in their finery, they riveted the paps, who bombarded them with dazzles of flashes and clicks.

At Sardi's she lit up the after-party, flitting her way through chatter and smoke, making butterfly landings at red-checked tables. She bantered with reporters and whispered with the Rostens, all the while dancing with Marlon Brando. Their affair had ended months ago, but their potent chemistry shone, helpfully diverting attention from Arthur Miller.

Lurking in the background was Jayne Mansfield—the "poor man's Marilyn Monroe" and the lead in George Axelrod's current Broadway hit *Will Success Spoil Rock Hunter?* Mansfield starred as Rita Marlowe, a simpering blonde with "golden curls, a fantastic behind, and delusions of grandeur." Despite having written *The Seven Year Itch,* Axelrod made no effort to conceal his real subject—Marilyn. *Itch* had launched him into fame—thanks largely to Marilyn—and now he was mocking her on Broadway. But that

didn't matter. She'd just won the role of her dreams. On opening
night Marilyn kept her cool, even when she ran into Axelrod. "I
saw your play," she said, with a stone fox look that chilled him to
the bone.

Already losing faith in Sheree North, Fox scooped up Jayne to
be their next replacement Marilyn. Toward Jayne, however, Marilyn showed no anger or ill will. In fact she barely noticed her at
the party, though Jayne clearly noticed Marilyn. Stuffed in a sheath
of silver brocade, hair bouffant blonde and lacquered with Elnett,
Jayne hovered over Marilyn's chair looking every bit the fangirl.

At midnight, Marilyn joined Brando for a radio interview with
NBC. They sat round a table crammed with microphones, ashtrays, and demitasses of black coffee, answering questions about
Lee Strasberg and the madness behind the Method. When asked
about her status at Malin Studios, Marilyn hesitated and said
she was observing as a student. That's when Brando stepped in.
"She's an actress," he corrected her in his soft-spoken way. "She's
an actress."

✒ As 1955 drew to a close, Milton began looking ahead: they'd
fly to Hollywood, settle business for a few days, then start filming
Bus Stop in Phoenix. He'd rent a bungalow with Amy and the baby,
Marilyn would hop between their place and Chateau Marmont.
But Marilyn was in no hurry to leave New York. Preparing for *Anna
Christie* was far more important to her than any film role. With so
much of her life up in the air, she could barely think about up-
rooting again or what would come next. Arthur—whose divorce
proceedings had just begun—was still living at the Chelsea. Where
would he be during filming? What about her friends, Norman and
Hedda, Eli, and Sam Shaw? And she was still settling into her

beloved flat on Sutton Place, preparing for her second Christmas in New York.

Jimmy Haspiel took her holiday shopping at Saks, where she lingered over the tie counter for hours. She chose a dozen ties for Arthur, in stripes and solids, silks and cottons. As usual, Jimmy carried her bags. On their way out the door, he stuck a sprig of mistletoe in her hair and kissed her.

Arthur was touched by the box of beautiful ties, Marilyn loved the handmade card he gave her. It read, "Don't worry, I'm more depressed than you."

It had been eight months since she'd started her work at the Studio, eleven since the launching of MMP, and over a year since she'd fled California with two suitcases and a cheap black wig. Her dream life was about to become her reality.

❧ Snow fell over Manhattan on December 23, blanketing the city in white. The next day, Marilyn gave her first and only Christmas Eve party. In typical Marilyn fashion, she decorated her living room, hired a guitarist, and completely forgot about the food. When she called the Greenes the day of the party to ask for extra plates, she realized she still hadn't thought of a menu. So Kitty cooked up a vat of beef stew and drove it to Sutton Place with her husband, Clyde. "You and Kitty go right in there and sit down," Marilyn told Clyde, who was struggling at the door with pots and stacks of china. "Fix yourself a drink and join the party."

Twenty guests crowded round Marilyn's table that night, including Arthur Miller, whom Kitty immediately disliked. "I had a sixth sense about him that he wasn't a hundred percent sincere. . . . And maybe I should have said it."

"I hope she doesn't marry him, Clyde," Kitty told her husband on the drive home. "He thinks he's too wise. If he marries her I think he's gonna destroy her."

"That's their business," said Clyde, with typical masculine reticence. "As long as they're happy. . . ."

On December 31, 1955, Marilyn's dream finally came true. Thanks to Milton's negotiations, Fox was ready to meet her on her own terms. The new contract included story approval, director approval, and cinematographer approval. She was allowed to make films with independent producers, and her salary was boosted to $100,000 per film. At twenty-nine she was now the highest paid actress in the world.

The sun shone brightly on December 31, and the fallen snow began to melt. Milton, Amy, and Jay and Judy Kanter met Marilyn at Sutton Place to celebrate New Year's Eve. They toasted their victory with Dom Pérignon, leaping in the air, giggling, falling into each other with peals of laughter: "We beat them! We beat them! We beat them!"

Stars

"In contrast to the old Marilyn, in her present incarnation she is a liberated soul—happy, cooperative, friendly, relaxed. Actually, it is as if she had undergone a psychoanalysis so successful that the analyst himself was flabbergasted."

PETE MARTIN

On January 4, 1956, Jimmy Haspiel dropped the *Morning Telegraph* at Marilyn's doorstep—the first public announcement of her triumph over Fox: BATTLE WITH STUDIO WON BY MARILYN. ACTRESS WINS ALL DEMANDS. "The bitter battle is over: Marilyn Monroe, a five foot five and a half inch blonde weighing 118 alluringly distributed pounds, has brought 20th Century Fox to its knees."

Marilyn's career was no longer at odds with her personal growth. By insisting on creative control, she could avoid the hack jobs that embarrassed and cheapened her. At a time when studio executives wielded absolute power, this was revolutionary. The Los Angeles *Mirror News* celebrated Marilyn's victory as "one of the greatest single triumphs won by an actress." By the end of January, she'd be on the cover of *Time,* which praised her as a "shrewd businesswoman." Not only had Marilyn won her autonomy—she was making history.

Milton held down the fort at 480 Lex, handling calls, planning photo shoots, and scheduling appearances. "Director approval is very important," he explained in a post-victory interview. "A great deal is in a director's hands. For example, creative ability. The right director can put a lot more into a picture than the words on the script he's given to shoot." In the midst of the media storm, they acquired the film rights to Terence Rattigan's play *The Sleeping Prince*—with Laurence Olivier as director and costar, produced by MMP.

This was their biggest coup yet—and Marilyn was behind it. She'd heard that Rattigan had been shopping his script around. She'd also heard that he was languishing in New York on a layover to LA. Springing into action, she had a message delivered to LaGuardia: "Have Mr. Rattigan meet me for cocktails. Barberry Room, 4:30 p.m."

Only one hour late, she strode in wearing dark sunglasses flanked by Jay Kanter, Milton Greene, and Irving Stein. But she barely needed them—in her own quiet way, Marilyn did all the negotiating herself. She had a bad cold, and Rattigan told her she sounded like Tallulah Bankhead. (Marilyn beamed and recounted the incident proudly to reporters.) Once she had Rattigan in her thrall, she lowered her sunglasses, batted her wide eyes, and baby-whispered: "Do you think there's a chance Sir Larry would do it with me?"

Laurence Olivier—"Sir Larry"—flew straight to New York and scheduled a meeting with Marilyn for February 7, a cold, wet Sunday. They'd planned to meet in his hotel suite—but he hated to force Marilyn out in the freezing rain: "It's such a bad day; we can't make her come here. We'll go see her."

When Olivier, Rattigan, and Jay Kanter arrived at Sutton Place it was Milton Greene who answered the door. Marilyn was hiding in the bedroom, terrorized. It took Milton two hours to coax her out while the men waited in the parlor. Laurence, a stickler for punctuality, let it slide.

He hadn't met her, but he was already beguiled by her—in screen tests she'd been so adorable, so witty and attractive. Not only did he desire Marilyn, he needed her. They were both bewitched by the idea of each other. At fifty, Olivier feared sliding into a rut and hoped to refresh his career and image. He wanted her sexy glamour; she wanted his gravitas. "One thing was clear to me," he recalled years later. "I was going to fall most shatteringly in love with Marilyn. She was adorable, so witty, and more physically attractive than anyone I could imagine. Look at that face—she could be five years old!"

After a quiet summer and even quieter fall, Marilyn was seen about town again. She attended an *Anne Frank* performance with Laurence Olivier and brought him backstage to a starstruck Susie Strasberg. She made a sparkly splash at *The Middle of the Night* premiere in white ermine coat, long black dress, and dangling diamond earrings. Kim Novak was particularly impressed, turning around at intermission and craning her neck to stare. Milton wined and dined Olivier, taking him out for fancy nights on the town with Amy and Marilyn. "It was a happy time," recalls Amy. "Larry adored Milton; Larry adored me; and he and Marilyn were totally flirtatious with each other. She giggled a lot—she'd always be leaning towards him like teeheeheeeheeeeheee. They were openly flirting.

He'd pay her crazy compliments, or tease her, like 'The tip of your nose is funny,' and she'd slap him and giggle. She loved it. She would light a cigarette and he'd be up lighting the cigarette for her. Or she'd be drinking champagne, and he'd say, 'Oh, my dear, your glass is empty' and get up very gallantly. I mean, honey—it's Olivier."

On February 9, Marilyn, Rattigan, and Olivier held a press conference at the Plaza Hotel to announce MMP's hottest new project. It was official: Marilyn had earned the respect of "the greatest actor in the English-speaking world." She had taken control of her career, and was about to make the two most important films of her life.

Over 200 reporters swarmed their table. They immediately started with the same tired themes. "One question put to Marilyn was did she still want to play *The Brothers Karamazov*," recalled one journalist. "She said, 'I never intended to play *The Brothers Karamazov*. I want to play Grushenka in *The Brothers Karamazov*.' Another reporter asked her nastily, 'How do you spell Grushenka?' Thinking he had trapped her and that she was too stupid to know. And she, with a very superior smile and a twinkle in her eyes, said, 'You can look it up in the book.' At that the reporters laughed and their questions were less sarcastic, less loaded, less angled to make a patsy—a fall girl—of her."

Olivier praised Marilyn as a "brilliant comedienne," lighting her cigarettes in his courtly manner, affably taking a backseat to let her shine. They made a handsome, elegant couple: he in his Savile Row suit and pocket square, Marilyn in black, her hair swept up at the sides with bobby pins, accentuating the cameo curves of her neck. Sometimes she'd drape a tuxedo coat over her shoulders, or lean intimately close to the reporters, chin cupped in her velvet-gloved hand. Elsa Maxwell noted with approval that Marilyn didn't imitate Olivier's "clipped British tones," speaking instead with her own "quiet naturalness."

But Elsa thought she got the clothes "all wrong" for the occasion. Marilyn had chosen a skintight slip, which looked especially vampy in the clear light of day. In the middle of the press conference, one spaghetti strap broke, causing a gasp in the crowd then uproar. "I need a safety pin," Marilyn yelped. After a few minutes of mass scrambling, a reporter procured a pin and handed it to Marilyn, who spent the rest of the conference holding her dress up with both hands "just so the press won't be disturbed."

Amy insists that it wasn't a publicity stunt: "I saw the strap, and it sure as hell wasn't loose when she left the dressing room. She was mincing and posing as she always did, with one shoulder always perched higher than the other—then the strap just popped. It wasn't that she cut the strap, but she was secretly pleased."

Accident or not, Marilyn had upstaged Olivier. He seemed to take it in stride, but Amy saw it as a turning point: "At that point in time, I think Larry realized he may have made a mistake. Because it was going to be a circus."

Broken dress straps were nothing. Working with Marilyn meant weeks of skipped alarms, wardrobe fiascos, line edits, late-night tears, and frantic phone calls. How would his British, by-the-book stoicism clash with her voluptuous lawlessness? But with Marilyn, it was always the unexpected that worked like a charm. "I've lived long enough to know that life doesn't always stick to the rules," wrote Elsa, who'd been watching from the rafters with glee. "The perfectly impossible and absolutely ridiculous keep happening all the time."

❧ Thrilled as she was to work with Olivier, preparing for *Anna Christie* was a bigger priority. Like Eleonora Duse, Marilyn acted straight from her core. She had a habit of throwing up on set before film takes. Sometimes she'd get migraines or embarrassingly trembly hands. "A stage role is totally different," Lee assured her. "You're on the stage; you have the lights; the audience is dark; nobody talks. You remember all those technicians and everybody standing around smoking and laughing back in Hollywood? You were very much aware of all that distraction." On the stage she'd have that curtain of protective velvet that only comes up when you're ready for it. But was Marilyn up to the intense immediacy of the stage?

On February 17, Marilyn was finally ready for her Studio debut. She woke up that morning with a pounding heart and a horrible case of laryngitis ("I could only croak and whisper"). Malin Studios was packed that night. Paula fanned herself in the front row, draped in black shawls and a long golden chain laden with good luck trinkets. "I'm going to have a heart attack," she groaned to anyone who would listen. But if anyone was having a heart attack that night, it was Marilyn: "I couldn't feel anything. I couldn't remember one line. All I wanted to do was lie down and die. I was in these impossible circumstances and I suddenly thought to myself 'Good God what am I doing here?' Then I just had to go out and do it." After blacking out backstage from anxiety, Marilyn shot all her nervy vulnerability into the scene. "So far I'm less shy on the stage than I've ever been in front of a camera," she would tell Pete Martin weeks later. "I have less trouble remembering my lines."

"Her painful nervousness lent a tension to the scene that seemed right. Everybody who saw that says that it was not only the best work Marilyn ever did," Ellen Burstyn remembers. "It was some of the best work they'd ever seen at the Studio, and certainly the best interpretation of *Anna Christie* anybody ever saw. She achieved real greatness in that scene."

Applause is traditionally a faux pas in the churchlike solemnity of Malin Studios. But this time Marilyn received a standing ovation. She immediately burst into tears.

◈ January and February were landmark months for Marilyn. She'd won her yearlong battle with Fox. She'd soon be working with dream directors Josh Logan and Laurence Olivier. She was once again the Press Darling—only this time for her talent, not her breathy voice and bombshell curves. She'd proved to the world her merit as an actress—and with *Anna Christie,* she'd proved it to herself. It made sense that Cecil Beaton, photographer to Picasso, Greta Garbo, and Queen Elizabeth, was now seeking her out.

On the designated date of February 19, Cecil paced his Japanesque suite at the Ambassador. He'd been chasing Marilyn for weeks—would this elusive blonde butterfly ever show up? Assistant Ed Pfizenmaier still remembers the moment Marilyn breezed through the door: an hour late, bag flung over her shoulder with two black dresses and a pile of makeup. "She came in the door," he said, "and the first thing she did was discard her shoes, which I couldn't believe. So immediately Cecil and I looked at each other with big eyeballs, and we could tell for some reason this was going to be a good day. I kind of adore someone who throws her shoes off and gets right into it," he added. "In other words, she wanted to work."

"We started out very proper with the legs to the side and everything else," said Ed. "And then suddenly all hell broke loose and she did her own thing. Romping and twisting and throwing her body around. She finally wound up half on the floor and half on the sofa. Cecil and Marilyn were just laughing, howling at each other."

For the third time that year, Marilyn clicked with a photographer who really got her. Cecil delighted in Marilyn's childlike aura, relishing the paradox of her whimsical glamour. To him she was a "Rhine maiden," an "innocent sleepwalker," an "abandoned sprite," an "overexcited child asked downstairs for tea." Cecil wrote in his diary, "I was so impressed by her sort of gaiety and variety of moods that I just wanted to catch that. . . . I just found myself so in sympathy, so amused and so delighted that all I could do was run around clicking in her wake."

The hours flew by without a single break. Marilyn flounced and frolicked, puffed on a daisy like a cigarette, played with a plastic bluebird, sipped ginger ale from an old-fashioned champagne coupe. In the span of one photo shoot—with no costume changes— Marilyn demonstrated her impressive range. She could play the vampiest vamp, then shift back into soft fawn mode with the baby bird at her cheek. ("Dostoevsky knew what he was doing," Beaton observed. "Marilyn knows what she is doing too. She would be a good Grushenka.") Thanks to her diet of raw steak and champagne, she'd toned up and was—according to Amy—slim as a "noodle." Winter walks in the city had brightened her eyes and perked up her skin. She'd never looked so refined, so soft-focus pretty.

"She did everything he wanted her to do," recalled Ed, "from laying down in the bed swathed in a sheet and him standing over shooting straight down at her. In those days we had 10,000 watt bulbs shining off the ceiling . . . and she was just like a purring lion under those lights. I don't know if it was one of her better days, or a good day or what, you know you hear so many bad reports, the sensationalism, but I certainly didn't experience any of that. And I think the photographs, Beaton's photographs, show it, that's the proof of the pudding. When you look at them, everyone remarks she looks so happy, gay, healthy, and everything. Contrary to what everyone says that she was difficult and hard to work with, I found her just a delight to work with, not difficult at all—I don't know where people come from—we just had a magnificent time."

The feeling was mutual. Marilyn adored the experience, and treasured one of Beaton's photos as her all-time favorite: She's lying in bed on her back, eyes wide, lips parted, clutching a pink carnation in one hand. Cecil wrote an article about it months later and gave Marilyn a copy along with the carnation photo. She framed it in a triptych, and kept it bedside for the rest of her life.

℘ All along, Marilyn's goal had been director approval. Now that she had her pick, who would she choose for *Bus Stop*? "Milton and Marilyn and I made a list of the twelve directors she would work with," remarked Amy, who was part of the decision as well. "She made it a point that she would no longer work with directors who were on the lot and had nothing better to do."

"One of the directors we had on the list was Charles Chaplin," explained Amy, "which of course everyone at Twentieth fell down kicking and screaming over. But I've got news for you: He would have been wonderful with Marilyn and vice versa. But that was also Milton—Milton saw nothing but heights for this woman— he shot much higher than she even in her wildest fantasies. His dreams for her were beyond her scope."

Eventually they agreed on Josh Logan: one of the rare Hollywood directors who understood the Method and respected it. He'd studied at the Moscow Theater with Stanislavski and was no stranger to insomnia and hospitalizations. He even tolerated Paula, who was now part of the package and Marilyn's on-set acting coach. Best of all, Josh had also directed on Broadway—most recently *Picnic* and *South Pacific*. "You can't forget, at this time Marilyn was in love with New York, was in love with New York theater, and Logan was a superstar there," explained Amy. "So again she started with 'I don't think I can; this man won't see me; why would he want to work with me, etc.' Then Milton arranged a meeting with Josh, who was a fine Southern gentlemen. Josh was thrilled with the idea that Marilyn would talk to *him*."

From the moment he met Marilyn, Logan was impressed. "I had no trouble communicating with her, understanding her, or getting her to understand me," he said. Having worked in Hollywood and New York, he immediately understood Marilyn's frustrations. "They were making fun of her, teasing and baiting a delicate and intelligent animal. They refused to see that she wasn't dumb, she wasn't an animal, but a highly intuitive artist. Everyone thinks she's stupid, and she's not. She has a brain far above the normal person, and she has developed the powers she was born with far above most people even with formal education."

Despite that winter's flurry of excitement, Marilyn still had time for the Monroe Six. When Jimmy Haspiel's birthday approached, the Six presented her with a card and envelope already stamped and addressed. "All you have to do, Mazzie," they explained, "is sign the card and put it in a mailbox, it's for Jimmy's birthday next week."

Marilyn was caring and generous, but no master of the ordinary—signing a card wouldn't be enough. Instead of giving Jimmy an impersonal birthday greeting, she invited him to join her on a cab ride through town. "Well, the taxicab came to a halt at the curb of 58th Street, and the moment had arrived. I remember I looked into her face and said, 'So long,' and as I added the words 'Norma Jean,' I turned my face away from hers, unexpected emotions overtaking me, and I couldn't actually look at her! I had already opened the cab door for my escape, and as I was rising out of the cab, I heard a sort of whispered 'Jimmy' behind me, and my body, which was in motion leaving the cab, reversed the motion. As I sat back down into the seat, Marilyn put her arms around me and hugged me very tightly, whispered into my ear, 'Happy Birthday, Jimmy,' and then she kissed me."

Decades later Jimmy Haspiel reflected on the cab ride: "What had happened was that instead of being ordered to do something, like with the card from the Six, it had to actually come from her, or it wouldn't have been real for her." That was Marilyn—impulsive, adorable, and always authentic—like a winsome "happy birthday" hot and sweet in your ear.

 By the last week of February, Marilyn was preparing to bid New York good-bye. Production for *Bus Stop* was scheduled for early March. Inevitable, unavoidable Hollywood was calling, with its stage sets, swimming pools, and fraught memories. This time she couldn't resist.

She wasn't the least bit nervous about her future projects. She wasn't intimidated by working with Sir Laurence Olivier, or by Kim Stanley's stellar performance in the Broadway version of *Bus Stop*. "It doesn't bother me in the least," she told Pete Martin. "It'll be two different characterizations by two different people, and I'm looking forward to it. Maybe I feel this way because I've gotten older inside. Remember, I said inside, not outside. I'd like to think of my life as having started right now. Somebody asked me when I was born and I said, 'Just recently, in New York.'"

Days before her departure, she visited dress designer John Moore. "I'll be back," she promised him, "when the picture is over. New York is my home now. Hollywood is just a place to work in."

On February 22, Marilyn met Elsa Maxwell for lunch at Waldorf Towers. This was a special occasion—a sort of good-bye interview—and Elsa had set white calla lilies on the black lacquered table, ordered oysters, caviar, and several bottles of Dom Pérignon.

Someone got wind that Marilyn was dropping by, so Elsa spent the morning fielding phone calls and barring the door from curious men. "One by one they had discovered they simply had to see me about something important," she chuckled. "Not at all curiously, the only time they had free was midday. True to form, she arrived over an hour late. She wore the same improper clothes she had worn to her press conference with Olivier, the low-cut black velvet suit with the dress supported by tiny shoulder straps, dangling earrings and with her blonde hair flying . . . I wanted to say, 'Oh, Marilyn, my dear, those clothes! They're not right for noonday!'"

Self-described as "short, fat, and dumpy," the seventy-three-year-old Elsa Maxwell had little in common with Marilyn on the surface. But her "laugh at yourself before anyone else can" motto was straight out of Marilyn's book. Brash, luxe, and extravagantly feminine, Elsa hoarded bottles of Joy just like Marilyn. (She'd even roamed the fields of Grasse with Jean Patou himself, coining Joy "the costliest perfume in the world.") Like Marilyn, Elsa was born poor, and like Marilyn, she felt like she was uneasy with marriage, feeling instead that she "belonged to the world." Marilyn adored Elsa's flamboyance, her pet skunks and pink piglets, her etiquette books with advice such as "Serve the dinner backward, do anything—but for goodness sake, do something weird."

Elsa had been rooting for Marilyn since the very beginning. Fiercely loyal, she loathed Marilyn's rival Jayne Mansfield almost as much as she loathed Elvis Presley and Nikita Khrushchev. She admired the way Marilyn pushed through her fear and was looking forward to crowing over her victory: "She's exciting because in spite of having the guts (no politer word will do) to gamble on herself the way aggressive business executives do, she's still shy and uncertain. . . . In a world today there are far too few exciting people. Everybody wants to play it safe, to get as much as they can for as

little as possible. It's good to meet someone who tilts at windmills—
or movie titans—who risks everything rather than be swept away
on a golden tide." Two "desperately serious" court jesters, beating
back the golden tide one lunch at a time.

The next day, Norma Jean Baker officially changed her name
to Marilyn Monroe.

℘ Before she left New York, Marilyn had one last interview
with her old friend Earl Wilson. She wanted to work in the bedroom—he could talk to her while she packed. In her black velvet
toreador pants and white tennis sweater, Marilyn was vibrant,
running around barefoot showing Earl new dresses, hopping up
to answer the phone or look up lines in a book. She fluttered
around the chaotic room, chairs strewn with minks, scripts, and
slips. With nowhere else to sit, Earl stretched himself out on her
pink taffeta bedspread, shoes and all.

Underneath the bubbly playfulness was a woman who knew her
worth. When Earl congratulated Marilyn on her triumph over Fox,
she corrected him and called it a "compromise."

"A compromise!" Earl was stunned. "Aren't you underestimat-
ing and understating it? Didn't you win a big victory?"

"It was a compromise on both sides," Marilyn said. "I do not have
story approval, but I do have director approval. That's important.
I have certain directors I'll work for and I have trust in them and
will do about anything they say. I know they won't let me do a bad
story. Because, you know, you can have a wonderful story and a
lousy director and hurt yourself." She named John Huston and
Billy Wilder, who'd expertly guided her through *The Asphalt Jungle*
and *The Seven Year Itch*.

"And I love George Stevens and Kazan even before I make a
picture with them!" She tossed her hair, grinning like a minx again.

And what next? She wanted to travel—London, Paris, Rome, even Russia. She quickly assured Earl that New York would be her real home—and she was hoping to buy a house "somewhere in the 60s . . . or 70s . . . or 80s . . . or somewhere."

"That girl has fought tremendously," Earl concluded, "and against frightening odds, to achieve her present eminence in pictures. . . . In her career she's found an answer, though incomplete, to her fears."

⌘ The night before she left for LA, Marilyn and Milton lounged around Sutton Place doing what they loved most—drinking, giggling, plotting, and playing with clothes. Marilyn tried on high-necked silk blouses, floppy black hats, and a fitted brown suit (it still had pins in it) for the flight the next day. Milton looked on, cocktail in hand, slumped in a chair, legs flung over the side.

They chatted about *Bus Stop,* the future of MMP, what going back to Hollywood might mean. Their year in New York was ending just the way it started—Marilyn and Milton, Milton and Marilyn.

That night, Jimmy Haspiel and Monroe Six member John Reilly stopped by to bid their Mazzie farewell. They brought seven glossy prints for her to autograph—that haunting picture John had taken on January 7, 1955, her first "official" night in New York. She'd been leaning against the wall of Marlene Dietrich's elevator, lips closed, a barely visible tear gleaming in her eye. Marilyn disappeared into her bedroom with a pen, while Jimmy and John chatted with Milton.

"Thank you for being so loyal," she signed one, and "thank you for your loyalty" on another, and "thank you for your loyalness"— offering six variations on a word that meant the world to her. But Jimmy's was different: "To Jimmy, Thanks for your friendship and devotion, Marilyn." Thrilled to be singled out, he slid the print in his coat pocket and walked the twenty blocks to East 30th Street, grinning all the way home.

At dawn, a limousine drove them both to the airport. Marilyn dressed in New York black with creamy costume pearls; Milton ready for Hollywood in shades and a light taupe suit. She was giddy, rolling down her window, leaning out to wave at Jimmy and the Monroe Six, who followed in a cab.

"At the airport," remembered Jimmy, "I became something of a human prop for the crowd of press photographers. While I was taking a shot of Marilyn, and she was posing especially for me, the press photographers shot the whole thing." It was plastered all over the *New York Sunday News* the next day: Marilyn beaming at her teenage fans, lit up with warmth and gratitude. Glowy and clear-eyed from the cold Eastern winter, she shone with self-possession. She'd charmed the implacable Sir Laurence Olivier. She'd landed her dream role as *Bus Stop*'s Cherie. She had the Strasbergs behind her and a year of Method training at the Actors Studio under her belt. And she had won victory over the Fox execs, who had insulted her and devalued her only ten months earlier. Somehow, she had found her center, found herself, after fourteen months in the city of her dreams.

Seventeen

The Return

*B*ack in LA, the American Airlines terminal teemed with paparazzi and journalists, eager to capture Marilyn's triumphant return. In her sleek new suit and black leather gloves, she strode past the cameramen with grace and poise. She left the press dazzled and reeling with questions: "What happened in New York?" Certainly, Marilyn returned strong, confident. But what was this strange alchemy—what had really changed, and was it all positive?

She'd be up against a lot—Miller-Monroe rumors had already begun to surface in gossip columns and Walter Winchell had just proclaimed her "darling of the left intelligentsia." While Mainstream Hollywood acknowledged her success, it often did so begrudgingly, still sore over her supposed "art-house pretensions." Even directors who loved her—like Billy Wilder and John Huston—were dismissive of the Method and the highbrow roles she planned to tackle. Had she alienated her fan base? Was she ready to start her first film since suspension, and how would Fox welcome her back?

Preproduction for *Bus Stop* would begin in two days, and there was plenty to be nervous about. After a year away, she'd be flung back into the world of production sets—page boys and runners dashing in and out with messages, scripts, and photo proofs. Hairdressers, masseuses, and ever-present publicity teams. Unmade beds at Chateau Marmont, costume blowups and last-minute script switches.

Luckily, Marilyn wouldn't be facing it alone. Milton rented a house in Westwood with Amy, baby Josh, Marilyn, and Kitty and Clyde Owens. "It was kinda hectic and pretty good too," remembered Kitty. They woke at six, worked all day on the rushes, and taxied back in time for Kitty's home-cooked dinners. Marilyn would beg for scrambled eggs rolled with capers. "Stop," Milton would plead. "You gotta be thin, thin, thin!"

This was the kind of work Milton loved, experimenting with lighting, camerawork, and costume. As the unofficial director of photography, he took charge of Marilyn's makeup—and as usual, the wheels in his head were already turning. Like Marilyn, Cherie slept all day—she'd have to be pale—but even in its whitest shade, Max Factor Pan-Cake wouldn't deliver the anemic pallor Milton was looking for. So he dusted Marilyn with baby powder—not just her face but her neck, chest, and arms. Marilyn hesitated at her pasty reflection. *Bus Stop* was her comeback. Was this the look she wanted to show the world: dull, doughy, and dredged in flour?

Marilyn soon came to realize Milton's "aspirin and black coffee" look was perfect for a nocturnal saloon girl like Cherie. Director Josh Logan was impressed. He knew the pressure she was under to stay pretty, the whispering that she'd alienate her male fans. "Marilyn's attitude toward her makeup and costume was courageous," he praised. "Incredible, really. Here you have a well-established star. She was willing to risk her position with that makeup many stars would have considered ugly. Every day we got a message from Buddy Adler or somebody else, telling us to change the chalk makeup. I kept saying trust her. And Marilyn wasn't afraid. She is never afraid to commit herself if she believes she is right."

Much to Marilyn's delight, Cherie's wardrobe was full of creative possibilities. Instead of the stiff lounge-singer gowns she'd worn in *Gentlemen,* or those ridiculous *Show Business* getups (half stripper, half tropical bird), she experimented with ripped fishnets and sleazy lame coats trimmed in monkey fur. She scoured secondhand shops for tattered and tired corsets and blouses—perfect for a honky-tonk chanteuse singing "That Old Black Magic" on a bus station tabletop. Billy Travilla designed a nightclub costume that she tore and darned hastily—just the way Cherie would. She ripped off the spangles and sewed them back on with the skill of a child. She attached scraps of black fishnet to darken the bodice. Perfect for "a ratty looking girl with a sense of direction."

Impressed with Marilyn's initiative, Josh encouraged her to take an active role in developing the character. He invited her to meetings with Buddy Adler and George Axelrod, and together they'd brainstorm over coffee or lunch. Soon, even the skeptical Axelrod perked up when Marilyn spoke. "We've got to get that in the picture," he'd say to Josh after a meeting, or "we've got to get that movement of hers."

"It's important to realize that Marilyn conceived the conception of Cherie herself," said Josh years later. "All I did was help her crystallize and help her get it on film. This conception of an uneducated girl with an Ozark accent and a fantastical crazy dream—well, it was in Bill Inge's original play script, of course, and it was in George Axelrod's movie script—but Marilyn gave it flesh and bones and heart. She put her own flesh on the character, and made the tawdriness, the pathos, the honesty of the girl so believable."

During one early meeting, they tried the Stanislavski trick of summing up the plot in one single sentence: "Will this girl who wants respect ever get it?" That's when Logan began to understand this wasn't just an actress playing a part: "Her crisis with Fox, her cross-country move—even her romance with Arthur—this was the story of Marilyn's life."

With a sympathetic director, a meaningful role, and Milton Greene behind her, everything looked promising. But once filming began on location in Phoenix, Marilyn's anxiety shot back up. After fourteen months looking inward in New York—books, therapy, Lee Strasberg, and Malin Studios—she was thrown back into the world of stage lights, call times, and stuffy trailers. She hadn't faced a movie camera in fifteen months and was flooded with insecurity. Lead Don Murray was too young—would his baby face make her look like a crone? Hope Lange's hair was too blonde—she'd have to dye it darker so she wouldn't steal Marilyn's thunder. All this under a media blitz in blistering Arizona heat.

But this time, Marilyn found herself surrounded by a team of supporters. Milton kept an eye on lighting and camerawork, patting her arms with baby powder between takes; Amy helped her read over her lines at night. Josh Logan was always attentive and kind. "Josh adored her," observed Amy. "He would no sooner raise his voice to Marilyn than kick her." Acutely aware of Marilyn's fragility, he looked out for her on the set and kept a protective eye on her interactions with the cast. "Whenever Marilyn and I got alone together," claimed her costar, Don Murray, "Josh would be behind the set listening to our conversations. He was very eager for us to get along, and if there was any kind of argument going to start he wanted to be there to jump in and stop it."

In Logan, Marilyn found a permanent ally. Not only did he coddle her; he was completely invested in their project. He understood her weaknesses and, more importantly, her strengths. "One thing Marilyn has beyond anyone today," he said, "is that when the camera starts to roll, she keeps on going and as long as I don't stop her she'll keep going. She keeps on getting better—she always stayed with the Ozark accent. What I did in *Bus Stop* was learn to put a camera on Marilyn when she was creating, not to cry cut, not to cut her off when she was beginning to secrete the emotion. We'd start rolling a scene and then she'd stop and it seemed like she forgot the line but we kept the camera on her and the assistant director fed her the line or I'd hand her a prop and mess up her hair and she'd keep going and I didn't jangle her by yelling cut and starting all over. You yell cut and right away the cinematographer wants to fix her up and the mood is broken."

Like Marilyn, Josh wasn't afraid to break the rules. He wanted extreme emotional close-ups: an inch above the chin to show some stoked-down fear, that space between the brows to show a subtle longing. But the technology wasn't there yet. With a regular CinemaScope six-inch lens, you couldn't shoot closer than seven feet. So he persuaded the cinematographer to try three-inch diminishing lenses, the kind usually saved for close-ups of teacups or calling cards. It worked, and Marilyn was delighted, thrilled to be part of a cutting-edge technique. Josh didn't care if they saw the fuzz of hair on her arms or the powder caked on her face or the veins in her eyeballs. Neither did she.

Once Josh had won her trust, Marilyn began to relax on set and even have fun. Cowboys, rodeos, pizza parlors, neon streetlights, mountains in the background—there was a dreamy, kitschy magic that lit up her sense of spontaneity. She'd leap about during the fireworks, or hop on Don's shoulders to get through an impromptu parade. Josh looked on, beaming in paternal admiration as Marilyn raced around the set like an enthusiastic puppy. "She has a way of getting excited before I'd finished a sentence and race away," he said, "full of enthusiasm and vitality to try the idea out and I'd have to say, 'Hold it, Marilyn; I haven't finished yet.'"

Always tolerant, Josh defended Marilyn's chronic lateness, insisting she had a "different sense of time." "It's not conceit," he insisted. "It's not a desire to annoy or harass other people. She thinks about the scenes and gets lost. One day in Phoenix we were waiting for the "magic hour," a movie phrase to denote a time of day when the sun is going down and there's enough light in the sky to show distances and give an effect of night. It lasts about five minutes. Marilyn was in her dressing room. We sent the [assistant director] over for her seven minutes early. As the minutes ticked away, I kept calling, 'Where's Marilyn; where's Marilyn?' No sign of her. Milton Krasner, the cameraman, kept cursing, 'We'll miss it, we'll miss it!' Finally at two minutes to go, I ran up to her room, and she's sitting in front of the mirror. I pulled her up and said, 'Run!' and we ran to the scene. 'Even though my name is Joshua,' I told her, 'I can't stop the sun.' The next time we had a magic hour, I got her there an hour and a half before."

Not everyone was entertained by Marilyn's antics. Even Josh admitted that she was oblivious of her castmates, falling into trances, or what he called "brown studies." When the time came to film the bedroom scene, she insisted on playing it nude and showed up in a terrycloth robe that she wriggled off under the bedsheets. She was pretending to sleep, and Don was supposed to lie next to her, shaking her awake gently. "Wake up, Cherie, its nine o'clock, no wonder you're so pale and white!" Only he flubbed his lines to "no wonder you're so pale and scaly." The camera had to be reloaded, and Don lay on the bed mortified, waiting for

Marilyn to react. She wiggled closer to him whispering: "Don, you made a Freudian slip. You said scaly instead of pale. That's very good. That means you're getting the emotion of Bo, subconsciously. You were thinking of snakes—do you know what a phallic symbol is?"

"Yeah, I do," Don muttered. "I've got one!"

But even Don had to admit that Marilyn was on form. "Let me say that according to people who had worked with Marilyn, *Bus Stop* was her best-behaved movie," he conceded years later. "They say she was more on time for this than for any other picture. She had Milton with her, who was very helpful. She had Josh, who was gently persuasive. . . . Psychologically it seemed to be a terrific period in her life."

Instead of being bullied, Marilyn was respected and, even more important, a key part of the creative process. "Marilyn herself conceived the basic approach to Cherie," said Josh Logan. "What I did, well, I helped her get it on film. Her approach emotionally gave us all the key to the music we played in the film. She stimulated every one of us. We were all 'sent' by her, inspired by her. She inspired all of us to do our jobs better."

After Phoenix, they left for their next location—the Idaho mountains with their snowdrifts and subzero temperatures. Several cast members caught the flu, including Marilyn, whose acute bronchitis landed her in the hospital, shutting down production for a week. By now Arthur was in Reno to begin the mandatory two-month residency that would expedite his divorce. "I can't do it," Marilyn phoned from her hospital room. "I can't work this way. Oh, Papa, I can't do it." She wept into the phone, lamenting her lack of training as an actress, her inability to "pretend." "All I know is real! I can't do it if it's not real!"

But the Stanislavski-trained Logan knew all about the real. He knew that Marilyn had to maintain constant contact with her character, a delicate current that could be broken while she waited for electricians to relight the set or wardrobe girls to fix her costume. Sometimes she'd wander away from him while he gave her instructions or direction on a scene. Instead of being annoyed, he recognized that an idea had been triggered, and she needed the silence and space to explore it. So when Marilyn announced in the midst of a scene, "Can I have a moment to think?" he let her "seek the reality behind the lines."

Her most difficult scene was the one with Hope Lange, whispering in the dusk about her fears and tawdry past. Josh saw her struggling through the big blocks of speech, pausing, her face screwing up as if she were about to vomit. "Every technician on the set thought she was fluffing her lines, blowing up," he said, "when she was feeling her way through the emotions of the lines. She knew her lines verbatim—she goes along as an actress but has the extra mind of the critic, a censor—and if she doesn't measure up, she'll stop and make a face of nausea, but this means she's on the verge of being good. It didn't mean she'd forgotten her lines or blew a scene and [that I'd have to say], 'Let's do it again.' I never stopped the camera—we had to print ten times as much film as we'd have done otherwise but we got her going that way."

Huddled up next to Hope on that rickety bus, she shivered in her cheap coat, hands red with cold. She spoke of the Ozarks' quieter horrors, of her menacing Pappy, and "going with boys" since she'd been twelve years old. She said Bo was the first boy who ever wanted to marry her—aside from her cousin Malcom, who "turned out real bad." She wasn't sure what love really was, but she longed for a man to look up to and admire. "I've just gotta feel that whoever I marry has some real regard for me," she said with a sigh, a melancholy haze falling over her face, "aside from all the love stuff." She could have been talking about Joe or Arthur.

Marilyn threw herself into Cherie with all the weight of the Method behind her. "She was pathetic, tawdry, pitiful, bedraggled," remarked Josh, "yet you never felt sorry for her. She was all these things with a subtle comic accent—and yet you didn't laugh at her. And she got across the tiredness, the weariness of it all—the weariness of her life as a small-time singer, the pathos of it when she sings her poor little song, 'That Old Black Magic,' and nobody listens to her."

In the last scene of *Bus Stop,* Cherie slumps over the bar, her face resting sideways on the counter. Bo hovers over her, his chin cradled in the crook of her neck. "Cherie, I like you so much the way you are, it doesn't matter how you got that way." As Marilyn sits up, some flecks of saliva pull away from her mouth—just the sort of thing retouched during edits. Josh insisted on keeping them: "I said her saliva was from her emotion, mouth open, hand on mouth. To me this was one of the great acting moments of intimacy and feeling in all filmic history." Marilyn agreed.

Bus Stop was Marilyn's first film under her new contract with Fox, her first after learning the Method with Lee, and possibly the most rewarding role of her life. It wasn't easy, with the intimidating script, the fluctuating weather, both leads' battling bronchitis and bouts of pleurisy. Yet somehow they pulled it off, ahead of time, and even more astonishingly, under budget. Marilyn and Milton were perfectly in sync—no pills this time, not even booze. "At that point in their lives those two human beings were so clean," explained Amy, "because they loved what they were doing. They would wake up and couldn't wait to get to the studio. It was a happy time."

Josh Logan would later call this time Marilyn's Golden Period, and it was. "With her declaration of independence in 1955, she became a different person," Zolotow noted. "She played Cherie in a tender area that lies between comedy and tragedy. It is the most difficult thing to do. Very few motion picture stars can do it. Chaplin achieves it. Garbo achieves it. And you know . . . I believe she has something of each of them in her—she is the most completely realized and authentic film actress since Garbo. She is pure cinema."

〜 At last, Hollywood agreed. "Hold onto your chairs, everybody," wrote the critic Bosley Crowther in the *New York Times,* "and get set for a rattling surprise. Marilyn Monroe has finally proved herself in 'Bus Stop.'"

"Speaking of artists," wrote Arthur Knight in *The Saturday Review,* "it is beginning to appear that we have a very real one right in our midst . . . Marilyn Monroe effectively dispels once and for all the notion that she is merely a glamour personality, a shapely body with tremulous lips and come hither blue eyes. . . . For Miss Monroe has accomplished what is unquestionably the most difficult feat for any film personality. She has submerged herself so completely in the role that one searches in vain for glimpses of the former calendar girl."

Josh took vicarious pleasure in Marilyn's success: "To some extent she was getting even with the sadistic half-wits who had humiliated her during her early years in pictures." Even the harshest critics couldn't help admiring Marilyn's stellar performance. When Fox execs brushed this kind of praise off, accrediting her obvious talents to a man, Josh wouldn't have it. "People would tell me, 'Well Josh, you got something out of her nobody else did.' I told them I didn't get anything out of her that wasn't already there."

Her time in New York had paid off. Marilyn had delivered the performance of her life.

Eighteen
Mazzie

"I'm bored with people who go around offering
psychological explanations for everything."

ELSA MAXWELL

On June 3, Marilyn returned to New York to marry Arthur. But
the relationships she formed in Manhattan were complicated. Were
the Strasbergs using her fame? Was the constant psychoanalysis
dredging up too many sinister memories? Did Laurence Olivier
consider her an equal, or did he want to sleep with her? (He wanted

to sleep with her.) Would her relationship with the Greenes ever sour, and would MMP continue to flourish? Who was Arthur, this lanky, reticent writer, and would his saintly support and quiet protectiveness last?

❧ Marilyn married Arthur on July 1, 1956, in the Katonah hamlet of Westchester County. "Arthur didn't have a black suit," recalled Amy, who guided Marilyn through the wedding preparations. "I don't think he owned a suit. So Milton made a call, brought six suits over to the studio, and outfitted Arthur head to toe. Marilyn, of course, had wanted to wear white and carry calla lilies and a long white train. I convinced her to wear beige—I mean this was her third time—the jig was up. I got her the Dalco shoes that I always got her—very high heel with pointed toe, parchment hose. Bendel's was the only one that had parchment hose at the time, and I sent her on her way."

Kitty baked an elaborate cake with swags of white icing, topped with the wedding ornament Amy and Milton had used three years earlier. Amy wore a beige lace top with white organza overlay, Hedda wore an A-line dress the color of sugared sand. Marilyn's dress of champagne chiffon was designed by Norell, with Amy's wedding veil dipped in tea to match. Lee Strasberg stood ready to give her away.

"Lee and Milton and I were sitting on the bed with her," revealed Amy years later, "and she turned to Milton and said, 'Tell me I'm making a mistake, and tell me you don't want me to do it, and I won't do it.' And Milton of course said, 'I can't do it for you, Marilyn. You have to make the choice yourself.'"

"Would you please close the door," she begged. "I need to speak to Milton alone."

"I was in there for a good fifteen minutes or more," remembered

Milton, "and I was walking around by the window, and she was sitting on the bed and had tears in her eyes, and said 'Milton, should I marry him?' I didn't know what to say. If I say no it's wrong, if I say yes it's wrong. I was there for her—I promised I'd always take care of her. When she called me in that room, that was a very important moment in both our lives. She had a stronger feeling than I did—'Yes, I'll marry you. I'll say no to him and marry you.' Yes, she would have, I think so. That I think would have happened."

Finally the door opened. "Lee and I just stood there very quietly," said Amy. "Finally Lee said, 'Yes or no?' And then she looked at the three of us and shrugged her shoulders, and smiled very cynically and said, 'Oh, what the hell, we can't disappoint the guests.' And she took my hand and said go out and light the candles and tell everyone out there I'm coming."

Milton put the glass under Arthur's foot, everyone yelled, "Mazel tov!" and Arthur lifted the veil and kissed the bride.

It was Milton, not Arthur, who stepped on the glass and crushed it. "Doomed," Amy whispered to a shell-shocked Lee, "before they even take the vow."

❧ Twelve days after her wedding, Marilyn boarded a London-bound plane to begin filming *The Prince and the Showgirl*. With Laurence Olivier as director and costar, this would be the first film that MMP produced, and Marilyn and Milton's ultimate coup. Olivier's hopes were just as high. He'd hitched his wagon to Marilyn and had quite vocally planned to fall "shatteringly" in love with her.

But potential issues loomed—not the least of which was Olivier's negative attitude toward Method acting. ("All this talk about the Method, the Method!" he'd groan. "WHAT Method? I thought each of us had our own method.") He was utterly unequipped to deal with this new, intuitive style. Meanwhile, Lee

Strasberg had been prepping Marilyn to distrust Olivier, to question his directing and to rely on Paula for help.

As a director, Olivier was the stark opposite of the warm, receptive Josh Logan, who let Marilyn's imagination run wild, allowing for retake after expensive retake. Best of all, Josh listened to Marilyn and continued to champion her after *Bus Stop* wrapped. For months he'd been writing to Olivier, warning him that Marilyn marched to the beat of her own drummer: "She's not a domesticated animal. She's a wild, untamed animal." But Olivier wouldn't accept feral behavior, no matter how talented. He expected Marilyn to adapt to his brisk, no-nonsense, and very English production set.

"From the first," remembers set photographer Jack Cardiff, "it was evident that Marilyn was going to be a problem for Larry on the film. . . . Marilyn had this ghastly obsession with Method acting and was always searching for some inner meaning with everything, but Larry would only explain the simple facts of the scene."

Marilyn liked to connect with a character, inching toward it then walking away like a lioness circling her prey. But Oliver didn't believe in digging deep, in finding the inner motivations and secrets of a character. He could be witheringly dismissive, patting her on the head like a child one day or sneering, "Just be sexy, Marilyn" the next.

"She went through so many agonizing times with Larry because he was, to her, a pain in the arse," said Jack Cardiff. "She never forgave him for saying to her, 'Try and be sexy.' I think she resented him. She used to call him 'Mr. Sir,' because he had been knighted."

As she shrank from Olivier, Marilyn hid more and more behind her buffer, Paula. Olivier was baffled by the cryptic prompts from Paula ("Think of Frank Sinatra and Coca-Cola!") or "More like a bird, Marilyn, more like bird!" Paula would spend hours getting

Marilyn ready, only to find she'd prepared her for the wrong scene. When she wasn't monopolizing Marilyn, Paula was harassing Olivier, helpfully informing him that his performance was "artificial." Eventually, he had two security guards pick up Paula and carry her off the set.

Oddly enough, Milton began to admire the Strasbergs in their own strange way: "Paula had a way out, like Lee had a way out: 'It's not an oil painting; it's a watercolor.' There are ten different ways you could take that."

Like the Strasbergs, Milton had his own way of working with Marilyn, such as cranking up the music to coax genuine tears. "She wouldn't take any glycerin in her eyes; it was always real tears. It's the vibrations of the music that made her tears stronger. So I walked over to Larry and said, 'Make the Bach louder.' Larry was ready to kill me. 'There's only one director,' he said."

By the end of filming, director and actress were in full-fledged war. Olivier was fed up with it all, fed up with the crazy hand-shaking warm-up moves, the tranquilizers and the meltdowns, the blank stares when she missed her lines, the trembling lips whenever he criticized her. He was exasperated that Marilyn demanded real caviar and champagne during the dinner-party scene, rather than making do with the apple juice and dyed-black bread balls they always used. After two days of retakes she ended up costing him several bottles of champagne and masses of Fortnum and Mason beluga at $12 a jar. He refused to attribute this to her commitment to authenticity, concluding instead that Marilyn was simply trying to torture him. Even her stomach troubles, he claimed, were "psychological warfare."

Equally troubling was Arthur. He and Marilyn had never really lived together, and now they were thrown into a chaotic pressure cooker, causing the cracks in their marriage to become painfully visible. From the very beginning, he isolated Marilyn from the rest of the set, urging her to refuse invitations, and was quoted in the *Daily Mail* as having said, "Thanks, England, thanks for leaving us alone."

"Arthur began to show up every day in the dressing room and he was disruptive," fumed Amy Greene. "No matter what Larry told Marilyn to do, Arthur had an opinion about it. Finally one day Larry told him to get the fuck off the set or he'd have him thrown off. . . . I mean, what was he doing there? I went antiquing, I went to museums, anything to stay out of Milton's hair. He went back to her dressing room, closed the door, and sulked for the rest of the day."

Not only was Arthur making it impossible for Marilyn to bond with cast and crew, he was quite deliberately driving a wedge between her and Milton. He'd always been jealous of Milton, and this jealousy only increased as the distance between himself and Marilyn seemed to widen. So he lashed out with petty insults, insinuating that Milton was spending MMP funds on antiques or frittering away valuable set time.

"So Arthur was stirring the pot," Amy complained, "because he knew it was a disaster between the two of them and he was hanging on for dear life. He knew that whatever idea he had in marrying her, it never materialized, and she felt the same. She was deeply unhappy, because it was another failure in her life."

Meanwhile, Marilyn was taking more pills than ever before. She'd increased her nightly dose of sleeping pills to the point where she needed a stimulant to wake up. She'd never taken amphetamines before, so Milton tried to start her on the less addictive extended-release variety. But Marilyn demanded the heady kick of instant release Dexamyls, which often made her so jittery she'd have to dose herself with barbiturates. She'd started slipping gin in her morning tea and asked Milton to keep her Thermos spiked on set. Milton said, "I was always worried she'd drink too much.

Olivier and I had a rule where we would never drink until six o'clock. So I'd pour a little less than she asked. I don't even think Miller knew about it. It didn't hurt her.

"When she had a problem," remembered Milton, "I solved it. She'd have a weekend with Arthur," said Milton, "and everything would get screwed up, and she'd be disorganized. She'd come in on Monday exhausted, bloated, and out of it. I'd give her a shot in the ass of vitamin B when she was tired. I secretly had two costumes made, because when you come in Monday you're bloated, then by Wednesday you're skinny again. She never knew the difference. That's how well I knew her." But despite all efforts, he was losing MMP and, even worse, his best friend.

In a foggy state, medicating her medication, Marilyn clung to Miller more desperately than ever. "This is none of your business; it's personal," she snapped when Milton gently questioned her outbursts or tears. Paranoid that Milton was "siding with" Olivier, Marilyn worried that Arthur was the only one protecting her. The stress of production left her bond with Milton vulnerable, and Arthur took advantage of that.

By the middle of production, Milton sensed that his hold over Marilyn was slipping, and that everything they had worked toward was spectacularly unraveling in a period of weeks. So he threw himself into salvaging the only thing he could: the film. For her sake he was affable and cordial with Olivier; for her sake he brushed off Miller's sneaky asides. As a playwright, Arthur had no understanding of film production—but he thought he did. When Marilyn fretted about going over budget, Arthur dismissed her concerns with ridiculously inaccurate statements. "What do you care? It's Warner Brothers' money." Milton, who usually bit his tongue around Arthur, finally exploded: "Schmuck! It's our money!"

If there was any hope for Milton and Marilyn, it dissolved at that point. It was the beginning of the end for MMP.

It was also the end of the Olivier-Monroe partnership. Their own insecurities got the better of them both. By the time the film wrapped, Olivier had turned into a tyrant, seizing control of the cutting and editing. Marilyn's pet project was no longer her own— it had deteriorated into a burden she dragged herself through each day. Olivier was equally miserable. Later, he'd claim that Marilyn had aged him fifteen years. Decades after her death, Olivier would still refer to her privately as "that bitch."

"Give the odds of 37-23-37 to one that they'll never film together again," quipped a reporter from *The Sun*. That day, Marilyn packed her bags, boarded a plane, and left Europe for the last time.

❧ After *The Prince and the Showgirl* wrapped, Arthur continued to insert himself in MMP. Friends were shocked to find him at his desk—not working but neatly snipping newspaper clippings and pasting them in scrapbooks. Others witnessed him huddled up with Marilyn and her dressmaker, deliberating over swatches of satin: turquoise, champagne, kelly green, or burgundy? It was shocking—a man who scorned glamour and fashion neglecting his own work to fuss over dresses. Of course, Arthur knew this left little room for Milton—that was the whole point. By January 1957, Arthur had successfully torn them apart. The Milton and Marilyn partnership was over.

"I went through that split up with Milton and Marilyn," said John Eula, "and it was tragic. Milton never believed that she would do what she would do, so he just sat there and did nothing about it. He never believed Marilyn would leave him, because he really was such a breadwinner for her, such a guiding light, such a foundation. The goddamned fool didn't understand that her husband had taken her away long before. Would you want your wife being owned forty-nine percent by somebody else?"

"I heard Milton on the phone and they were both crying," wrote Amy, who witnessed the terrible breakup. "These two people should have been together through thick and thin. Nothing—nothing—should have put them apart."

On February 17, 1957, Milton Greene met with Marilyn to negotiate the end of his contract with MMP. Arthur stood by like a sentry, flanked by his lawyers and ready for battle. But Milton only asked for half of his investment: $100,000.

"That's all you want?" Arthur asked.

"Take more," Marilyn whispered to Milton, her voice about to break.

"No," said Milton firmly, looking her in the eye. "Let me be the only one in your life never to take more."

It was the last time she ever saw him.

ᐁ The spell that started in late 1954 was broken. Unlike *Bus Stop, The Prince and the Showgirl* opened to mixed reviews and poor box office counts. MMP was destroyed. Cut off from Milton, Marilyn descended rapidly into a darkness from which she never fully recovered.

After her Olivier fiasco, Marilyn took a break from career to focus on marriage and family. But inertia proved far more harmful than the stress of filming. She and Arthur returned to Sutton Place, and bought a flat at 444 East 57th Street. There were wood-paneled elevators and white-gloved door attendants, but inside it looked haunted, dismal, and eerily hotel-like. She'd brought her white baby grand, her books, and beloved Sinatra records. She kept the fridge stocked with dozens of Piper-Heidsieck splits. But the bedroom was boxy and bare as a cell, with only a queen-sized mattress, a rickety gray nightstand, and a black Bakelite telephone she threw on the floor. There was a sad dining alcove, barely used, huge dingy mirrors propped on modular sofas, and pale carpeting marred by stains from the dog. Walls kept bleach-white and blank, no paintings of flowers and bulls, no 59th Street Bridge—just a gloomy view of buildings across the street. Not that it mattered: Marilyn covered each window with blackout curtains, sealed shut day and night.

Her world shrank; she grew lonelier each day. She passed undisciplined, unhappy hours in a haze of breakfast cocktails, phone calls, and temper tantrums. She'd wake around noon, shrieking "No! Don't!" when her maid tried to open the curtains, then sweetly order a Bloody Mary from her cook. Entire days were spent in bed, spinning Sinatra records, calling DiMaggio on the phone. One year into her marriage and she was already mourning Joe, obsessing over him ("Joe used to take me for the best Italian dinners"), asking her maid to cook lasagna, as if ricotta and tomatoes would bring him back. Arthur rarely dined with her, so Marilyn ate in bed, staining the sheets with red sauce, Hollandaise, and gravy.

Meanwhile, Miller hid in his study. When he did emerge, he had more interest in chatting with the cook or secretary than his own wife. It was pitiful—if he suggested a movie or party she leaped up like it was Christmas and spent the day fussing with makeup and clothes. Half the time he'd cancel, opting instead for another evening of brooding, avoiding his wife, and struggling over a play he could not seem to write. Their next four years were punctuated by miscarriages, overdoses, and chilly stretches of silence before ending in a Mexican divorce in 1961.

Untethered to marriage or home, Marilyn had to revive her career, which unfortunately meant moving back to Los Angeles. She bought a house in Brentwood and nailed a plaque to the door inscribed CURSUM PERFICIO, Latin for "My journey ends here." For Marilyn, Hollywood had always been "just a place to work," but this Spanish hacienda was pure LA, from the "telephone room" to the kidney-shaped swimming pool she never used once. She flew to Mexico to buy authentic handmade furnishings—woven blankets, scallop-trimmed benches, ceramic tiles for her kitchen—most of which remained in their cardboard boxes. She bought paintings but never hung them, leaving them propped against bare bedroom walls alongside Saks bags full of still-tagged clothes. A house, not a home—half furnished, half lived in, half a life.

According to Marilyn's housemaid, Eunice, leaving New York was her fatal mistake. Had she stayed in Manhattan, Eunice repeatedly claimed, Marilyn would have lived. Away from New York's creative cocoon, Marilyn's confidence withered. Her East Coast friends never deserted her. The Rostens and Shaws sent her postcards and presents, calling her weekly or daily, nurturing her to the end. But Marilyn needed more. Beset by gallstones, sinus infections, insomnia, and worsening endometriosis, Marilyn's dependency on barbiturates and painkillers soared. She fell in with a deluded, celeb-obsessed shrink who pushed even more pills and kept her dependent. Cut off from the only friends who understood her, she spiraled into loneliness.

"I was walking through La Scala restaurant in Beverly Hills," remembers her Studio friend Jack Garfein, "and she's sitting there with her secretary Pat Newcomb, and I said, 'Marilyn, it's Saturday night and you're with your secretary,' and she said 'Why, what would you want me to do, Jack?' I said, 'Well, you know what you should do—move to Paris—live there and they'll give you a parade down the Champs-Élysées.' The wit, the humor, the touch of reality: She said, 'Well, Jack, would you leave your wife to go with me?' And of course, I didn't answer, but my look was obviously that I wouldn't do that. So then she said to me, 'You know, Jack, remember when we went shopping for clothes, I was changing in the room and you were helping me change—you said something to me, Jack—it stayed with me all my life. You know, when I went through difficulties with Arthur, many times I thought of what you said to me in that room. Do you remember?' Of course, I didn't—like most men, when we're taken by a woman, we say things. . . . And I said, 'Yes, I remember.' She looked at me and said, 'You're lying, Jack; you don't remember.' Obviously I said something that came out, her presence inspired me, and that was important to her—with all the games, and changing the dresses, in the end she saw that I was just a man, that whatever I said that was important to her came out of me but obviously didn't stay with me. I was on a ship crossing the Atlantic coming back from Europe when I heard about her death, and the first thing I thought of was what the hell did I say to her?"

Epilogue

*I*n July 1962, Amy Greene woke from an unusually bad dream and turned to Milton:

"Marilyn needs you."

"What are you talking about?"

"In my dream she's alone, she doesn't have anybody she can trust. She was sending me signals to tell you to go to Los Angeles."

"You know we're leaving with Sally Kirkland in three days to cover the Paris collections. I can't do that."

"Milton, for once in your life listen to what I'm saying. She needs your help. Get on a plane, don't take the assignment. *Go* and help her."

So he picked up the phone and called her for the first time in five years.

"You know," she said, "I'm right back where I was before MMP.

They're giving me the worst roles. It's like the last ten years never happened. I'm right back to where I don't want to be."

"Don't do it," Milton urged. "If you want me to come out there, I'll leave today."

Of course, Marilyn assured Milton she'd be fine—that he had to go to Paris for the fashion show, that she'd call in a few weeks and they'd all meet for dinner or drinks at La Scala or the Mocambo. Milton had saved her eight years ago, and despite all that had happened, he was ready to do it again.

But Marilyn never made that call. Perhaps she was guilty about the way she'd treated him years before. Perhaps she was embarrassed—by her fear, her neediness, her inability to make a relationship stick. Perhaps she was ashamed that at thirty-six she was once again Zanuck's plaything. So Marilyn packed her pain down. She gave a few sunny interviews, posed for photo shoots on the beach, and hinted at new career moves on the horizon. On Sunday, August 5, she died alone, clutching the phone in an unmade bed full of phenobarbital and chloral hydrate.

Milton never believed that Marilyn killed herself—none of her real friends did. "She took sleeping pills," Milton insisted, "sipped champagne, then forgot how many pills she'd taken." Toward the end of his life Milton began to think there hadn't been an accident at all, that there were others involved, but he didn't know who. Accident or murder, could he have changed things?

"You were right," he moaned over and over to Amy. "I should have gone to her."

"All we demanded was our right to twinkle."
MARILYN MONROE

Notes

Chapter One

3 *"What the hell'"* Joshua Greene, *Milton's Marilyn* (Munich: Schirmer/Mosel, 1994), 25.

5 *"Not even a verbal one"* Shelley Winters, *Shelley II: The Middle of My Century* (New York: Simon & Schuster, 1989), 28.

5 *Before Dylan left* Ibid., 29.

11 *"Or they maintained an aloofness"* Greene, *Milton's Marilyn,* 17.

15 *"and it bothers me"* Marilyn Monroe and Ben Hecht, *My Story* (Boulder, CO: Taylor Trade Publishing, 2006), 175.

18 *"If it's ever a question"* Rita Garrison Malloy, "Marilyn, Oh, Marilyn, *Motion Picture,* November 1954, 63.

19 *"I've never seen anyone"* Ibid.

20 *"I'm gonna be the head"* Scott Feinberg interview with Amy Greene.

20 *"drive-in hamburger joints"* Maurice Zolotow, *Marilyn Monroe* (New York: HarperCollins, 1990), 57.

Chapter Two

25 *"Recently somebody asked me"* Pete Martin, *Will Acting Spoil Marilyn Monroe?* (New York: Doubleday, 1956), 100.

30 *"We both liked to feel"* Helen Bolstad, "Marilyn in the house" *Photoplay* (September 1955).

35 *"I used to make her pancakes"* Christopher Nickens and George Zeno, *Marilyn in Fashion: The Enduring Influence of Marilyn Monroe* (Philadelphia: Running Press, 2012), Kindle edition.

39 *"I'd just get out of the room"* Greene, *Milton's Marilyn,* 37.

39 *"She was fascinated"* Anthony Summers, *Goddess: The Secret Lives of Marilyn Monroe* (New York: Open Road Media, 2012), Kindle edition.

40   *"She said nobody"* Ibid.

40   *"Isadora Duncan Week in Connecticut"* Ibid.

Chapter Three

50   *"I told her I was afraid"* Eli Wallach, *The Good, the Bad, and Me: In My Anecdotage* (New York: Harcourt, 2005), Kindle edition.

51   *"The time she came backstage"* Ben Gazzara, *In the Moment: My Life as an Actor* (New York: Carroll & Graf Publishers, 2004), 72.

54   *"there was nothing cheap"* Milton Berle, *Milton Berle: An Autobiography* (New York: Applause Books, 2002), 266.

55   *"It was fun to watch"* Greene, *Milton's Marilyn.*

57   *She took his arm* George Carpozi, *Marilyn Monroe: Her Own Story* (New York: Belmont Books, 1961), 8.

58   *"You could win the battle"* Greene, *Milton's Marilyn,* 44.

Chapter Four

62   *"But I thought"* Truman Capote, *Music for Chameleons* (New York: Vintage, 2012), Kindle edition.

63   *"Well, she said"* Ibid.

Chapter Five

75   *"I'm continually off balance"* Martin, *Will Acting Spoil Marilyn Monroe?,* 58.

75   *"When I worry about that"* Ibid., 67.

75   *"She's running around without a top on"* Ibid., 14.

77   *"You know, those are the times"* Sam Shaw and Norman Rosten, *Marilyn Among Friends* (New York: Henry Holt & Co., 1988), 107.

Chapter Six

89   *Robert Stein found the afternoon* Robert Stein, "Do you want to see her?" *American Heritage Magazine* November/December 2005.

93   *"Eventually the party"* Elaine Dundy, *Life Itself!* (New York: Virago Press), 2012, Kindle edition.

Chapter Seven

106   *"She wanted so badly"* John Gilmore, *Inside Marilyn Monroe: A Memoir* (Los Angeles: Amok Books), 2007, Kindle edition.

107   *"We're her family now"* Ibid.

110 *"aroma of sex"* Les Harding, *They Knew Marilyn Monroe: Famous Persons in the Life of the Hollywood Icon* (Jefferson, NC: McFarland & Company, 2012), Kindle edition.

111 *"Gee, I thought you'd be much fuller"* Ibid.

112 *"Remember you can sit"* Stanley Buchthal and Bernard Comment, *Fragments* (New York: Farrar, Straus and Giroux, 2010), 81.

113 *"It was like she wanted to trade"* Gilmore, *Inside Marilyn Monroe*, Kindle edition.

113 *"And if they fired her"* Ibid.

Chapter Eight

127 *"Well, I don't know"* Michelle Morgan, *Marilyn Monroe: Private and Confidential* (New York: Skyhorse, 2012), Kindle edition.

127 *"I think we all respected"* Gazzara, *In the Moment*, 89.

128 *"He obviously had a mad, fatherly crush"* Ibid., 245.

Chapter Nine

129 *"There was another page"* James Haspiel, *Marilyn: The Ultimate Look at the Legend* (New York: Henry Holt & Co., 1991), 66.

133 *"Do you live around here?"* Norman Rosten, *Marilyn: An Untold Story* (New York: Signet, 1973), 55.

134 *"even Greta Garbo"* Ibid.

134 *"It was like"* Ibid.

135 *"So many lights in the darkness"* Buchthal, Fragments, 71.

139 *"My body is my body"* Ibid., 53.

139 *She vowed* Ibid.

140 *"It frustrated and hurt me"* Ibid., 107.

140 *She'd walk* Shaw, *Marilyn Among Friends*, 87.

142 *"So Pete would empty his pockets"* Haspiel, *Marilyn: The Ultimate Look*, 63.

142 *"Is that you, Marilyn?"* Rosten, *Marilyn: An Untold Story*, 15.

143 *"I think that is why"* Haspiel, *Marilyn: The Ultimate Look*, 65.

144 *"She is in complete control"* Morgan, *Marilyn Monroe: Private and Confidential*, Kindle edition.

Chapter Ten

149 *"How little these glamour girls"* Elia Kazan, *Elia Kazan: A Life* (New York: Alfred A. Knopf, 2011), Kindle edition.

149 *"Art was a good dancer"* Ibid.

149 *"The female resentment"* Arthur Miller, *Timebends: A Life* (New York: Grove Press, 2013), Kindle edition.

155 *"that I might be slipping"* Ibid.

156 *"It was the very inappropriateness"* Ibid.

156 *"America was still a virgin"* Ibid.

159 *"From life on the streets"* Ibid.

Chapter Eleven

164 *"Because, darling"* John Strasberg, *Accidentally on Purpose: Reflections on Life, Acting, and the Nine Natural Laws of Creativity* (New York: Applause Books, 2000), Kindle edition.

165 *Lee manned the grill* Ibid.

167 *"I don't think you're fat"* Ibid.

Chapter Twelve

179 *"Each popping cork"* Rosten, *Marilyn: An Untold Story*, 16.

180 *That was an appealing part* Shaw, *Marilyn Among Friends*, 18.

181 *The salesgirl unzipped Marilyn* Ibid., 15.

183 *"She'd been so proud"* Shaw, *Marilyn Among Friends,* 162.

183 *"There seemed to be"* Eve Arnold, *Marilyn Monroe* (New York: Harry N. Abrams, 1987), 40.

184 *"For shoes"* Ibid.

184 *"Marilyn, I see all your movies!"* Rosten, *Marilyn: An Untold Story,* 17.

185 *"You go back"* Ibid., 19.

185 *"Don't be nervous"* Ibid.

186 *"She was in control"* Arnold, *Marilyn Monroe,* 41.

188 *"It sounded as though Eisenhower,"* Ibid., 46.

188 *"She rode it all"* Ibid., 47.

189 *"Her hair was tangled"* Ibid., 49.

Chapter Thirteen

194 *"What Marilyn was doing"* Haspiel, *Marilyn: The Ultimate Look,* 109.

196 *"She never got the time thing"* Rosten, *Marilyn: An Untold Story,* 24.

196 *"I know she's smart"* Sandra Shevey, *The Marilyn Scandal* (Berkeley, CA: Berkeley Publishing Group, 1990), 238.

196 *"Take out clauses"* Ibid.

196 *"Eli, you're going to be working"* James Goode, *The Making of the Misfits* (New York: Limelight Editions, 1963), 69.

197 *"I followed her up Broadway"* Morgan, *Marilyn Monroe: Private and Confidential,* Kindle edition.

198 *"It was a high moment"* Rosten, *Marilyn: An Untold Story,* 26.

198 *The next day's gossip column* Ibid., 28.

198 *"Both girls"* Shaw, *Marilyn Among Friends,* 158.

198 *"That inner child"* Ibid.

199 *"Hurry, take a cab!"* Rosten, *Marilyn: An Untold Story,* 32.

199 *"There was more meaning"* Shaw, *Marilyn Among Friends,* 192.

199 *"She stood before this vision"* Rosten, *Marilyn: An Untold Story,* 28.

200 *"I've had these dreams"* Shaw, *Marilyn Among Friends,* 146.

200 *"If you had asked me"* Shevey, *The Marilyn Scandal,* 312.

203 *"She stared into space"* Rosten, *Marilyn: An Untold Story,* 52.

204 *"Actually the whole thing"* Miller, *Timebends,* Kindle edition.

207 *This wasn't really her style* Haspiel, *Marilyn: The Ultimate Look,* 97.

Chapter Fourteen

211 *Marilyn leaned forward* Gilmore, *Inside Marilyn Monroe.*

212 *The policeman kept her company* Haspiel, *Marilyn: The Ultimate Look,* 65.

212 *"For Miller, a level of frosty detachment"* Miller, *Timebends,* Kindle edition.

213 *"He felt, but he didn't tell"* Barbara Leaming, *Marilyn Monroe* (New York: Three Rivers Press, 2000), 174.

216 *"Marilyn was all but drenched"* Haspiel, *Marilyn: The Ultimate Look,* 92.

216 *"Well, Jimmy, don't let it bother you!"* Ibid., 93.

217 *"I saw Mamie Van Doren"* Ibid.

218 *"Looking at her"* Capote, *Music for Chameleons,* Kindle edition.

219 *"This was one unhappy lady"* Greene, *Milton's Marilyn,* 54.

219 *"Everybody carried them"* Ibid., 72.

220 *"When she lived with us"* Ibid., 74.

221 *"I have a feeling"* Buchthal, *Fragments,* 73.

221 *It was the ultimate nightmare* Ibid., 75–77.

222 *"At that moment"* Strasberg, *Accidentally on Purpose,* Kindle edition.

Chapter Fifteen

227 *"It would be a full quarter of a century"* Haspiel, *Marilyn: The Ultimate Look,* 117.

229   *"It was easy to be intimidated by Marilyn"* James Grissom, *Follies of God: Tennessee Williams and the Women of the Fog* (New York: Vintage 2016), Kindle edition.

229   *"This was a girl"* Ibid.

229   *"People looked at me onstage"* Ibid.

230   *"But to do* Anna Christie" Gilmore, *Inside Marilyn Monroe,* Kindle edition.

230   *"She wanted to be taken seriously"* Grissom, *Follies of God.*

230   *"Arthur read the part"* Miller, *Timebends,* Kindle edition.

234   *"That's their business"* Greene, *Milton's Marilyn,* 58.

234   *"We beat them!"* Ibid.

Chapter Sixteen

236   *"A great deal is in a director's hands"* Martin, *Will Acting Spoil Marilyn Monroe?,* 110.

236   *She'd also heard* Ibid., 111.

236   *Once she had Rattigan* Ibid.

238   *"At that the reporters laughed"* Ibid., 122.

244   *"All you have to do, Mazzie"* Haspiel, *Marilyn: The Ultimate Look,* 111.

244   *"As I sat back down"* Ibid., 112.

245   *"What had happened"* Ibid.

245   *"Hollywood is just a place"* Martin, *Will Acting Spoil Marilyn Monroe?,* 128.

248   *But Jimmy's was different* Haspiel, *Marilyn: The Ultimate Look,* 124.

249   *"While I was taking a shot of Marilyn"* Ibid., 125.

Chapter Seventeen

259   *"They would wake up"* Greene, *Milton's Marilyn,* 72,

Chapter Eighteen

268   *"Would you want your wife"* Greene, *Milton's Marilyn,* 86.

Epilogue

269   *"These two people"* Green, *Milton's Marilyn,* 88.

269   *"Let me be the only one"* Ibid., 86.

274   *"Don't do it"* Ibid., 91.

274   *"You were right"* Ibid., 92.

Bibliography

Arnold, Eve. *Marilyn Monroe*. New York: Harry N. Abrams, 1987.

Banner, Lois. *Marilyn: The Passion and the Paradox*. London: Bloomsbury, 2012.

Berle, Milton. *Milton Berle: An Autobiography*. New York: Applause Books, 2002.

Buchthal, Stanley, and Bernard Comment. *Fragments*. New York: Farrar, Straus and Giroux, 2010.

Capote, Truman. *Music for Chameleons*. New York: Vintage, 2012. Kindle edition.

Carpozi, George. *Marilyn Monroe: Her Own Story*. New York: Belmont Books, 1961.

Dundy, Elaine. *Life Itself!* New York: Virago Press, 2012. Kindle edition.

Gazzara, Ben. *In the Moment: My Life as an Actor*. New York: Carroll & Graf Publishers, 2004.

Gilmore, John. *Inside Marilyn Monroe: A Memoir*. Los Angeles: Amok Books, 2007. Kindle edition.

Goode, James. *The Making of the Misfits*. New York: Limelight Editions, 1963.

Greene, Joshua. *Milton's Marilyn*. Munich: Schirmer/Mosel, 1994.

Grissom, James. *Follies of God: Tennessee Williams and the Women of the Fog*. New York: Vintage, 2016. Kindle edition.

Guiles, Fred Lawrence. *Norma Jean*. New York: McGraw-Hill, 1969.

Harding, Les. *They Knew Marilyn Monroe: Famous Persons in the Life of the Hollywood Icon*. Jefferson, NC: McFarland & Company, 2012. Kindle edition.

Hanks, Tara. *The Last Misfit*. Tarahanks.com

Haspiel, James. *Marilyn: The Ultimate Look at the Legend*. New York: Henry Holt & Co., 1991.

Kazan, Elia. *Elia Kazan: A Life*. New York: Alfred A. Knopf, 2011. Kindle edition.

Leaming, Barbara. *Marilyn Monroe*. New York: Three Rivers Press, 2000.

Martin, Pete. *Will Acting Spoil Marilyn Monroe?* New York: Doubleday, 1956.

Miller, Arthur. *Timebends: A Life*. New York: Grove Press, 2013. Kindle edition.

Monroe, Marilyn, and Ben Hecht. *My Story*. Boulder, CO: Taylor Trade Publishing, 2006.

Morgan, Michelle. *Marilyn Monroe: Private and Confidential*. New York: Skyhorse, 2012. Kindle edition.

Nickens, Christopher, and George Zeno. *Marilyn in Fashion: The Enduring Influence of Marilyn Monroe*. Philadelphia: Running Press, 2012. Kindle edition.

Rollyson, Carl. *Marilyn Monroe: A Life of the Actress*. Jackson, MS: University Press of Mississippi, 2014.

———. *Marilyn Monroe Day By Day: A Timeline of People, Places, and Events*. Boulder, CO: Rowman & Littlefield, 2014, Kindle edition.

Rosten, Norman. *Marilyn: An Untold Story*. New York: Signet, 1973.

Shaw, Sam. *The Joy of Marilyn: In the Camera Eye*. New York: Exeter Books, 1979.

———, and Norman Rosten. *Marilyn Among Friends*. New York: Henry Holt & Co., 1988.

Shevey, Sandra. *The Marilyn Scandal*. Berkeley, CA: Berkeley Publishing Group, 1990.

Spoto, Donald. *Marilyn Monroe: The Biography*. New York: Cooper Square Press, 2001.

Stapleton, Maureen. *A Hell of a Life*. New York: Simon & Schuster, 1995.

Steinem, Gloria. *Marilyn*. New York: Henry Holt & Co. 1986.

Strasberg, John. *Accidentally on Purpose: Reflections on Life, Acting, and the Nine Natural Laws of Creativity*. New York: Applause Books, 2000. Kindle edition.

Strasberg, Susan. *Marilyn and Me: Sisters, Rivals, Friends*. New York: Time Warner Books, 1992.

Summers, Anthony. *Goddess: The Secret Lives of Marilyn Monroe*. New York: Open Road Media, 2012. Kindle edition.

Wallach, Eli. *The Good, the Bad, and Me: In My Anecdotage.* New York: Harcourt, 2005. Kindle edition.

Winters, Shelley. *Shelley II: The Middle of My Century.* New York: Simon & Schuster, 1989.

Zolotow, Maurice. *Marilyn Monroe.* New York: HarperCollins, 1990.

Acknowledgments

I am grateful to the following people for interviews, for access to documents, and for their correspondence: Kathleen Gray, Darryl Rooney, Greg Schreiner, Scott Feinberg, Joshua Greene, Carl Rollyson, Melissa Stevens, and Anne Orteig. For access to the Norman Mailer collection and Maurice Zolotow collection, I thank Elizabeth Garver and Richard Watson at the Harry Ransom Center.

Susan Strasberg's *Marilyn and Me* was a key document in writing this book, as were Eve Arnold's *Marilyn Monroe,* John Gilmore's *Inside Marilyn Monroe,* Norman Rosten's *Marilyn: An Untold Story,* Shelley Winters' *Shelley II,* and James Haspiel's *Marilyn: The Ultimate Look at the Legend.* In addition to these texts were several filmed interviews, including Scott Feinberg's interview with Amy Greene, Kim Morgan's interview with Jack Garfein, and the informative website everlasting-star.net.

I owe many of the physical details to Marilyn's devoted photographers, who left a stunning visual record of her year in New York City.

It is a pleasure to thank my agent, David Kuhn, as well as Sarah Levitt, Nicole Tourtelot, William Lo Turco, Kate Mack, Jessie Borkan, and Nate Muscato. Many thanks to everyone at Flatiron Books, especially Colin Dickerman, Whitney Frick, James Melia, and Amelia Possanza. Bob Ickes and David Lott have my sincerest gratitude for their patience in handling endnotes and edits, and many thanks to Henry Kaufman for his expert legal read.

Last, I thank my family for their consistent and kind encouragement.